SKY'S THE LIMIT

BUILDING BUSINESSES TOGETHER

Shah, Chase your dreams

BO GHIRARDELLI AND NICOLAS CARY

Sky's The Limit

ISBN 979-8-9913741-0-1 (paperback)
ISBN 979-8-9913741-1-8 (hardcover)
ISBN 979-8-9913741-2-5 (ebook)
ISBN 979-8-9913741-3-2 (audiobook)

Book Design: Clarity Designworks

Contents

Disclaimer

As an entrepreneur, you will receive advice from lots of people, and none of them will perfectly understand you and your business. It's your job to filter the advice you get and decide what to keep and what to ignore, including from this book.

This educational material provides general information related to the law designed to help entrepreneurs think about their own legal needs. However, legal information is not legal advice. This book does not provide legal advice and the authors are not lawyers. Although we go to great lengths to make sure our information is useful, we recommend you consult a lawyer if you want legal advice, or do your own research. Similarly, this book does not provide financial investment advice. You may explore Skysthelimit.org's community to find volunteer legal or investment experts who may be willing to provide pro-bono (free) support.

Authors' Note

At the time this book is published, we the authors, Nic and Bo, have personally volunteered thousands of hours and helped over 200 entrepreneurs launch and grow their businesses across four continents. And through the nonprofit organization we founded 14 years ago, Skysthelimit.org, we have helped tens of thousands more.

We love entrepreneurs. They get us and we get them. We've been entrepreneurs since childhood, like many of you reading this book. Entrepreneurs are the backbone of society—they feed us, clothe us, build our homes, take care of our children, clean our teeth, wash our cars, and provide so many other products and services that make our lives better. For us, a life worth living is one that empowers as many entrepreneurs to achieve their full potential as possible, while we enjoy the growth, excitement, learning, tribulations, and successes along the way. That's why we wrote this book.

Entrepreneurship isn't taught in schools. We think this is a travesty. The good news is that we know anyone can learn entrepreneurship, anyone can start a business. It is just like learning a new job, sport, or instrument—you need to practice it to get better.

The subtitle of this book is "Building Businesses Together" because entrepreneurship cannot and should not be done alone. Too many founders are isolated, lonely, thinking they need to do everything themselves. We've tried that miserable route. There is a better way. Include people in building your business—friends and family members, mentors, advisors, industry peers, employees, and more—and we've found you will be happier and more likely to achieve your goals for your business. Ultimately though, when including other people, you will need to decide which advice, insights, strategies, and tactics you will—and won't—use. It's your business at the end of the day.

Skysthelimit.org has over 80,000 entrepreneurs and volunteer business mentors signed up on our digital platform, accessible from your laptop, desktop, iOS or Android. It is a richly diverse community: when most members join, three quarters are in the "idea" stage of starting a business while the other 25 percent join with a business already running, nearly 70 percent are women, 80+ percent BIPOC, majority low-income, and representing every kind of business from fashion to food to beauty. For nearly a decade, we've partnered with top Fortune 500 companies like Accenture, PNC Bank, and Goldman Sachs to match their employees as volunteer supporters of entrepreneurs—a digital marketer in New York helping an entrepreneur launch their first Instagram ad campaign for their fashion line, a banker helping an entrepreneur with their pitch to raise money, and so many other examples.

This book was designed to help earliest-stage entrepreneurs launch and grow their businesses together with a group of peers and mentors. This book is for both groups—the entrepreneur and the mentor. The book covers a lot of areas and includes Discussion Guides for you to use together, along with Checklists to help you stay focused on the right things while you build your business. The earliest days of launching a business are chaotic, exciting, painful, and filled with a spectrum of other emotions.

For entrepreneurs, we hope this book will increase the chances of you accomplishing your goals for your business, while avoiding pitfalls and wasting your precious time. For mentors, we hope this gives you context and a playbook for supporting entrepreneurs, while you build mutually beneficial relationships that you can have for an hour or a lifetime, filled with inspiration, learning, and personal growth.

To the entrepreneur in all of us

Introduction

Ask a dozen entrepreneurs to describe their entrepreneurial journeys and their answers will probably include both the difficulty and the excitement. We won't lie: entrepreneurship is hard, mostly because there are so many concurrent variables. If you've opened this book because you're an entrepreneur or thinking about becoming one, we're here to help and we've got your back.

In the pages that follow, we offer our take on the steps to becoming a successful entrepreneur. We wholeheartedly recommend seeking guidance and advice from a mentor and talking through your own experiences with other entrepreneurs. We share our perspectives, rooted in helping tens of thousands of early-stage entrepreneurs launch businesses, while having built some businesses ourselves.

Bo Ghirardelli's entrepreneurial journey began one Christmas season when he was a child. Bo, along with his brother and father, went out to cut down a Christmas tree in the woods of Northern California. Bo asked about a vine-like plant hanging on most of the trees. Bo's father explained that it was mistletoe, the plant that's traditionally hung in doorways during the holidays; when two people find themselves under the mistletoe, they're supposed to kiss—an ancient tradition! "People buy mistletoe?" Bo asked. "They sure do," Bo's dad said. Bo convinced his brother to climb the tree and gather as much mistletoe as they could. They set up a table on the sidewalk in front of their house in Oakland, CA and sold bunches of mistletoe wrapped in ribbon to all the neighbors—a serial entrepreneur in the making.

Nicolas Cary earned his first buck harvesting clams by hand in the shallow waters of Gardiners Bay on Long Island. As a young adult, he learned about inventory management (keeping his clams secured in a dive bag), customer support, sales, and just in time delivery—by dropping clams off to neighbors on his fixed gear rusty Schwinn bike. Nic's entrepreneurial journey took a more serious turn in high school when he and a friend helped design websites for law firms, a sandwich company, and even became back-to-back website-building champions in a statewide competition in Colorado.

Fast forward a decade when Bo and Nic met on the first day of college. They quickly became inseparable friends, and when they graduated, they traveled to India to volunteer as teachers. They shared a desire to help young people and noticed that while many young people have both the drive and the ideas to start a business, they lack the network and knowledge to do so. Nic and Bo are passionate about the importance of mentorship, philanthropy, and how technology can enable incredible impact at scale to help support the next generation of entrepreneurs around the world. And Skysthelimit.org was born.

Who This Book Is For

In 2014, Skysthelimit.org began with a mission to connect underrepresented young adult entrepreneurs in the United States to information, expert support in the form of volunteer mentors, and customers. We know that talent is distributed equally, but opportunity isn't. We connect hard-working, earliest-stage entrepreneurs with opportunity, and in turn they create local jobs, new income streams, and wealth for their families and communities.

We believe in the power of entrepreneurship and business ownership to change lives. In the last 10 years, more than 80,000 entrepreneurs have joined Skysthelimit.org, and they've helped us learn what new entrepreneurs need. This book covers 14 different areas of starting and building a business. Each chapter covers timeless content while highlighting stories of how entrepreneurs have succeeded. We envision the book delivering value for entrepreneurs and volunteers who mentor them.

Our mission is to build meaningful relationships between entrepreneurs and their supporters. While the book speaks primarily to entrepreneurs, mentors can also use it as a guide for conversations with mentees, making it easier for them to work together.

One of our founding principles is *always be learning,* so entrepreneurs at any stage of their journey should find something new to learn in these pages. However, our main reader is the first-time entrepreneur in the early stages of their journey. These entrepreneurs have an idea and are getting ready to launch their business or may have launched their business recently and are looking to grow. They're typically young adults, but there's an entrepreneur in everyone, and it's never too late to put your talents to the test. **Entrepreneurs** should read this book and walk away with:

- Practical knowledge to apply to their business.
- A sense of how they can use the Skysthelimit.org platform and programming to build relationships and their business.

Skysthelimit.org recruits mentors among employees from Fortune 500 companies like Accenture, Goldman Sachs, and PNC. The volunteer mentors are interested in skills-based volunteering and come from all career stages, departments, and industries. After reading the book, **volunteer mentors** should:

- Understand how to start a business and gain ideas, frameworks, templates—and most importantly, the right questions to ask—to support entrepreneurs.
- Have a sense of how they can use the Skysthelimit.org platform and programming to build relationships with entrepreneurs.

If you are a corporate decision-maker (or influence decision makers) within CSR, ESG, foundations, or employee engagement, reading this book can help you understand how Skysthelimit.org delivers impact and employee engagement at scale.

How to Use This Book

We present a lot of tools and concepts in this book, and they all work together but we can only present one at a time. We've done our best to present them in the order that you'll use them, and you'll see that they build on each other.

We recommend reading the opening six chapters to grasp the foundational ideas of entrepreneurship. After that, feel free to jump around to the topics that you need most to grow your business now—at the beginning of each chapter we mention when you might need the topic. At the end of each section, we've included Discussion Guides that offer a list of questions to help you accomplish the tasks associated with the topic. Mentors and mentees can use these Discussion Guides as a starting point for mentoring conversations.

Some of the words and phrases in the book may be new to you. We've defined those words within the text. As much as we prefer plain English, we use jargon for key concepts that really matter for business—terms that other entrepreneurs, customers, investors, and lenders may use that you should be familiar with. We define these to make them accessible.

Talk to any entrepreneur or small business owner and you'll quickly learn that starting a business requires a lot of work. Generating a business idea is a great starting point, but an idea doesn't become a business without effort. Some budding entrepreneurs understand the effort necessary to create a business, but they might not be familiar with the many steps required to launch a business venture. If you're willing to put in the effort to build a business, you're going to want to know the steps needed to reach your goals.

Let's get started!

Note on Fundraising

Finding the money to start your business likely sits at the top of your to do list. Trust us, we've seen so many entrepreneurs spend all their time here before preparing properly. Asking for money shouldn't happen until you've spent time working on who you are as an entrepreneur, who your customer is, how your idea solves your customer's problem, what your product or service is, how you'll reach your customer, and how you'll run your business. Even better, we want to help you fund your business from sales with a healthy profit so you only have to raise money from investors if you decide to. While that may be impossible for some businesses, we suggest you try before you spend all your time and energy fundraising. We suggest you read one or two of the early chapters in the book before flipping to Chapter 13, Funding and Financials, to learn about fundraising.

CHAPTER 1

Entrepreneurial Foundations

When Should You Read This Chapter?
Whether you have already started a business or are simply thinking about it, read this chapter before going on to the others. Learning about the principles that provide the foundation for entrepreneurship will help you think about why you want to be an entrepreneur and provide guidelines for making decisions about how to run your business.

Who do you think of when you hear the word entrepreneur? Jay-Z? Elon Musk? Taylor Swift? Oprah Winfrey? Tyra Banks? Mark Zuckerberg? Shaquille O'Neal? Do you think of yourself? If you're reading this book, you should add your own name to the list. And you don't have to create a huge tech company to be an entrepreneur. In fact, well-known entrepreneurs who run big companies are a small percentage of entrepreneurs as a whole in the United States and beyond.

According to the Small Business Administration[1] (SBA) there are slightly more than 33 million small businesses in the US, and they make up 99.9 percent of all US businesses. Entrepreneurs who run a company with fewer than 20 employees make up 89 percent of those small businesses. Small businesses are far more important to the growth and

1 https://www.luisazhou.com/blog/small-business-statistics/#:~:text=99.9%25%20of%20businesses%20in%20the%20US%20are%20small%20businesses,-(SBA%202023%20Small&-text=Of%20the%20majority%2C%2098%25%20have,have%20fewer%20than%2020%20workers

sustainability of the economy than people think—they are the backbone of nearly every economy around the world and provide most of the jobs and innovation our society needs. Small businesses provide jobs for more than 61.2 million people in the US, accounting for almost half of all workers across the country. And they generate 44 percent of the US economic activity, known as the gross domestic product or GDP. And remember, all big businesses started off as an idea.

We define entrepreneurship as creating value for a group of people in a way that sustains a profitable business. That sentence makes it sound easy, but it's not. To be clear, 20 percent of new businesses fail in the first year and the failure rate increases over time, with only about 30 percent of businesses making it to year 10. But you don't have to be part of that statistic. While we don't believe get-rich-quick business ideas really exist, we do believe that laying solid entrepreneurial foundations allows you to build meaningful businesses that achieve your goals over time. We're sharing our experiences in the hopes that they'll help you achieve your dreams for your business, and in this chapter we discuss the foundational principles we adhere to.

Why Do You Want to be an Entrepreneur?

In 2010, Simon Sinek's TED talk "How Great Leaders Inspire Action" went viral, becoming one of the most-watched talks in TED history. Drawing from the theories presented in his book, *Start With Why,* Sinek (addressing employers with regard to employees) explains that people are motivated and inspired to do something when they first identify why they do it. After defining your why, you can then move on to the what and the how.

We believe entrepreneurs should also start by defining their why. Being an entrepreneur can be as hard as it is rewarding; there are challenges, risks, long-nights, and sometimes loss. Knowing why you chose to step onto the entrepreneurial path will keep you going when you run into hurdles and obstacles along the way.

The reasons people become entrepreneurs mostly fall into a few categories:

- The desire for financial and personal independence, whether that means making extra money, being their own boss or ambitiously trying to create generational wealth.
- The desire to solve a problem in their community or themselves in the form of something they wish existed for them.
- The desire to improve a product or process by doing it better than their employer.

We suggest you tap into the deep emotion that will inspire and sustain you. To do this, write in a journal or talk with a peer or mentor, and ask yourself why you want to be an entrepreneur five times. This process, known as The Five Whys, is adapted from a tool developed at Toyota (the car company). Toyota used this exercise to solve problems in vehicle design, and many businesses have used it since to solve problems not only in product design, but also in customer service and employee management. The process looks something like this:

1. Why do you want to be an entrepreneur?
   I want to set my own hours and my own rules about how much I earn.
2. Why do you want to set your own rules?
   When I've had jobs working for other people, they set the hours and that often conflicted with spending time with my family. They also established how much I could earn, and there was a cap on salaries and raises.
3. Why do you want to spend more time with your family?
   I grew up in a single parent household where my mom had to work two jobs to make ends meet.
4. Why do you want to earn more?
   Although she worked hard, we lived paycheck to paycheck often worrying about paying the rent. I want it to be different for my children.

5. Why do you want a different life for your children?
I want my children to feel secure and safe and not feel alone like I often did. I don't want my children to worry about me like I worried about my mom. I want my children to have a childhood.

You may fear judgment or criticism from people who know you—especially if you're the first entrepreneur in your family or circle of friends—but talking about your business idea makes it real. Call a supportive friend or family member and talk to them about your motivations for your business. This will help you get feedback from people who know you best, and you'll start to get comfortable talking about your business! You can also join Skysthelimit.org and connect with another entrepreneur or volunteer. Write down notes from your conversation.

Understanding—and remembering—why you want to be an entrepreneur will give you a boost of motivation when the work gets tough or you begin to doubt all your choices.

DISCUSSION GUIDE

- Why do you want to be an entrepreneur/build this business? List as many reasons as you can; the more reasons you have, the higher your motivation to achieve your goals.
- What are the financial or lifestyle goals that being an entrepreneur could help you achieve?
- How will you know that your business is a success? Write a one-sentence description of your ultimate goal. *Example: Ultimately, I will consider myself and my business successful when I achieve 10,000 happy customers and $1 million in profits.*

Becoming an Entrepreneur

Now that you know why you want to be an entrepreneur, it's time to think fully about the idea you want to bring to the world. We like to use a framework called effectuation.

As jargon goes, effectuation sounds rather academic, and maybe even a touch pretentious. But in reality it's not as intimidating as it sounds. Effectuation is a framework for thinking, a self-led investigation—it's *how* you decide *which* idea to work on as an entrepreneur. It's similar in spirit to the most widely-recognized marketing campaign of all time: Just do it.

Cognitive scientist Dr. Saras Sarasvathy developed effectuation as a result of hundreds of hours of conversations with 27 entrepreneurs about how they make decisions and take action in the face of an unpredictable future—which is where most entrepreneurs operate. Shifting from planning mode to action mode is one of the most important parts of not only starting, but also successfully running a business over time. So it's helpful to know that you can return to effectuation whenever you need to make a decision about your business.

So how does it work? Effectuation walks you through a logical thought process to evaluate the situation you're dealing with. It helps you determine the real nature of your idea and the risks of pursuing it, rather than what you'd *like* to be true in a best case scenario. It takes you from dream mode to action mode, with some potential for harsh truth along the way. There are five key elements involved:

1. **Evaluate your means:** Expert entrepreneurs launch businesses that take advantage of who they are, what they have, what they know, and who they know.
2. **Know your goals and limits:** Successful entrepreneurs think about how much they can afford to lose (otherwise known as their risk tolerance) in terms of time and money to launch and sustain their business.
3. **Learn and adapt:** Expert entrepreneurs expect to make mistakes, have bad luck, and confront failure along the way. They use these

experiences to learn what works, examining what didn't go well to find clues for what they should do differently in the future.

4. **Earn commitments:** Expert entrepreneurs get feedback and commitments from potential customers and key partners as early as possible to reduce the risk of investing their own resources in the business. This can lead to new means and new goals, starting the cycle over again.
5. **Believe:** Expert entrepreneurs believe in themselves and their vision, that they can create a world where their business is successful. They stay focused on what they can control, and tend to ignore what they can't control.

Effectuation in Action: Renee's Restaurant

Perhaps the best way to animate effectuation is with an example. Let's say Renee wants to open a restaurant and acts on her idea. First, Renee considers her resources or means: She has $2,000 saved that she can use for startup costs. She knows how to prepare 10 superb dishes, but she's never worked in a restaurant, so she lacks knowledge and experience on the operations side. On the plus side, a dozen people have said if she opens a restaurant, they will come once a month, but she knows those aren't firm commitments.

Now let's take a look at her goals and limits. Renee does not want to take on debt, but she *is* willing to risk losing the $2,000 in savings because she really wants this idea to work. If she opens a restaurant and doesn't immediately have enough customers to pay the rent, the worst-case scenario is that she has to work three jobs to cover her costs. This is not an outcome that Renee can tolerate, and thus it's becoming clear that her idea may not match her risk appetite.

Now let's look at Renee's interactions. She has about a few thousand followers on social media, but most of them don't live in her area, so they couldn't visit her restaurant regularly. Interestingly, the same people that said they might come to Renee's restaurant also expressed interest in having Renee cater dinners for them in their home. It's becoming clear that perhaps Renee's idea of opening a restaurant isn't a good fit for her. She needs more experience and maybe even a business partner or investor to help her open a restaurant. However the effectuation process has revealed a new opportunity: a catering business.

In the last step, Renee can remove some of the risk from her idea by approaching some potential customers for her catering business idea. Perhaps they have a specific event in the coming months they would pay a deposit for, or even a few recurring dates in the next year. As a result of this process, she realizes that the first version of her business should be a catering business that she can start from her home to practice her recipes and prepare to create amazing food to eventually launch her restaurant. It's lower risk, matches her goals, and aligns with what her prospective customers already want from her.

Notice how after going through the process of effectuation, Renee's idea took a different turn. Her entrepreneurial journey may now look like: catering from home, then shifting to a food truck, and then opening a restaurant one day with a partner. Effectuation helped her decide what to do with the resources she has right now and how to grow her business as her resources increase.

If Renee hadn't gone through the effectuation process, she may have concluded that she shouldn't start the restaurant at all. After all, the risk was too high and she wasn't willing to take on debt. But in the spirit of "just do it," she found something she *could* do, once she took into account the means, goals, interactions, and commitments she did have access to.

Good Ideas Versus Bad Ideas

Renee's story is a good example of the three main areas where effectuation usually helps entrepreneurs.

1. It will help you go from idea to sellable product or service with proven customers.
2. It helps you seek and select partners or mentors that can support you in your business.

3. It provides a foundational technique for making decisions about your business.

In addition, effectuation helps entrepreneurs separate good ideas from bad ideas. In entrepreneurial terms, a good idea tends share these things in common:

- It solves a real specific problem.
- It is a problem that is shared by customers you can actually reach or have access to.
- You're able to pre-sell those customers or gain firm commitments from them.
- You have the potential to scale your idea.

On the contrary, a bad idea solves a generic, nonspecific problem for an overly large or poorly defined group of people. Bad ideas are often already addressed by big companies with lots of resources—ones who can afford to take the hit if things don't work out. Bad ideas are things like new diet supplements (highly regulated), restaurants (extremely competitive and low margins), or an app to sell used goods (platforms already exist). Good ideas can emerge from bad ideas as you narrow the definition of the customer and the solution. For example, a pop-up salon for female domestic violence victims or a textbook exchange for students.

In Renee's case, her customers are working mothers who want good food, but they don't have the time to cook. Rather than solving the generic problem of people needing to eat (fast food does this pretty well), she has 10 people who have committed to engaging her catering services at varying levels. A couple of them want her to cater monthly dinner parties, a few others would like her to cook for them twice a week in their home. With these commitments, Renee has enough resources to start her business.

Practicing effectuation will help you learn to make decisions on what to do next in any scenario, so put it to the test and practice, practice,

practice! With your idea effectuated, you're ready to learn about the entrepreneurial principles that will help you stay on your path to bringing that idea to life.

DISCUSSION GUIDE

- What is your business idea or goal?
- What relevant skills & experience do you have to help you build this business?
- What relevant resources (e.g., equipment, money, etc.) do you have to help you build this business?
- What relevant connections, relationships, people, and followings do you have who will help you build this business?
- What are concrete examples of what you can afford to lose while starting this business? How much time? How much money? What else are you willing to lose?
- How will you show your potential customers and/or partners your idea? Can you make a list of 5 to 10 potential customers and/or partners who you can reach out to and see if they are interested in your business idea? Can you get commitments (verbally or in writing) from them?
- When trying to get commitments from customers or key partners, what did you learn? How can you adapt?
- Effectuate: Is there an approach you can take that is more aligned with the experiences, resources, and connections you already have? Is there another idea or approach you can take that will be less risky? Do you believe in the approach you're taking to building your business?

Entrepreneurial Principles

As an entrepreneur, you never stop learning, and your education begins by learning a few foundational principles that will apply to your business whether you are a solopreneur (that's an entrepreneur who works alone) or have your sights set on building an empire. The principles themselves have one thing in common: learn, learn, learn. If you take away one idea from this book, that's it: learn, especially from your customers.

We've identified six principles that offer a foundation for building your business and can guide you when you're making decisions. You can think of the principles as your business compass—they'll be your North Star when you're deep in the woods with a particular challenge or opportunity. The most successful entrepreneurs do the following, and we do, too:

- Adopt a growth mindset.
- Apply the 40/40/20 Rule.
- Persevere and stay focused.
- Learn from your best teacher: your customer.
- Use the scientific method to evaluate decisions.
- Bootstrap to pay for your startup costs.

Let's take a deeper look at each one.

Growth Mindset

A growth mindset means you believe that you can grow and improve with practice. Entrepreneurs face many obstacles to start a new business. A growth mindset can help you solve problems and tackle obstacles, while encouraging you to see your current skills and talents as traits that can grow with time and effort. The opposite of a *growth mindset* is a *fixed mindset.*

Someone with a fixed mindset might think that only certain people are born to be entrepreneurs, so when it comes to being a successful founder, you either have it or you don't. On the other hand, a growth mindset allows you to see entrepreneurship as a skill that can be improved over time through mentorship and practice, trial and error. At Skysthe-limit.org, we have seen countless times that entrepreneurship can be learned through practice.

You can develop a growth mindset by shifting your thoughts and beliefs around ideas such as failure, comfort zones, and continual learning.

Fail but Grow

Failures and challenges are simply part of the learning process and opportunities for growth. If you don't like to fail, you should think twice about starting a business. As entrepreneurs, we learn through failure, but failure does not define us. Michael Jordan said: "I've missed more than 9,000 shots in my career. I've lost almost 300 games. Twenty-six times I've been trusted to take the game-winning shot and missed. I've failed over and over and over again in my life. And that is why I succeed."

Leave Your Comfort Zone

Staying in your comfort zone—doing tasks that come easy to you or bring you good, predictable results—is, well, comfortable, but if you never leave your comfort zone, you'll never discover your potential nor grow. Be willing to take risks, even small ones, to push the edges of your comfort zone.

Take Time to Reflect and Focus

Because of our hectic, busy lives, taking the time to reflect and refocus can feel wasteful and counterproductive. And yet, an old Zen saying suggests, "Sit in meditation for 20 minutes a day; unless you're too busy, then you should sit for an hour." Take the time to think about your goals, plan how you'll reach them, and reflect on the actions that are working and those that are not. When you take the time to reflect, you shift from reactive to proactive and choose to focus your energy on the actions that will have an impact on the success of your business.

Keep Learning

There are opportunities to learn and be inspired everywhere. While the amount of data can feel overwhelming, learning keeps your mind fresh. Try to spend at least a half hour reading or listening to a podcast each day that will expand your horizons.

Seek Feedback

Feedback from respected peers, customers, and mentors can reveal what you don't know and areas for improvement—sometimes called blind spots, like the places you can't see from the side mirrors of a car. You want to keep an open channel with your customers to make sure your product or service meets their needs and solves their problems. Likewise, discussing your business practices with peers and mentors can save you time and errors. Most of all, remember their criticism is about your business—it's not personal. And also remember—you can't please everyone all the time, you need to filter feedback through your understanding of your main customers and business.

Learn From the Process

There's a saying *the journey is the reward,* and this defines the idea of learning from the process. Of course you want to achieve your goals, but the lessons learned during the process of reaching those goals will impact your success in achieving your next set of goals. This part of the growth mindset pulls together all the previous parts.

The Fixed-Mindset Trap

As you adopt the growth mindset, be on the lookout for your fixed-mindset triggers. When faced with hurdles, constructive feedback, or lower-than-expected results, it's easy to feel insecure, fearful, or defensive—the opposite of the curiosity and willingness to learn that a growth mindset requires. It's also in those moments that we tend to fall back on our habits—good or bad. Be aware of your triggers and habits and be quick to correct them in order to remain focused and thrive with a growth mindset.

The 40/40/20 Rule

Your time is your most precious asset, and your business has a better chance of succeeding if you apply a structured method to allocate your time to your tasks. Many entrepreneurs refer to the Pareto Principle, also known as the 80/20 Rule, which states 80 percent of your output is the result of 20 percent of your effort. We've refined and developed our own 40/40/20 Rule and recommend that you spend:

- 40 percent of your time selling to your customers (learn more in Chapter 3, Customer Development)
- 40 percent of your time improving your product or service for your customers (learn more in Chapter 4, Product and Service Development)
- 20 percent of your time learning how to improve your business, and working on the operations, from your website to accounting to strategy (learn more in Chapter 9, Operations)

You'll improve your product or service by talking to your customers—this is why it is *so* critical to spend a lot of time trying to sell your product or service even from an early stage! When you're developing your product or service, you want to think both creatively and critically about what makes your product or service unique (we write about the Unique Selling Proposition in Chapter 2, Product-Market Fit). Consider the problems you are solving and why customers should pay for your offer.

Salespeople live by the motto, *always be closing* (well, for 40 percent of the time). The time you allot for selling includes improving your marketing and sales channel (see Chapter 5, Marketing and Sales), actively pursuing leads, and meeting with potential customers and partners.

With an active growth mindset, you want to spend time learning how to improve and grow your business. As detailed later in this chapter and the next, you want to test your ideas quickly and methodically to create a constant feedback loop—and that feedback drives the improvements to your product or service.

Focus, Focus, Focus (Persevere and Stay Focused)

Our editor for this book said the number one reason people don't finish writing their books is because they have too many ideas and jump around from one to the other. The same is true of entrepreneurs: too many ideas either leave you procrastinating as you try to choose one or exhausted as you try to manage all of them.

We all have the same number of hours in the day and as discussed in the principles of a growth mindset and the 40/40/20 rule, you need to allocate your time appropriately to keep moving toward a successful business. Focusing on one business at a time will ensure you deliver value for your customers, while spending your time working toward the success of one venture. This doesn't mean that you can't eventually have multiple businesses—that's quite common for entrepreneurs, particularly those entrepreneurs who have built robust teams and systems to the point their businesses can run without them in the day-to-day operations. These are ideas we discuss in Chapters 9 and 12, Operations, and Building a Team.

First you need to decide which idea to concentrate on. As described earlier, effectuating your idea involves thinking about your means in relation to the idea, talking to potential customers about their problems, and matching your idea (solution) to their problem. You may learn during effectuation that a different idea is actually better for your business than your original idea.

Many entrepreneurs have the attention span of a goldfish and are quick to be enthusiastic about a new idea. If that's you, it may seem boring to focus on one thing and say no to the other 99 that cross your path, but it's one of the most effective ways to achieve your entrepreneurial goals. Less time spent on other projects means more time spent on your true vision and more time spent working toward that success. And in the Cycle of Starting a Business, you may just find that another idea you had is better for you now than the one you started with.

Your Customer Is Your Best Teacher

If you look back to our definition of entrepreneurship—creating value for a group of people in a way that sustains a profitable business—the question that should come to mind is *how do I know that I'm creating value people want?* Talk to your customer. You'll read that time and again in these pages, but you don't have a business without customers; your business (your product or service) and your customers are two sides of the same coin. Learning from your customer about what they want, about what you're doing well and where you need improvement, will help guide your business to success.

Scientific Methodology for Entrepreneurship

Once you've settled on an idea through effectuation, you want to test it with the market. We suggest you apply the scientific method to your idea. Don't worry—you don't have to go back to seventh grade or wear a lab coat.

There are six basic steps to the scientific method (we've included the technical terms for those steps in parentheses). Translated to business terms it might look like this:

1. Start with a hunch that something might work, or that you've identified a valuable business idea or problem that needs solving. (Define the question.)
2. Create a prototype, business idea, or outline that you can show to other people. (Make a hypothesis.)
3. Do market research and get commitments from your network—will people buy this, do they need it, do they think this is a problem? (Gather evidence.)
4. Make changes and improvements to your idea based on the feedback you've gained. (Analyze the data you've gathered.)
5. Sell it to them again. (Draw a conclusion.)
6. Repeat!

For your business, the scientific method guides you through the process of **testing your idea** (whether that's for your product, a marketing campaign, or a job posting), **gathering evidence** (are people responding positively to it or not, and how do you know), and **adapting your idea** (making changes that reflect the evidence and feedback). This cycle is repeated again and again and helps you respond quickly to the marketplace. It saves you from spending a lot of time and resources to create a product or service that you believe is perfect, only to discover no one wants it because it doesn't solve their problems or meet their needs. Usually this happens because you didn't talk to your customer enough along the way to have learned that earlier.

Of course, having ideas, building prototypes, and getting feedback from customers is all well and good, but how will you pay your startup costs? Let's take a look at an approach called bootstrapping.

Bootstrapping

Most entrepreneurs don't have a lump of cash to start their business. They need to be creative with their resources and more often than not, rely on themselves to cover those initial startup costs. Many entrepreneurs—including Richard Branson, Steve Jobs, and the founders of Airbnb, Mailchimp, Shopify, and GoPro—started their business by bootstrapping. The term comes from the idea of pulling yourself up by the straps on your boots (back in the day, boots had straps) and means using the few resources you have to start your business. The concept can be misleading and has even been criticized because some entrepreneurs have bigger, stronger boots than others (like having a parent or relative who's willing to invest in their idea or college degree in business). Many entrepreneurs from low-income communities don't even have the boots to begin with, just like they don't have a family and friends network who can loan them money to start their business. Likewise, they may lack the skills or experience to approach potential customers. But these are just obstacles to navigate, and Skysthelimit.org exists to help you solve these problems by offering many online resources and a mentor network.

If you're building your business with your personal savings and cash from first sales, then you are a bootstrapper. Sites like Kickstarter and GoFundMe are founded on the concept of bootstrapping: you use the resources you have to create a sample product and build out the campaign, then people buy your product/service before it's ready. That's the feedback discussed in both effectuation and the scientific method. You use the money they pay in advance to bring your idea to life and then deliver it.

Using your own resources to launch your business also means that you take on all the financial risks and responsibilities. As you effectuate your business idea, you define the amount of financial risk you're willing—and can afford—to take. Bootstrapping also comes with advantages; since you answer only to yourself, you have full control of your business and can move forward as quickly or slowly as you like without having to meet expectations of an external investor. With careful planning and budgeting, bootstrapping can be an excellent way to start your business. Ideally as you build your business you will find partners and investors who can help support you (we discuss that in Chapter 13, Funding and Finance), but your first and top investor will, of course, be YOU!

Perfection is a trap. "Good enough" is an entrepreneur's mantra.

Launching a "good enough" service or product that has some value as soon as possible—and then talking to customers and getting their feedback on how to improve—is much better than waiting to build the "perfect" service or product. Perfection often masks itself as procrastination; you put off launching or you tinker with the details or tell yourself you have to wait for the full moon when Saturn and Jupiter are aligned, but the longer you keep your idea in your head without getting feedback from your customers, the riskier your business idea gets. Done and shipped is better than perfect—"perfect" doesn't exist!

DISCUSSION GUIDE

- Do you have a growth mindset?
- Of the ideas behind a growth mindset—Fail but Grow, Leave Your Comfort Zone, Take Time to Reflect and Focus, Keep Learning, Seek Feedback, Learn from the Process—which one is most challenging to you?
- How can you apply each of the growth mindset ideas in your business?
- Do you divide your time following the 40/40/20 rule? If not, where do you need to spend more time or less time?
- Can effectuation help you narrow your focus down to one business idea? What is that idea?
- Are you talking to your customers (or potential customers) on a daily basis to get feedback and learn how to improve?
- What assumptions or hypotheses have you made about your idea? Have you tested it with the scientific methodology described above?
- As a bootstrapper, what resources do you have, either your own or from your network?

What Business Will You Build?

As you reach the end of this chapter, we hope you're excited about being an entrepreneur, have found clarity around your idea by answering the questions in the discussion guides, and feel ready to get started. Taking the time to go through the thought processes outlined in this chapter before launching your entrepreneurial endeavor goes a long way to setting you on the path to success.

CHECKLIST

- ✓ Define your why.
- ✓ Tell a friend or family member about your motivations for your business.
- ✓ Practice effectuation.
- ✓ Review the entrepreneurial principles.
- ✓ Get a notebook or find a place to write down all your business notes.
- ✓ Schedule a specific time block to work on your business in the next month—and put it on your calendar.
- ✓ Apply the scientific method and lean approach to your idea.
- ✓ Set up a call with a peer or your business advisor to go through the questions in the Discussion Guide.

CHAPTER 2

Product-Market Fit

> **When Should You Read This Chapter?**
> We believe understanding Product-Market Fit is critical to confirming the existence of paying customers for your product or service idea. This chapter helps entrepreneurs just starting out as well as those who are struggling to succeed or who want to expand their offer—essentially, this chapter is for everyone!

Entrepreneurship is about action. Bringing your business to life means thinking about *what* you want to build and thinking about *how* to make it a business. It's worth thinking about how you will make money to sustain your business early on. You make money when you create and offer something—a product or service—that people want to pay for. The sweet spot where your idea matches the customer's desire is called Product-Market Fit and modern business planning begins here.

We've found, as you read about in Chapter 1, Entrepreneurial Foundations, you'll learn far more from testing your ideas with customers instead of spending a lot of time writing a 100 page business plan. That doesn't mean you fly by the seat of your pants. When we think about a new business idea, we write down our answers to a few core questions that guide all the activities of running a business. We begin with two questions to create a Product-Market Fit Plan:

- What's the idea?
- Who is the customer?

At this point, you probably haven't talked with any customers, so your initial answers are based on assumptions you make. In our experience, the best way to improve your assumptions is to talk with potential customers, a process we detail fully in Chapter 3, Customer Development. We detail the product development process in Chapter 4, Product and Service Development.

The Bias Trap

The more evidence an entrepreneur has that there's demand for their idea, the less likely they'll fall into the bias trap—believing they know something the market doesn't. The best way to avoid the bias trap is to talk to as many customers as you can: potential, past, and present. Even there, listen carefully because it's easy to hear what you want to hear.

Product-Market Fit (PMF)

Remember our definition of entrepreneurship: figuring out what you can make or do (product/service) that is valuable enough for a group of people (customers/market) to buy at a profit for your business. The relationship between the two—product/service and customers/market—is called Product-Market Fit (PMF). PMF is a spectrum from no fit to perfect fit. Companies that succeed have some degree of PMF. Your company falls somewhere on the line depending on how well your product meets a given group of customers' needs. To move farther to the right on the spectrum, you have two variables you can tweak: one is your product—you can change what you're offering for a given group of customers. And second is your customers—you can offer the same product to a different group of customers. Making a change can suddenly increase (or decrease) your PMF. The closer you are to perfect fit, the better your chances of success.

Testing Your Idea

Because it's based on assumptions, your first PMF is preliminary. You've effectuated your idea (see Chapter 1, Entrepreneurial Foundations) and applied the scientific method, but once you define the preliminary PMF, you need to test your key assumptions *before* you build your product/service. (We fully discuss product development in Chapter 4, Product and Service Development.)

In the early stages of your business, you should be focusing far more on proving the existence of a market opportunity than creating a sample product or service. Your efforts to talk to customers—to identify and find the right customers to talk to—are paramount to your success.

In 2011 entrepreneur Eric Ries wrote *The Lean Startup*, which applies a software development framework called Lean to starting a business. Ries suggests that entrepreneurs create the Minimal Viable Product (MVP)—the simplest, feature-free version of your product (or service) that you can create while maintaining its usability. Ries, and many entrepreneurs who have used the Lean approach, believe it will save entrepreneurs time and resources by letting them test and develop their ideas in small increments, making changes as they go rather than building something nobody wants.

For example, Skysthelimit.org started by working one-on-one with young first-time entrepreneurs in Morocco to write a business plan. This was the MVP before developing a platform, curriculum or mentor network. Like the scientific method, the Lean approach can save you time and resources by letting you test and develop your ideas in small increments, making changes as you go rather than building something nobody wants. Lean Methodology requires you to ask customers to test your idea, iterate quickly based on their feedback, and then act on the information to make changes to your product or service. After some repetition, you will have something that already has satisfied customers. That said, however, while MVP is an enduring concept in business, it may not be the best route for new entrepreneurs.

The problem we, and other present-day entrepreneurs, see with Lean is that an MVP is an untested solution. Lean puts the cart before the horse. People want solutions, but they want solutions that solve their problems. Entrepreneurs can discover solutions and talk with customers about them before building anything. Bootstrapping entrepreneurs need to spend their resources wisely; understanding the needs and demands of their potential customers before they build a solution allows them to do so.

Perhaps building an MVP was the most efficient way to test the market 15 years ago, but that's no longer the case. Social media, websites, and the internet offer so many possibilities to talk to your customer, learn about their problems, and determine the demand for a solution. For the cost of a domain (see Chapter 7, Website and Technology), you can create a landing page that explains your product or service concept and see how many people respond. You can run targeted ads on social media to gauge interest and collect data about your customers. You can use AI to create a digital prototype. If people are clicking and signing up for your newsletter, that signals interest in your offer without even having a product or service yet.

What's more, the people who share their contact information with you are exactly the people you can reach out to for surveys, interviews, and pre-sales. If we've said it once, we'll say it a dozen more times: learn, learn, learn from your customer before you build anything. Putting your customer first, ahead of your offer, is the modern entrepreneur's key to success.

The steps to creating a valid, verified PMF are listed here. Look back at the work you did for effectuation and bring that forward as you write your PMF and determine where your idea falls on the product-market spectrum. You'll learn more about your customer and your product in the next two chapters, so you can repeat this exercise later as you gather more information.

1. Think about the problems your customer has and the solution you offer = Product-Market Fit Plan.
2. Identify your differentiation, simple vs. complex for example.
3. Test your product/service with your potential customers *before* you actually develop it.
4. Create your first version or prototype, keeping in mind the problem it solves for the customer.
5. Determine your price point based on market expectations (and make sure to cover your production costs).
6. Start selling (or at least showing) your product or service to your customers.
7. Conduct follow-up interviews with customers for feedback and improvement on your product, learn who's buying, what they want, what they're willing to spend.
8. Iterate your product/service to satisfy the market or change the market to one that wants your product.

Let's go through the process behind these steps.

Analysis Paralysis Trap

While we do recommend you analyze and evaluate your product and the market, there is a thing as too much analysis—known as *analysis paralysis*. For many entrepreneurs, especially those who are perfectionists, this trap looks and feels like doing the right work, but they're really stuck spinning their wheels, analyzing all the data but procrastinating on taking action.

We believe the best data comes from talking with your customers. If they are willing to buy your product/service, you are headed in the right direction; if they are not willing to buy, it's your job to figure out how to make your product or service more valuable at the right price-point, i.e., price too high or too low, features missing, they can find a better solution elsewhere. Adjust and change your offer accordingly and try to sell it again.

Map Your Preliminary PMF

Your preliminary PMF presents the starting point for your assumptions and will change as you talk to your customer to learn about their problem and improve your idea based on the information you learn. The preliminary PMF has two data points:

- Idea (product/service)
- Market (presumed customer)

Let's say you have a vision for a global clothing company. You see yourself designing clothes, traveling to source fabric, setting up a factory that employs local people to produce the items, and selling online. Maybe a celebrity wears your creation to an international music award event, and sales skyrocket.

We love to aim high, but before you write the business plan for your global conglomerate, think about who will buy your first product—that's your Product-Market Fit Plan. Too many entrepreneurs fail because they begin too many steps ahead, starting out too big or not having thought about the PMF. Once you have a well-defined PMF, you can create an actionable plan for producing your product/service, selling it to your customers, and, if you want, growing your business. Like most things entrepreneurial, your PMF will change as you learn more about your customer's desires and grow your business.

DISCUSSION GUIDE

- Who do you think your customer is?
- What problems do you think your customer has?
- How do you know they are facing those problems?
- Of the problems your customer has, which problem do you solve?
- What solution do you offer to that problem?

Unique Selling Proposition and Advantage

The first steps guide entrepreneurs to think about how their idea can be a business by answering questions about the concept, the features and advantages their product/service offers, and how their offer is different from other similar products/services in the market. The advantages identified become the Unique Selling Proposition (USP).

Your USP can be better, faster, or cheaper than the competition. We discuss focusing on the benefits you offer to the customer in Chapter 5, Marketing and Sales. Typically, you can be two of the three—better and faster, but not cheaper; faster and cheaper, but not better; or better and cheaper, but not faster. How are you different from your competition? Think broadly about this question: are you easier to work with or offer better customer service? Do you have newer/better/different equipment or methods?

Your advantage can be just about anything. Perhaps you have a lawn care service and you have the newest version of lawn mower that not only cuts the grass and minces it into mulch (cutting down on waste and fertilizer costs) but is also battery powered, so it's both silent and environmentally friendly. With your silent mower, you can cut your customer's lawn without disturbing their neighbors. Your lawn care is probably better than the competition, but is it also faster or cheaper? You have a state-of-the-art mower so it could be faster but perhaps you need to recover the investment costs of the mower. Or, since the mower is electric, perhaps your service can be cheaper because you don't have to pay for gas to fill the tank.

Make a list of all the problems you think your customer has, then think about which of those problems your offer helps them solve and how. Are you better, faster, or cheaper? As you think and make assumptions about your customer's problem and desire, also think through the advantages and your USP. Then you want to talk to your customer to confirm your assumptions. In Chapter 3, Customer Development, we outline questions to ask your customer to learn about and understand their problems—with that understanding, you can create a viable product or service.

DISCUSSION GUIDE

- What are the advantages and features of your product/service, your Unique Selling Proposition?
- How could your offer be better than other solutions available?
- How could your offer be faster than other solutions available?
- How could your offer be cheaper than other solutions available?
- How are you different from your competition?

Determine Your Price

We can probably all agree that we need money to live, and generating an income and profit is often one of the reasons for becoming an entrepreneur. An entrepreneur usually needs to replace the income they would otherwise earn from a traditional job working for someone else. Figuring out how much to charge for a product or service can be one of the hardest aspects of entrepreneurship, and once again, it is an iterative process.

Pricing doesn't happen by pulling a number out of thin air when you're selling to a customer. It happens through thoughtful consideration of the value of the solution you offer, the cost the market will sustain (meaning how much the customer is willing to pay), the costs of producing the solution you sell, and how much profit you'd like to make. When you talk to customers about your product/service, they'll want to know how much you charge to determine if your price aligns with the value they perceive you offer. Here we're presenting the minimum you need to consider with pricing; we talk about pricing in depth in Chapter 4, Product and Service Development, and fully discuss budgeting, bookkeeping, and accounting in Chapter 10, Accounting and Bookkeeping.

The Hidden Cost Trap

We believe in value-based pricing and so we explain pricing through that lens throughout this book. At the same time, all entrepreneurs have expenses and want to make a profit, so you need to make sure the price you establish will cover those expenses. Though we created a nonprofit organization with Skysthelimit.org, we still have expenses to cover to run our organization. We pay developers and designers to build our app and have sales and marketing costs to attract both mentors and entrepreneurs, as well as funders like corporates and donors. Even if you are a solopreneur who offers dog sitting services, you'll likely spend some money on marketing, whether that's your smartphone to promote yourself on social media or fliers you print and hang up on the bulletin boards of your local veterinarian and pet supply stores. Then, maybe you need to purchase special leashes to walk more than one dog at a time or dog treats to keep the pooches on your good side. When you're starting out, especially in an online business or a service that requires little equipment, it's easy to overlook small expenses, not to mention the value of your time. We talk more about bookkeeping in Chapter 10, Accounting and Bookkeeping, but for now you can keep a list on your phone or in a small notebook of the time and expenses you spend on your business.

DISCUSSION GUIDE

- What value does your solution offer to customers?
- Can you place a dollar value on that solution?
- What do other people offering a similar solution charge?
- How much time do you plan to spend building/creating/selling your product or service?
- Do you use equipment you already own to make your product or conduct your service?
- What price will the market support for your product or service?

Key Assumptions and Iteration

Your key assumptions are the starting point of your business—you have an idea for a product or service, and you assume people will pay you for that product or service. You assume there are people who have a problem that your product/service solves. Your Unique Selling Proposition assumes that your product or service solves the problem better/faster/cheaper than someone else's.

Entrepreneurs are not always aware they're making assumptions, an idea we covered in The Bias Trap earlier in this chapter. Using the lawn care service as an example, an entrepreneur may drive around a neighborhood of a few hundred homes with manicured lawns and assume that half of those homeowners would hire them to care for their lawn—but that may not be realistic. They need to consider how many other lawn care service providers are already satisfying the customers in that neighborhood and how many homeowners mow their own lawn. It may be more realistic to assume that 10 percent of the homeowners would hire this new lawn care entrepreneur. In their enthusiasm for their idea and potential, entrepreneurs often assume the potential market is grander than it really is.

Early in the process you must ask, *are your assumptions correct*? The sooner you speak to potential customers to verify your assumptions, the sooner your business will be off the ground. (We give you a full process for interviewing customers in Chapter 3, Customer Development.) You can begin to test your assumptions with internet research. Again, with the lawn care service, you could search for the number of homeowners in a given neighborhood and the number of lawn care companies in the area, but don't stop there. You need to talk to real people. You can begin with people you know who either are, or know, potential customers. Ask them if they use a lawn care service, are they happy with the service and why or why not. If they don't use a lawn care service, what will convince them to do so? Maybe you drive through the neighborhood on a Saturday morning when people are outside and stop to ask if they use a lawn care service.

You could also test your assumptions in a less proactive, more passive way. Post a paper or digital flier on local bulletin boards and see what kind of response you get. Highlight your Unique Selling Proposition and when potential customers call you, ask questions that help you confirm your assumptions or iterate your offer.

The feedback from your customer interviews should enable you to improve your product/service to bring you ever closer to a perfect fit. If, however, during interviews with potential customers, you find that no one wants your product/service, that doesn't necessarily mean your idea is awful, but rather that you need to redefine your market and customer—maybe you're trying to sell the right thing to the wrong person. Starting small even when you have big ideas helps you avoid costly mistakes.

The "I Hate Selling" Trap

All too often we hear entrepreneurs say, "I hate selling" (or the variation, "I hate marketing"). We say, "Stop selling! Solve problems and create value." People in the world have problems that you solve; bringing your solution to them is an act of generosity and helping, not sales.

Remember the 40/40/20 Rule includes improving, selling, and learning. If you struggle to sell your idea, you will struggle to develop a solid PMF. You need both effective sales and a viable product to reach the right end of the PMF spectrum. Sometimes people only have one or the other. In that case, you may want to consider bringing in a partner to make up for the skill or idea that you lack. See Chapter 12, Building a Team, to learn more about working with a partner.

DISCUSSION GUIDE

- What are your assumptions about your customer: Who do you believe your customer is? Is your customer willing to pay the price you're asking?
- How will you test your assumptions with your customers?
- After talking to your customers, what will you change about your product or service?
- Will you raise or lower your price?
- Does your solution match the problem the customer has?
- If not, do you need to make changes to your solution or try to reach a different customer?

Product-Market Fit Plan

We like to write our assumptions and feedback in a simple grid that captures everything we think so far about our idea. It looks like this:

Customer	Problem	Solution

The Product-Market Fit Plan is an initial evaluation of your business idea. It clearly displays the customer you serve and how your idea solves their problem. In the next two chapters, we do a deep dive into the customer and the product.

CHECKLIST

- ✓ Write down the advantages and unique selling proposition of your product/service.
- ✓ Identify your differentiation.
- ✓ Design and execute your product/service testing experiments to determine if customers want what you are thinking of selling.
- ✓ Create your first version or prototype.
- ✓ Determine your price point based on your production costs and market expectations.
- ✓ List your assumptions about your customer and the market potential.
- ✓ Test your assumptions by conducting interviews with potential customers for feedback and improvement.
- ✓ Learn who's buying, what they want, what they're willing to spend.
- ✓ Iterate your product/service to satisfy the market or change the market to one that wants your product.
- ✓ Write your Product-Market Fit Plan.

CHAPTER 3

Customer Development

When Should You Read This Chapter?
Knowing and learning from your customer is a core concept of how we think about entrepreneurship. This chapter should be read as soon as possible, regardless of how far along you are in creating your business.

Conceptually, we've explained Product-Market Fit and the steps to move your idea to the right of the PMF spectrum. The activities of Product-Market Fit are Product Development and Customer Development, and they are intricately entwined in every step of the entrepreneurial journey. You can't develop your product without your customers, and you can't develop your customers without your product. To fully understand each, we present them one at a time, beginning with the customer, because it is your customer's feedback that will impact the product you eventually sell.

The "Market" part of PMF represents the customers who will buy a product or service. But what—or who—is a customer exactly and why does an entrepreneur care? A customer is a person (or another business) with a problem that you can solve. Entrepreneurs who deeply understand their customers are much more likely to succeed, whereas entrepreneurs who have only a simple, superficial, general understanding of their customers need to invest time here. Remember, it's 40 percent of the 40/40/20 Rule.

As we outlined in the previous chapter, Product-Market Fit requires testing your product/service by showing it—ideally selling it—to customers, listening to their feedback, making your product/service better by adding or eliminating features, and then taking it back to the customer, selling and/or listening to feedback, improving, and repeating this process as your business grows.

If your customer doesn't like your product/service, meaning no one is buying it or placing early orders, you have two choices:

- Change your product
- Look for a different customer

How do you know when to pivot and when to persevere? You return to the Product-Market Fit sequence and either present a different product to the existing potential customer or present the existing product to a new potential customer. But that brings us back to the question: who is your customer?

In this chapter, we suggest writing a customer profile or "persona" that includes demographics and psychographics. We then guide you to think about different types of customer segmentation. Finally, we discuss writing a customer problem statement to determine if your idea solves the problem your intended customer has.

Customer Profile or "Persona"

You want to describe your customer so you can answer the question, *who will buy what you're selling?* During your entrepreneurial journey, you'll often hear or read about your ideal customer, your target audience, your customer profile, or persona; each of these terms describes the person who will buy what you're selling. The "person" the words define is fictional but the qualities they have are real. The terms come up when you read articles or listen to podcasts about marketing, building an email list, or creating new products. If you buy advertising, the ad salesperson will ask. If you hire a designer for your logo, website, or brand collateral, they'll ask, too. Who is your customer?

Every time entrepreneurs or companies, big or small, have a new idea or a significantly different iteration of their product or service, they go back to the customer to make sure assumptions they're making about the customer's problem and the size of the market are true. The better an entrepreneur understands their customer and the problems the customer wants to solve, the more specific they can be in their customer profile and the better they can design and develop their product. In the beginning, entrepreneurs make assumptions about their customers—who they are and what they need—then they test those assumptions by interviewing the customers. Let's look at the steps to creating a customer profile.

Who Is Your Customer?

Most businesses sell their product or service to more than one type of customer. For example, Skysthelimit.org thinks of four types of customers: entrepreneurs, volunteers, corporate partners, and individual donors. When you first begin working on a customer profile, think about a large, broad category that all your customers fit into. This could be by gender, such as women, or it could be by profession, such as teachers, hair stylists, or retired people. Like Skysthelimit.org, you may have more than one type of general customer. To begin, however, choose the one whose problem you can best solve. Our main focus is entrepreneurs, so we'll continue to use that as an example.

After you identify the general customer, you want to think about segmentation—that's a fancy marketing term that means dividing that broad customer group into smaller, easier-to-approach groups. For Skysthelimit.org, entrepreneurs is a huge group. There are idea-stage entrepreneurs, post-launch entrepreneurs, serial entrepreneurs, and more than a dozen others. When we think about the biggest segment we can help, we identify young entrepreneurs who have an idea but haven't yet started their business. So, idea-stage entrepreneurs is our first, or primary, segment.

The better you can segment your customers, the better you can solve their problems and market to them. Segmentation informs how you communicate with your customers when you tell them about your product or service. You want to highlight the features that solve their specific problem. (You can read more about marketing in Chapter 5, Marketing and Sales.) This, of course, adds complexity and effort to your business, so you want to start with your biggest, best customer profile first to maximize your returns. Over time, you can create additional customer profiles and associated marketing and sales efforts for each. But in the beginning, keep it simple and choose the single, best one.

The goal of creating a customer profile is to be super specific. The next step defines the demographics and psychographics of your primary segment.

DISCUSSION GUIDE

- Who is your customer, in a broad, general sense?
- Do you have more than one type of customer? If so, which one is the most important to you?
- What are the segments within your broad customer group?
- Of those segments, which one is the biggest, best segment that you help?

The Segmentation Trap

When entrepreneurs begin to think about their customers and the various segments they want to reach, they often think, *I can help all of them.* That may be true, but it's critical for any entrepreneur or business owner to be specific about their customer. The more specific the customer profile, the easier it will be to reach that customer.

Customer Demographics, Psychographics, and Mindsets

With your primary customer segment defined, you can now get specific: visualize them physically and write down details like their age, gender, ethnicity, residence, marital status, education, job, etc. Simple demographics like age, marital status, and income can be helpful to initially define and locate your customers but they don't offer insight to buying habits. To design viable products and services, entrepreneurs need to consider how people behave and what's important to them when dealing with the problem they're trying to solve. In addition to their demographics, describe your customer's pain, their problem, their passions, and desires, especially in relation to your product or service—we call these psychographics or mindsets.

Psychographics and mindsets identify people based on their emotional desires and expectations. Mindsets are a series of perceptions or beliefs people have about themselves—not necessarily about your product or service, although it can come into play. Mindset helps you determine why someone might buy your product or service. For example, if a customer has the mindset that they are trendy, they choose clothes that reflect that attitude. Entrepreneurs who understand the different mindsets within their target audience can adapt the way they talk about and sell their product to match the customer's mindset.

Mindsets are divided into five major categories:

- **Beliefs**: Find out what your audience believes in (community, friends and family, any activities, ways of thinking, etc.) and then see how your product/service can coincide with those beliefs and values.
- **Hopes and fears**: You can think of this in relation to your industry, but try to think big picture and talk with your loyal customers to understand what makes them feel fulfilled vs. disappointed.
- **Emotional needs**: Appealing to emotions is a great marketing tactic, but you need to know what emotional needs are at play in

the first place. The need for security, acceptance, affirmation, and self-esteem can be huge.

- **Expectations**: This is where you build trust with your customer. People like to know the products and services they purchase align with their values, ethics, and social constructs.
- **Brand perceptions**: In the early stages of your business, your customers won't yet have a perception of your brand, but as you gain customers, you can ask how they describe your product/service to others.

As you develop a description for your customer profile, adding psychographics helps you truly see who will pay for your product or service. You can learn about your customer's mindsets through interviewing them (we give you suggestions for doing this later in this chapter) and putting together focus groups, polls, or surveys—all of which you can do online. Then, when you write your ideal customer description, make sure you touch on all the points listed.

The right product at the right time is critical for every business, especially new businesses. Knowing what your customer wants can make or break the success of your company. The best Product-Market Fit limits the range of potential customers to the ones who are willing and able to buy your product.

Thinking about these questions helps you narrow the group of customers you want to reach and will be helpful when you begin marketing and want to figure out where these people hang out. You may believe your customer is all women but not all women have the same problems, so you want to narrow that definition. Maybe you believe your customer is any woman in their twenties, but you can narrow the description more to define your customer as women of color in their twenties who are single and attending community college. They are typically the first in their family to go to college and are looking for scholarships to help pay for tuition. The specificity helps you consider the problems they have, find potential customers to talk to about those problems, and target your marketing to them.

When you put the answers together in a paragraph it might look something like our description of the entrepreneurs we want to reach with Skysthelimit.org:

> *Skysthelimit.org entrepreneurs are between the ages of 18 and 29, mostly BIPOC located in a mid-size to large city, and all of them are passionate about launching their business idea. Generally, they make about $25,000 per year before they join Skysthelimit.org. They have skills and experience to build their product or deliver their service but need help creating a business around these skills. They generally need some structure around building a business, some good advice, people to bounce ideas off, a network of professionals who can support them, new customers to sell their products and services to, and some money to get their business up and running.*

DISCUSSION GUIDE

Describe your customer's demographic:

- In general, how would you describe your customer?
- How old are they?
- What gender do they identify with?
- What's their ethnicity?
- Where do they live?
- Are they married or in a committed relationship?
- Do they have children?
- What education do they have (e.g., high school, college)? Where did they go to school? What school do they attend if they're still in school?
- What type of job do they have? Or are they unemployed or a student?

- What's their income?
- Does your customer go to church, and if so, what church do they belong to?
- What kind of sports does your customer play?
- What hobbies do they have? What do they do for fun?
- Was your customer born in the US or did they immigrate from another country?
- How many people live in your customer's household?
- What is their political affiliation (e.g., Democrat, Republican, other)?
- What type of body does your customer have (tall, thin, short, robust, etc.)?
- What is your customer's clothing style (formal, urban, casual, etc.)?
- What does your customer spend most of their time doing (e.g., working, going to school, traveling, hanging with friends, playing video games, sports, etc.)?
- What kind of TV shows, movies, and music does your customer like?
- What kind of causes does your customer care about (e.g., animals, religion, politics, the environment, children, etc.)?
- What kinds of products or services does your customer spend lots of money on (e.g., housing, food, travel, self-care, clothes, etc.)?
- *Describe your customer's psychographics and mindset:*
- What keeps them up at night?
- What makes them happy?
- What are they afraid of?
- What do they believe in?
- What do they desire in life?
- What's the biggest challenge on their mind?
- What would change if their problem was solved?
- Write a paragraph that describes your customer.

The Friends and Family Trap

Interviewing your family and friends as potential customers doesn't count as good data for making business decisions. Your family and friends love you and want to see you succeed so they may buy your product and tell you it's wonderful. We hate to break it to you, but your friends and family aren't your customers. Even if they pay you for your product or service, their support isn't enough. We have seen entrepreneurs get a bunch of interest in their idea from their mom and their close friends, so they go out and spend a lot of money on building their company only to realize that no one else wants what they are selling. Family and friends are too nice—the market isn't.

Your first real customer will be outside of your family and circle of friends.

Customer Problems

What problems does your business solve for your customers? Successful businesses solve clear problems for their customers. For example, Skysthelimit.org customers (early-stage entrepreneurs) often have the following problems:

1. They don't know the steps to take to start their business or grow it.
2. They don't know where to get money for their business.
3. They need business experts who can help them solve specific problems for their business (like legal questions, or accounting for their money).
4. They want someone who can help them stay accountable to keep working on their business idea.
5. They need someone who is trustworthy, reliable and experienced who they can bounce ideas off of and who understands their particular business.

We know this because we talked to those types of entrepreneurs. In the beginning, we had some assumptions (right or wrong) about what early-stage entrepreneurs needed, then those assumptions were confirmed or we made changes based on feedback.

Likewise, when you come up with the idea for your business, you make assumptions about your customer and the problem you solve for them. As you get to know your customer better, you will gain more insight into their specific problem. Remember, Product-Market Fit is all about offering a solution to your customer's problem. Think of items or services you've bought; you made the purchase because you think that product or service will solve one of your problems. When you buy new jeans, they may solve the problem of replacing an old pair or may make you feel great because you've recently lost weight. When you eat at a restaurant, you think that food will taste great or satisfy your hunger.

If you want to make products and services that your customers will love, focus on how you can solve your customers' problems. To do this, you'll want to write a customer problem statement. A well-written customer problem statement should be as specific as possible and include the following:

- Identify your target market. This information comes from your ideal customer description.
- Define the size of the market. You can infer this from your customer's demographics in terms of where they live.
- Define the size of the problem. Is the customer's problem life or death, or something smaller?
- Define the current problem. This statement summarizes the first three data points.

For example: Customers who buy t-shirts in Oakland, CA are having trouble finding t-shirts that have both stylish cuts and trendy designs. Notice that this example does not talk about the solution, only the issue. It defines a specific customer group with whom you can build empathy.

It reflects the actual customer problem, which you can solve but it could have more details as you learn more about the customer's problem.

When you first write your customer problem statement, you may still be in assumption mode. Maybe you've done some online research about your customer, you've thought about the demographics and mindsets, but you haven't yet actually interviewed customers. You'll refine the problem statement after talking to the customer and reframing the problem based on their feedback.

For example, after you talk to twenty or so potential customers about their t-shirt problem, you can narrow the problem statement to be: Women in their twenties who buy t-shirts in Oakland, CA have trouble finding t-shirts that have stylish cuts and trendy designs that give them a sense of confidence when they wear them because they are flattering to a full-figured woman's body without looking like a baggy man's t-shirt.

Chances are your customer has more than one problem and if you defined multiple customer segments, each segment may have a different problem, or set of problems. Write a statement for each problem you can think of and rank them by putting the problems that your product/service solves best or the most at the top of the list.

The better you define the exact problem you believe exists, the more accurately you can test whether the problem truly exists for your customers. As we've written earlier, make sure your potential customers actually have the problems you think they do BEFORE you risk a ton of time and money on creating something no one wants. And remember, this is an iterative process—you will need to continuously seek out your customer's problems and make sure your products and services are actually solving them!

DISCUSSION GUIDE

- What is your customer's problem?
- Use the Five Whys method (see Chapter 1, Entrepreneurial Foundations) to add details to the problem statement.
- How urgent or pressing is your customer's problem?
- What problem(s) does your business solve?
- Does your business solve your customer's problem?

Competitors

Very few products are truly brand-new today. It's really hard to come up with something that no one has done before—and truth be told, even harder to sell something no one has done before. One of our mentors told us when we were just starting out, "If someone else is doing it, it means there's a market." And, as we wrote in Chapter 2, Product-Market Fit, your product or service has a Unique Selling Proposition that makes it either better, faster, or cheaper than the competition. Competition is a healthy component of a thriving economy, and you can learn a lot from your competition about the market and your customer.

When a customer considers buying from you, they're going to compare you to their existing solution provider (your competition). You need to know how you are different and be able to express your Unique Selling Proposition to the potential customer. Does your product use better quality ingredients or materials than the competition? Do you deliver exceptional high quality service in record time? Does your product/service cost less?

You want to know how your customer receives the product or service—this will be critical information as you read Chapter 4, Product and Service Development. In other words, are they ordering online or going to a store? You also want to consider direct and indirect competitors, with most of your focus on direct competition. Going back to the t-shirt shop in Oakland, direct competition might come from other online sellers or stores like Target or H&M, where the t-shirts don't cost much and may be trendy, but they won't necessarily be unique—chances are the customer will run into someone wearing the same shirt. Indirect competition would provide alternatives such as tank tops, hoodies, or long sleeve shirts.

The Competitor Trap

It's more important to focus on knowing your industry than obsessing over your direct competition. You want to be familiar with the products/services that customers can choose from, the size of the industry's customer pool, and trends in terms of developments or innovations. Your competitors are a good source of information but can also be a distraction. Learn from your customers and build your own understanding of your industry.

DISCUSSION GUIDE

- Who/what currently solves your customer's problem for them?
- Why do they buy from them?
- What does your competitor's current solution cost (time, money, reputation, etc.) your customer?
- What challenges exist with their current solution?
- How do these challenges make them feel?
- How loyal do they tend to be to this provider?
- Why would customers switch to you? (hint: this is your USP)
- What do you compete on? Price? Features? Quality? Location? Service? Something else?
- Write a brief description of your competition.
- What specific activities would you need to do to get customers to switch?

Customer Interviewing

We believe talking to your customer is one of the key factors of an entrepreneur's success. The earlier in your entrepreneurial journey you talk to your customer about their problem, the faster you'll create and improve your product and make sales. Considering how often we talk about getting feedback from your customer, you may be wondering how to do that.

We suggest talking to them in as many ways as possible: in person, online through surveys and polls, by asking for comments on a social media post, or in focus groups. There's an art and science to interviewing and interpreting feedback. Your questions need to lead the customer to provide the information you seek—that doesn't mean you'll get the answer you hoped for but asking good questions leads to insightful, valuable feedback that helps you improve your product/service.

Ultimately we're trying to convey that by really understanding your customer's problems and motivations, you will be more likely to get the feedback you need. That feedback should confirm that you have properly identified your customer, that you understand their problem, that your idea is viable and valuable and properly priced.

To gather this information, you want to ask open-ended questions, which are questions that require a full sentence answer, not simply a yes or no. For example, if you ask your customer, "Do you have trouble carrying your groceries home?" They can answer yes or no, and the conversation might end there. It is more useful for you to understand their problems in their own words, for example, asking them, "What's most difficult for you when you go grocery shopping?" Use the questioning style of the Five Whys as you did in the first chapter for your own motivations for being an entrepreneur. This line of questioning helps you get deep, informative answers.

Five categories of questions can guide the conversation and reveal useful information about the customer's problems. These categories and sample questions include:

- **Problem details**: You can provide a bit of context to lead the conversation. Your question will show that you have empathy for the customer and are curious about their problem. If they try to deflect or avoid the question, keep exploring, rephrasing if necessary.
  - What's the hardest part about being someone who ____________? (Fill in the blank with something that reflects the customer demographics and psychographics you defined earlier, such as "someone who has to take the bus to school," or "someone who wants to stand out in a crowd.")
  - » Tell me about the last time you had this problem. Explore specific actions and events in the past; don't ask about future intent or opinions.
  - » Why is this a problem for you? This gets to the root of the real problem they're trying to solve.
- **Emotions**: When the customer shares their feelings, you can again show empathy and also ask for specifics. For example, if they say they feel angry, you can ask who they're angry with or who they blame for the problem.
  - What emotions come up when you think about this problem?
- **Current solutions**: This question provides more information about the depth of the problem. If they tried to solve the problem more than six months ago, ask about a different problem. When they tell you what happened, ask lots of dumb questions.
  - When did you last try to solve this problem?
  - What happened?
- **Deficiencies:** The answer to this question reveals where the current solution could be improved.
  - What's not ideal about that solution?

- **Channels:** This question gives insight to how the customer makes decisions.
    - How did you discover that solution?

When you analyze the feedback a customer provides about their problem, you can compare that to your idea and determine the viability and value of your product/service as well as the validity of your assumptions about your customer. You may find the demographics or the problem you assumed for your customer are slightly different from what you thought. And all information and feedback are good because they help you better solve the customer's problem. At the end of your interviews, you may discover that your customer doesn't have the problem you believed they did. At that point, you have to decide to alter your idea to better meet the customer's needs or redefine your customer profile.

One last note, there's a tool known as active listening that is helpful in conversations like these. In active listening, the interviewer isn't thinking about the next question while the customer is talking; the interviewer is actively listening to the answer. When the customer stops talking, the interviewer repeats back what they heard the customer say and waits for the customer to give some affirmation that the interpretation is correct. Then, the interviewer asks a follow up question that takes the conversation deeper and allows them to gather useful information.

The following offers a list of potential questions to ask, dividing them by the purpose they serve. Keep in mind this is an example, you don't have to ask these specific questions, but rather questions that are appropriate to validate your business idea. The conversation is broken down into roughly four parts and reflects those questions mentioned above.

Warm Up

- Good morning. Thanks for taking the time to chat with me today. How's your week going?

Ask About the Problem

- Great. I know your time is valuable, so let's begin. What's the biggest challenge you're facing as a __________?
- When was the last time you tried to solve that problem?
- What happened?
- Why is this a problem for you?
- What emotions come up when you think about this problem?
- How much is this problem costing you now?
- How much would a solution be worth to you?

Current Solutions

- How are you currently solving and how did you find that solution?
- What isn't ideal about the current solution?
- What's the biggest challenge you're facing as a ________ with respect to ___________?

Wrap Up the Call

- *If the person seems like they are a target customer, ask:* I'm actually exploring a solution to [insert the problem they are most actively solving] problem. Can I contact you if we find a viable solution?
- I'm trying to understand this problem from a wide range of perspectives.
- Do you know 1 or 2 other people who are struggling with [insert the problem they are most actively solving] that I might talk with?
- Thank you, and thanks again for your time today.

After you interview at least 25 customers, you can analyze their answers. Look for common themes in the answers and compare their answers with the assumptions you made about your customer. As you review their problems and current solutions, what about your idea feels on track for potential customers? What needs to change in your customer description or your product idea? This is the iterative process of an entrepreneur: make assumptions about the idea and customer, talk to the customer about the idea, adjust the idea based on customer feedback.

DISCUSSION GUIDE

- Who are the 25 potential customers you will interview?
- What problems did your customers say they have? Make a list as the problems come up then group them by similarities.
- Did some people say they have the same problem? The more often the same problem comes up, the more likely it's a problem many people have—this is the problem you can focus on solving.
- As you review their problems and current solutions, what about your idea feels on track for potential customers?
- What needs to change in your customer description, or your product idea, to best reflect what you learned during the interviews?

This chapter is called "customer development" because an entrepreneur should never stop talking to the customer to develop that relationship, and to develop a person into a customer. While initial interviews focus wholly on the customer's problem, here are two other types of customer interviews that you'll conduct repeatedly during your entrepreneurial journey.

One is a testing interview, during which you show an early version of your solution. This could be a sketch, a 3-D animation, a video, or simply talking about your solution. This interview helps you understand the level of interest a customer has for your idea. It's always about getting feedback. You want to ask the customer open-ended questions about whether they think their problem will be solved by your solution. You then iterate your solution based on their feedback.

A third, the selling interview, happens when you have a working prototype or MVP. You show the physical object (or perform a shortened version of the service) to the customer and look to garner pre-sales. A customer ordering your solution is the best feedback you can get, but that doesn't mean you stop improving. Every time you speak with your customer you have an opportunity to learn, grow, and improve your product, service, and business. Don't miss that opportunity!

Your customer is half of your business equation. Your product/service is the other half. In the next chapter, we present the steps to develop and build your product/service and think about how to sell and deliver it to your customers.

CHECKLIST

- ✓ Write a customer profile based on your assumptions of their demographic and psychographic descriptors.
- ✓ Define the different segments your product/service can serve and consider both market and mindset segmentation.
- ✓ Write a description of the customer's problem as you see it.
- ✓ Make a list of at least 10 people who are potential customers.
- ✓ Interview those potential customers about the problem you believe they have and how they currently solve it.
- ✓ Present your solution and ask for their feedback.
- ✓ Analyze the feedback and update your business assumptions to reflect what you learned.

CHAPTER 4

Product and Service Development

When Should You Read This Chapter?

Like knowing your customer, developing your product or service is an iterative, never-ending process. Whether you're in the idea stage or already have a product available, read this chapter along with the other opening chapters as soon as you begin reading the book.

At its core, a business sells a product (food, clothes, candles) or a service (pet sitting, website design, hair styling) to a customer. Some businesses offer both, like a caterer who also offers diet and nutrition counseling or a hair salon that also sells shampoo and headbands. The activities and choices you need to think about for creating and selling a product or service have some commonalities and some differences. In this chapter, we've presented the things they have in common and broken them apart when they have type-specific concepts.

As you mull over how to get your product to market, there are six basic categories of tasks you can follow to develop your product from start to finish. These are the steps to creating your first viable product or service that customers will pay for and should be thought of as an ongoing cycle in which you will iterate, or continually improve your product.

1. Designing
2. Producing

3. Pricing
4. Selling
5. Delivering
6. Improving

We go through each step in this chapter. The thought processes and questions you considered in the previous chapters inform how you do the work here.

Creating Your Product or Service

Entrepreneurs love thinking and talking about new ideas, new solutions to old problems, new frameworks for old processes. In Chapter 1, Entrepreneurial Foundations, we suggest using effectuation to narrow those ideas down to the minimum viable product that will be the first product or service you launch.

Many entrepreneurs love the design phase. Here you tap into your creative energy to think about the look and feel of your product/service. You can see your product and how it works in your mind. You begin making sketches for the product or create a flowchart for the service you'll provide. You'll then speak with a few potential customers to get their feedback on the positive and negative features and incorporate that feedback into a prototype—a working or non-working example of your product or service.

Designing Your Product or Service

Whether a business offers a product or service, careful consideration and thought about the design of the thing the business sells is a critical and ongoing part of the development process. A product business offers a physical item, such as clothing, food, or a musical instrument, and requires design and manufacture of the product itself. As described in the next section, making a working prototype is part of the design process. A service business offers a combination of personal labor and expertise to deliver the desired work. A service requires your hands and mind. We pay for both; with products we consume the item, whereas with services, we consume the value the service provides us, which may be time saved or a new hairstyle.

In Chapter 1, Entrepreneurial Foundations, we presented effectuation as a thought process to evaluate your business idea and start acting on it. While it may seem easy enough to tell a customer, "Hey, I have this thing or can do this task for you and make your life easier," taking the time to design the product or service that truly solves your customer's problem helps you identify your unique selling proposition and differentiates you from your competition. By going through the design process, an entrepreneur often discovers they have more to offer than they initially thought. The goal of product or service design is to identify the features and differentiators of your product/service and how they work together to best solve the customer's problem. To begin, go back to the problem your customer described and then make a list of all the features of your product or every service you can provide:

- Think about your biggest services, strengths, and skills in your industry.
- Identify where you can provide a high level of quality.
- Find a focus that differentiates you from others offering a similar product or service (i.e. better, faster, or cheaper).
- Identify gaps in your knowledge and decide if it is worthwhile for you to teach yourself or if you'll need to hire someone.
- Create a detailed description for the value you'll deliver the customer.

Creating Your Pre-MVP

At this point, you can have that second round of customer interviews where you show them how you think your solution will solve the problem they described in the previous interview. This conversation is still about the customer's problem, but you also present your ideas on a solution. We think of this as the pre-MVP, sometimes called a prototype. The pre-MVP may be as minimal as a hand drawing or 3D mockup on your computer (a low-fidelity prototype). For a service, you may offer a written description of the services.

As you show your pre-MVP to potential customers, you continue to gather feedback about how closely your product/service solves their problem, so you can continue to iterate and improve it until you reach the point that you are ready to finalize your product.

With the feedback you receive from this second round of interviews, you can improve your product or service and then make a functional version of your product (a high-fidelity prototype), or you might offer a sample of your services, say a 15-minute polish change instead of a full manicure. You're now ready for the third round of interviews where you can begin to ask for pre-sales. You're still asking for feedback, still improving, but your product should be viable enough (remember Minimum Viable Product) that a customer can decide to make a purchase or not. The MVP should clearly demonstrate that you listened to and understand your customer's problem and have created a solution they can't live without.

Entrepreneurs often create three versions of their product/service, and there may be multiple iterations of the first two versions:

1. The first is a low-fidelity version (the pre-MVP) that provides enough information that a customer can offer feedback.
2. The second is a high-fidelity version (the MVP) that is a working product the customer can touch and try.
3. The third is the product itself that you can sell. This version incorporates all the feedback you received on the MVP and is a fully functional solution.

Your prototype will likely be far from perfect at the beginning—the goal is the minimal viable product—but it does need to be good enough for a customer to understand what it does and buy it from you. A well-designed prototype—product or service—will meet the customer's expectations and solve their problem. After several iterations, you'll reach a prototype that you can reproduce, either yourself or with partners, and then sell. Let's look at how to make a product.

A note on emerging technologies, particularly AI: There are many software tools being released at breakneck speed to help with design and prototyping. For design, you can use ChatGPT to describe your product or service idea and have it generate images (and videos) to show to potential customers. For prototyping, there are companies integrating generative AI with 3D printing and robotics to create prototypes at a fraction of the time and cost compared to just a few years ago. It used to take years to learn AutoCAD to design and manufacture new products—now you just need to describe what you want in a clear and specific way. Don't be afraid to explore and test these powerful tools, remember the Growth Mindset is one of the key ingredients to an entrepreneur's success.

DISCUSSION GUIDE

- What features of your product/service solve your customer's problem?
- How do you differentiate from your competition?
- In the initial interviews, what feedback did customers offer that inspired you to improve your product/service?
- What specific changes did you decide to make?
- What type of pre-MVP can you create to show to customers?
- Have you shown the pre-MVP to customers? If so, what is their feedback? If not, when will you do so?
- If you have shown your pre-MVP to customers and incorporated their feedback, have you made an MVP?
- What feedback have customers given you on your MVP?
- Do you feel ready to make the first saleable version of your product/service?

Making Your Product

Making—manufacturing—a product can happen in many ways and many variables come into making the decision of how you'll make your product. Manufacturing is the process of making goods by hand or by machine. Items used in manufacture may be raw materials or component parts of a larger product.

Entrepreneurs need to think about their resources in terms of time, skills, materials, and money. For example, do you have the skills and materials to make your product yourself? If you want (or need) someone else to manufacture your product, do you have the funds to pay for it? Can you do a pre-sale of your products to get the funds to pay the manufacturer? Do you even know someone who can produce your product, or do you need to find a manufacturer? There's a spectrum of effort and customization that we've divided into five categories.

Let's use an example of an entrepreneur who has noticed people who live in small spaces often don't have surface area for potted plants but would like to brighten up their home with plants. This entrepreneur has done their research to develop a Product-Market Fit and confirmed that there's a market for woven plant hangers. The options for making them are:

- **Vertical integration**: This means you build/grow all components yourself. For example, the entrepreneur grows and spins the cotton, then braids the thread into designs that they've created.
- **Handmade**: The entrepreneur buys the yarn, maybe even uses existing designs, but does the weaving themselves.
- **Custom manufacturing**: This is a manufactured version of a handmade item.
- **Partnerships**: The entrepreneur creates the designs but partners with other people or businesses to produce the woven plant hanger.
- **White label or private label**: The entrepreneur buys finished woven plant hangers and puts their name or logo on them.

We've made making your product sound easy, but manufacturing may be one of the most daunting steps when it comes to launching a business. How do you take the idea in your brain and create a physical product or an actual experience? You may have a business in which you will be creating the product yourself, like handmade jewelry, home-cooked foods, or artisan goods. You may have the need to outsource some parts of your production, like getting bulk T-shirts for your custom prints. You may need someone to help you fulfill the services you are offering. Figuring out where to get the materials and/or resources you need is challenging, but that's why we are here to help!

You've finalized your product design. You've done several iterations and improved a couple versions of your product, and you're finally ready to make a version you will sell. Below, we've put together some guidelines to help you make your final product. Once you review them, you can use the resources provided to find the right manufacturer for you or you can run a quick search for a manufacturer in your industry.

1. **Decide if you will be making the offering yourself or if you will be using external labor.**
    - Can you buy partial product parts? For example, you can buy t-shirts with a specific cut before printing a design.
    - Can you or will you be able to make any parts or components of your final product?
    - If you are not making it yourself, then where will you look for labor?
2. **List all equipment or resources you need to create your product or service.**
    - Is there any special equipment required to create your product?
    - Are there any special resources required to create your product? For example, if you're creating a food business, you might have some special ingredients you need to import.

- Know your product well enough to explain to suppliers exactly the specifications you need (e.g., sometimes a millimeter can cost you thousands!).

3. **Research platforms or marketplaces that provide easy, low-cost access to equipment and/or labor.**
   - **Time**: Consider how long they will take to manufacture your product. Communicate your timeline in advance and share your expectations early. Don't forget to take shipping into consideration here, as well.
   - **Volume**: Consider how much product they can make, are you a small business that needs 1,000 items or 100,000 per month. Make sure they have the ability and manpower to make as much product as you need. Most manufacturers have a minimum order quantity, known as MOQ.
   - **Cost**: Consider your manufacturing budget. Can you afford them? Don't forget to include a little wiggle room for the unexpected.
   - **Payment**: When do they expect to be paid? What are your payment options? Most factories require a down payment before production begins. The down payment is usually for tooling: 50 percent deposit and 50 percent on completion.
   - **Storage**: Consider where you'll store finished products, can the manufacturer store products? For how long?
   - **Distribution**: Consider what the manufacturer can do with finished products. Can they deliver directly to your customer? Can they deliver to you, or will you have to pick-up the finished product?
   - **Resources**: Consider if your manufacturer can handle the sourcing of materials, or if you will have to provide it.

- **Location**: Explore domestic vs. offshore suppliers. Explore your local suppliers who can typically provide better pricing, locally produced (less shipping costs/time) and ask for references for quality checks. Consider the advantages and disadvantages of each: high cost but better quality (domestic); low cost and more suppliers to choose from (offshore).
- **Contract or partner:** Consult Alibaba, Maker's Row, or Printful for manufacturers and sites like Upwork or Thumbtack for contractors and professionals to hire or partner with.

4. **Choose and commit.**
    - Sign and provide any applicable documentation.
    - Be aware of all fees.
    - Be aware of quality assurance steps.
    - Can you visit the facility?
    - Can they provide recent proof of inspections or third-party audits?
    - Will they subcontract work to other factories, or is all the work done in-house?
    - Be flexible, as your initial design may need modifications to be produced.
    - Build good relationships with your suppliers for better pricing, quality, and long-term sustainability.
    - Find an expert and/or cultivate a mentorship with someone in the same industry who can help you with the process, such as point out negotiation pitfalls, import regulations, taxes.
    - This is a lot of trial and error, so always make sure you can get a sample of your product before you commit to a full order.

The Partner Trap

Choosing the people or businesses to partner with is a risky but necessary decision. There are some ways you can reduce your risk here. When looking for a partner, do your research, ask for samples (which you can then use as prototypes to show your potential customers), talk to people and build a relationship, look for credentials and past evidence of success, seek references, trust your gut, and know when to walk away. Be clear about what you are looking for and write it down. When you are small and just starting out, make sure you don't spend all your money on products you haven't sold yet. It's also a good practice to pay on delivery, not ahead of time, or only make a deposit up front before you receive the goods. It's sad to say but if you are in business long enough you WILL get screwed at some point. We've been there and you'll have our sympathy when it happens to you, but keep your eye on the big picture, your vision, and don't let it stop you from carrying on.

Choosing the right manufacturer is a crucial step in your new business. They will control your most important component, your actual product. That includes the quality and a large fraction of your operating budget so make sure you arm yourself with research. Compare as many options as you need and always negotiate.

DISCUSSION GUIDE

- What kind of manufacturing will you use to produce your product?
- What kind of equipment or supplies do you need to make your product?
- Do you need any special equipment or supplies that might be hard to get? If so, where will you source these items?
- Do you need a partner for support with either labor, materials, or knowledge?
- Have you asked for advice in reviewing any contracts with partners or suppliers?

Preparing Your Service

It may seem easier or less costly to offer a service, and that's true in some cases that don't require special skills or equipment. However, many service-based businesses require skills and special equipment. For example, if you are a trained aesthetician and have decided to open your own location, you need to have the right tools and most up to date skills to provide your service. In the beginning, you may work out of your home or go to your customer's home to offer your services. As you build your client base, you may decide to rent a location that needs renovation before you can open your doors to business. The research and expense to open a service-based business can be as involved as for a product-based business. While you want to differentiate yourself from the competition, don't spend too much on things your customer doesn't care about. Rather than overspend, your Unique Selling Proposition can be your skills and your impeccable customer service.

Aside from skills and equipment, you may need proper insurance coverage (we discuss that in Chapter 11, Legal and Regulatory) or have an active license, such as a beautician license.

DISCUSSION GUIDE

- Do you need a location or special equipment to offer your service? If so, how will you find a location or purchase the equipment?
- Do you need any special supplies to offer your service? If so, where will you source them?
- Is there any special software you need to book appointments?
- Have you asked for advice in reviewing any contracts with partners or suppliers?

Pricing

Whether you start a product or service business, pricing can be challenging. Entrepreneurs seem to fall into two categories—their prices are too high or too low. We gave a brief introduction to pricing in Chapter 2, Product-Market Fit, and here we provide the full run down.

Price represents the value of your product or service and the goal is to establish a price that meets the expectations your customer has about perceived value. Notice that we wrote "your customer." Knowing your customer is critical to pricing. If you have Louis Vuitton prices at H&M, or vice versa, few items will be sold: two different products and brands, two different customers. Pricing is both an art and science, and it constantly changes as customer expectations and the market change.

Pricing Your Product

In addition to knowing your customer, you need to know how much it costs to make your product or offer your service. For a product, you have the tangible costs of the material and production of the product itself—plus the value of your time to create, sell, and manufacture it. For a service, you have the value of your time to perform the service and the cost of any equipment or material necessary to offer the service. We explain pricing a service in the next section.

To begin, we think of pricing in its simplest terms as napkin math—calculations so simple you could write them on a napkin—representing the Cost of Goods Sold (COGS). Once you've established your COGS, you can move on to value pricing, which we discuss later in this section.

cost of materials + cost of your time = cost of goods sold

You may have heard the phrase, *buy low, sell high.* You can't sustain your business if you sell your product for less than it costs to make it. COGS reflect the cost per unit, but that cost can vary depending on how many units you produce. Likewise, the cost of materials can vary depending on the number of units you buy. Suppliers do their own COGS calculations, and if you buy 100 units of something it will typically cost less per unit than buying one. For example, if up to 10 yards of fabric sells for $5 a yard, but more than 10 yards of fabric sells for $4.55 a yard, it makes sense to buy 11 yards ($50 for 10 vs. $50.05 for 11). This concept is known as economies of scale.

For your time, start with the dollar amount per hour you want to earn and be realistic about how much time you dedicate to your product. There's a video circling on social media about how much a pair of hand-knitted wool socks would cost. The wool itself has a set cost of $20, and it takes 25 hours to knit a pair of socks. The knitter calculated that to make $10 an hour they'd need to price the socks at $270! That's a fancy pair of socks; they would likely need to sell the socks at $540 a pair—and be able to sell over a dozen a week—to make it worth their time to turn this into a business.

As a starting point, think about the hourly rate you'd like to earn and multiply that by the number of hours you spend making or doing your product, then add that to the cost of materials. Looking back at our woven plant hanger, if a ball of twine costs $2.50, eight wooden beads cost $1 a piece, and the metal ring at the top is $1.50, the cost of materials is $12. Pretty simple math that you can write on a napkin. If it takes you three hours to make one plant hanger and you want to earn $15 an hour, the cost of your time is $45.

$12 + $45 = $57 Cost of Goods Sold
for one unit of your woven plant hanger

However, pricing doesn't end with the COGS—that would be cost-based pricing, which relies solely on data of the cost of the material and time. We want you to think about value-based pricing, or setting your prices based on the COGS plus the value your customer perceives when they purchase your product.

Value-Based Pricing

Value-based pricing means knowing your customer so well that you understand the features they value and how much they are willing to spend for your product/service. Unless they are buying a commodity (like grain or iron), customers rarely want to buy the cheapest thing. There are whole books written on the psychology of pricing but typically, when standing in front of three options, most customers choose the middle option. The psychology of pricing relies on the explanation that customers believe the lowest-priced offer is too good to be true or of poor quality, that the highest-priced offer is for wealthy people or simply overpriced, while the middle-priced offer is just right. (You can learn a lot about pricing from Goldilocks.) For the woven plant hanger, maybe $75 aligns with the customer's perceived value. Consider the following urban legend about pricing.

> *An entrepreneur had a jewelry store in the downtown shopping area of a small coastal tourist town. She had to go out of town and asked a friend to watch the store for the weekend. Her parting words were, "Don't worry if you don't sell anything. Business has been terrible this season." When she returned from the weekend, she asked her friend how the weekend had gone. "Great! There was steady foot traffic both days, and I sold almost everything." Stunned, the owner asked how she accomplished this. "I raised the prices," her friend said.*

If your prices are too low, your customers may be wondering about the quality of your product. Customers associate a higher perceived value with a higher price. As we mentioned, however, pricing is an art; if the friend had set the prices too high, the customers would have likely preferred to buy from a name brand high-end jeweler.

A customer also associates a value with the brand and the packaging. If you look closely at store brand items in the grocery store, you may find that two different brands are manufactured at the same plant and sold at two different prices. That's right—the lower-priced cookies, pasta, rice, beans, and detergents sold under the store name are often made by the same higher-priced brand manufacturer even though they are exactly the same thing.

In addition to COGS, an entrepreneur also must consider the fixed costs of starting and running the business, but we'll talk about those in Chapter 10, Accounting and Bookkeeping. For now, calculate COGS as a starting point for pricing. Like the other aspects of running a business, pricing is iterative and will change as you gather more information.

The Competition Trap

You want to be familiar with your competitors, the prices they ask, and the product/service they offer but make sure the people you see as competitors really are your competition. It's easy to fall into the trap of misidentifying your competition. The customers who shop at Walmart are not the customers who shop at Whole Foods, and both brands would be making erroneous assumptions about their customer if they considered the other their competition.

If you make hand-screened t-shirts, TJ Maxx isn't your competition. You want to compare yourself to other custom t-shirt shops either in your area or available online. And, even then, they may not be your competition. If you make t-shirts for 30-something moms, you don't want to compare yourself to another company that sells to 60-something Harley riders.

Your product price will ultimately determine your net profits, or how much your business makes. At the end of the day, profitable businesses thrive, and all others fail. In Chapter 10, Accounting and Bookkeeping, we present budgeting and financial management, and you'll want to refer to the pricing work you've done here, then.

Value-based pricing influences how you price your service, perhaps even more than with a product. Rather than a tangible thing being exchanged between you and your customer, you are selling your service, your expertise, and your own special way of solving their problem.

Pricing a Service

When an entrepreneur begins thinking about pricing a service, there are four factors to keep in mind:

1. The perceived and actual value of your service to your customer, modified by
2. the market price available to your customer for alternative or competing services, and
3. cost to deliver. (You want to make sure your price is more than your costs; more about the cost of providing a service later in this section.)
4. Then, compare your pricing to direct competitors—are you better, faster, and/or cheaper—and have a justifiable reason if you are considerably more or less expensive. (If you don't know of any direct competitors, that could be a sign to do more research.)

As with product pricing, an entrepreneur begins thinking about how to price their service with the customer in mind. What value does the customer place on the service being offered? When a customer starts looking for a service solution, they probably have a number in mind associated with how much value they believe that service provides.

For example, let's say you've interviewed your customer, and you know the value they place on a pedicure is $35, that's the going price in your neighborhood, and that price covers your time and expenses for things like files and polish. If they find a salon that offers a $15 pedicure, unless it's a special offer for first-time customers, they'll likely think the service won't be very good. Likewise, if they spot a $100 pedicure at a spa, they may dismiss it as overpriced or wonder if the polish has platinum flecks. That's not to say there aren't customers for the $15 or the $100 pedicure, but maybe they aren't your customers. First and foremost, you want to price your service based on the value the customer expects—and, of course, deliver that value.

Pedicures at a much lower or much higher price speak to pricing strategies. A higher price points to a premium pricing structure where the entrepreneur delivers high quality but knows there will be lower volume, i.e., fewer customers, but there's more profit per sale. The lower price points to economy pricing where the entrepreneur aims for high volume at a lower price, and a lower profit per sale.

Although a service business doesn't produce a product, there are often material costs involved with offering the service, which may be tools or supplies needed to offer the service or certifications or licenses required to run the specific type of business.

As with products, you want to look at your competition but make sure you compare yourself to the true competition. If you are a life coach just starting out, you will charge a fraction of someone like Tony Robbins. Compare your estimated hourly rate to your competitors to test whether your price matches the price your customers expect to pay. Are you

- **Charging more:** Are you using premium materials? Are your customers getting added value? Do you have a lot more experience and expertise? Make sure your customers know why they should pay more.
- **Charging less:** Are you simply trying to build a customer base? Make sure your customers know the prices are lower for a limited time. Feel free to modify or increase your prices a little to be on the safer side.
- **Charging just right:** This is okay too but remember that it is usually easier to lower prices than to increase them after your business opens. While some businesses with a captive audience, such as a ski resort or gym, can charge more, many product-based businesses need to drop their prices to attract new customer segments and sell more units.

Services tend to be priced in one of four ways, depending on the type of service provided. It would be odd for a hair stylist to charge hourly, although prices are probably calculated with an hourly fee in mind. Likewise, it would be unusual for a babysitter to charge by the project—the parents may never come home! Consider the following ways of pricing as you set your own prices and remember that the customer's perceived value of your service greatly influences the price you can charge:

- **Time-based pricing:** Charge for the exact time used to complete a service or in 15/30/60-minute blocks—lawyers even charge in six minute increments! Hourly rates are often used when you are pricing your expertise and seniority. A more experienced photographer with an extensive portfolio will generally be paid a higher hourly rate than a less experienced photographer. You should consider including your travel time as an extra charge.
- **Flat rate pricing:** Use your hourly rate to estimate how long it will take to perform the service. Charge a fixed price for each service listed on your menu/portfolio. If a project takes longer than expected to complete, you may risk losing money on the client. Consider including a cap on the number of hours involved so you can charge additional fees if the service runs over that time.
- **Tier pricing:** Allow customers to pay less for less or more for more. This is typical for service bundles like two sessions for $160 or four sessions for $280. Don't be afraid to change your pricing as you go either—it will take time to get it right, and eventually, you'll want to raise your prices as you get more experience and clients.
- **Variable pricing:** Allow customers to bargain and negotiate to set the price for each customer. In general, charging different prices to different customers should be based on some sort of repetitive reasoning. Like businesses vs individuals, 100 hours vs 50 vs 25 vs 2. A business cannot afford to lose its integrity and respect among customers.

The Low-Price Trap

Pricing your service is challenging because you want to strike a balance between what the customer expects to pay, that is the price the market supports, and the value of your time, while staying competitive and driving business. Make sure you charge enough for your service. One of the biggest obstacles that owners face when starting their first service-based business is not charging enough. This is especially true for those who are new to their business. Many service entrepreneurs undervalue themselves at first and charge too little to win customers. Entrepreneurs who charge per hour often set the hourly rate too low while those who charge per project often spend more time than planned and end up earning less per hour than they anticipated.

Most consumers don't value things they don't pay for. In blind taste tests, if a consumer is told something they are sampling is more expensive than the alternative, most of the time they will say it's better. The point is, selling something cheaper can be a good strategy, but you better have a lot of it. Make sure to charge your customers the VALUE to them of what you are selling, not the cost. Arm yourself with feedback from your customer interviews, research, and competitive prices. You can try to set your price and make your first three to five sales, then increase—even double—your rates.

DISCUSSION GUIDE

- When a customer thinks of your product or service, do they consider it low, medium or high value?
- Do your prices align with your customer's perceived value?
- Do you use premium or economy pricing for your service?
- If you sell a product, what is the COGS for your product?
- If you offer a service, how will you set your prices?
- Are your prices aligned with those of your true competitor?

Sell

We've written a whole chapter on marketing and sales where we discuss the process through which your customer learns about your brand and product/service, engages with you, and eventually buys from you. Within product development, we limit the discussion of sales to the physical aspect of presenting your product, accepting payment, and finalizing the sale. This is a piece of the whole customer journey (the time a customer spends with you to learn about your offer and make a purchase) but it is as important as all the other stops along the way. The easier you make it for your customer to buy from you, the more likely they make it through the entire checkout process. Selling a product differs from selling a service so we've divided them in this section.

Consider these aspects of the process:

- When do you sell your product?
- Where do you sell your product?
- How much can you sell?
- How does the customer pay you?
- What's your refund/return policy?

When and Where To Sell Your Product

Some products and services are seasonal. For example, you may spend nine months of the year creating holiday sweaters that you only sell in November and December.

There can be a difference between when you sell something and when you deliver it. If you sell tulip bulbs, you may accept orders year-round but only ship the bulbs in October.

While the market's seasons or your personal schedule may determine when you sell your product/service, where you sell it is easier to define. Where you sell your product/service ultimately impacts how you deliver it:

- Online Sales Options
  - Customers can order and pay for products on your website or schedule and even pay for services.
  - You can partner with external ecommerce providers like Amazon or Etsy for products or Upwork for services.
- Storefront
  - Customers can purchase your product or service at your own retail property.
  - You can partner with large or small retailers to resell your product or to allow you to offer your services in their space.

How Much Can You Sell?

It's easy to believe there's no such thing as too much business, but too many businesses have gone under because of an unplanned spike in demand or rapid growth for which they were unprepared. For example, during the pandemic, with so many people working from home, the demand for Zoom exploded overnight and the company had to adjust its services to meet bandwidth requirements.

Likewise, companies that respond to a temporary situation without making a long-term plan often fail. UK company Hopin, which hosted online events, died when the pandemic subsided and people started meeting in person again.

Entrepreneurs who sell a product may want to ask manufacturing partners for their minimum order quantity and their maximum production capability, so they have a full awareness of their sales capacity and can create a contingency plan should a product not sell well or sell out quickly. Before you have to deal with excess product, think about the type of price reduction you can offer to sell overstock, and before you run out of product, think about how you'll respond; will you accept backorders?

Payment Methods and Plans

If you have a brick-and-mortar storefront, at a minimum you'll want to be able to accept cash, credit, or debit cards. If you are collecting cash, you'll need a business bank account to have cash for "change," and you'll need a secure place to store your cash during business hours. In-store or online credit and debit payments are relatively easy to set up either through your bank or with a payment processor. Many allow you to use your phone as the point-of-sale mechanism, so you don't need the card reader, just a stable internet connection.

Most products sold by a small business are paid for in full at the time of purchase. Buy now, pay later (BNPL) is an increasingly popular payment method that allows shoppers to pay for their purchases in installments. Consider enabling this on your online store through a provider like Shop Pay Installments. You'll capture the millions of people who use BNPL to buy products online. If you sell high-priced items and are so inclined, you could accept payments in installments but then you are in the position of being a creditor to your customer and there's a certain amount of risk involved if the customer doesn't pay you.

A payment model that benefits your business is a subscription or recurring charge model. For example, Harry's offers a subscription where the customer receives a new razor every month, just about the time the old razor blade is dull. This provides guaranteed monthly income for the duration of the subscription.

As you're accepting payments, you can also start building a central database of basic information on customers and prospective customers, like name and contact information, so you can inform them of new products, offers, or sales.

Return and Exchange Policies

Especially in North America, customers love a good return option. For a small business, returns can be a nightmare. You believe you've sold an item and two weeks later the customer walks back in and asks for a refund or exchange. Or worse, you offer free shipping (which means you're paying for the shipping) and then the customer returns the item. You're out the cost of the shipping.

You can protect yourself by setting a limit on the timeframe within which a return can be requested. Make sure your return policy is clearly posted at the physical or virtual checkout.

Selling a Service

Selling a service is quite different from selling a product. If you're running a service-based business, YOU (or your team) are the product. That means you need to sell yourself just as much as your service and you'll need to educate your customers on both. You probably already know this, but people buy from those they know, like, and trust. So, after you find someone who has a problem, you want to convince them that you are the right person to help them. You'll need to educate your prospective customer and build trust.

Sometimes a service-based business does deliver a tangible item. For example, if you are a copywriter, you offer copywriting services, but you deliver a completed written piece to the customer. Rather than a manufactured product being the thing the customer buys, you make the "product" through the act of your services which the customer pays for. The value you offer is well-written copy. If the customer wants just any old copy they could ask AI to write it.

Use the steps included in Chapter 5, Marketing and Sales, and Chapter 7, Website and Technology, to produce valuable and useful content that educates your prospective client. You'll also want to share some of your best ideas via email or some other type of regular communication. Assuming the potential customer wants the service you are offering and has the money to pay for it, the only thing standing in the way of making the sale is trust. They need to believe that you are going to do the thing that you say you are. Help them understand that you provide high quality services and that they will be happy with the result using testimonials, success stories, and customer reviews.

Consider these aspects of the process:

- Where do you sell your service?
- How much can you sell?
- How can a customer book your service?
- How does the customer pay you?
- What are your terms of service?

Where Do You Sell Your Service?

The location where you conduct your service business depends on the type of service you offer. For example, if you offer website design or any service that can be done at a computer without direct contact with the client, you can work from home, a co-working space, or any place that you can take your computer. If you offer a physical service such as lawn care, massage, or pedicures, you'll need to go to your client's home or have a space where they can come for the service.

How Much Will/Can You Sell?

Entrepreneurs who offer a personalized service have a limited amount of time they can physically offer the service in, so they may sell their time months in advance of the actual service being delivered. If you find yourself with a growing wait list for your product or service, this is a sign that you could raise your prices or that it's time to hire contractors or employees to help you.

Consider how much time you have available as well as how much time you want to work. Remember to block off time for vacation, personal appointments, and any events that will leave you unavailable to work.

You may also choose to schedule your work seasonally. Perhaps you want to take summers off so you can spend time with your children. Or you offer a service helping college-bound students write their application essays. You work directly with clients only in the Fall months, so students have the applications ready to submit in January.

One of the best parts of being an entrepreneur is defining where, when, and how much you work.

How Can a Customer Book Your Service?

- Online Sales Options
    - Customers can schedule and pay for services on your website or through online scheduling apps like Calendly.
    - You can partner with external ecommerce providers like Upwork for services.
    - Phone: Do you have a business phone number? Some platforms like Google Hangouts can provide a free phone number, but lots of entrepreneurs just use their personal cell for business.
    - Email: Have you created a business email that you will check regularly? If it's important to your customers to professionalize how you present to them, a business email can be great. Skysthelimit.org runs on Google Workspaces, so our business emails all use Gmail.
- Storefront
    - Customers can purchase your product or service at your own retail property.
    - You can partner with large or small retailers to offer your services in their space.

Payment Methods and Plans

The payment methods and plans for services are like those for products. Along with the ability to accept cash, credit, or debit, you also need a business bank account and a secure location to store cash. As previously mentioned, card payments are now fairly easy to set up as long as you have a stable internet connection.

If clients book their time with you through an online scheduling app, you can ask them to pay for the service before it occurs or invoice them afterward. If it's a service that takes place in person, you can collect their payment when they have their appointment. Most services have standards for the type of service. Aestheticians tend to accept payment at the time of service. Online service providers such as copywriters or website designers may ask for a partial payment before beginning the work and then subsequent payments when milestones are met.

A powerful payment model that benefits your business is a subscription or recurring charge model. For example, when your customer buys a 12-month package of personal training sessions, they provide their credit card, and you charge them once a month, but the sale is for the full year. This provides guaranteed monthly income for the duration of the subscription.

As you're accepting payments, you can also start building a central database of basic information on customers and prospective customers, like name and contact information so you can inform them of new products, offers, or sales.

Terms of Service

Depending on the type of service you offer, you may or may not have a customer sign a contract—if someone comes into your shop for a manicure, you probably won't ask them to sign a contract; if you're designing a full brand and website for a client, you probably will. Even for the smallest offer you might want to have written terms of service available for consultation. Terms of Service typically define your policies for scheduling, payment, cancellations, no-shows, guarantees, and dispute settlement. If you have a website, your Terms of Service can reside there. If you have a storefront, you could keep a copy available for customers to read upon request at the reception.

Ideas are great, but without sales to accompany them, businesses will likely fail. As you can see, there are a lot of things that go into successfully selling products or services. The key is making the process as smooth and easy for the customer as possible.

DISCUSSION GUIDE

- Where will you sell your product or service? In-store, online?
- How will a customer pay you? Will you offer a payment plan? If so, how will you manage that?
- What is your return/refund policy?
- What are your terms of service?
- Does anything about your selling process differentiate you from your competition?
- How can you make the sales process a positive experience for your customer?

Delivering Your Product or Service

At this point in the product development process, you get to see the results of all the preparation you've done so far: a happy customer receiving your product or service. How you deliver your product continues to reinforce the positive experience your customer has with your business. One way to stand out in a competitive market is to look for ways to "surprise and delight" your customers, and the delivery of your product or service is a great place to get creative. Products and services can be delivered in some of the same ways, and there are a few that are specific to each. The list here goes from easiest type of delivery to most complex:

- **In person**: Both products and services can be delivered in person. The customer may come to you, or you may take your product or service to them.
- **In-store:** You may have your own retail space to sell your product or offer your service, or you may place your product or service in someone else's space.
- **Online:** If your product is something like a template or course, your customer could receive it directly as a download. Your

services may be delivered online in the form of a video call or the deliverable of the service you offer, such as a completed website.

- **Delivery service:** You might use a courier or messenger like UberEats or Deliveroo to deliver your product.
- **Print-on-Demand:** There are new companies emerging which allow you to put your design or logo on a range of stock products. You list the items you want to offer to your customers online, and when people order, the company will make/print your product and ship it to your customer. You make money on the difference you pay for making the product and the price you charge your customer—very little risk for you and no inventory management or shipping boxes constantly. At Skysthelimit.org, we use Printful for our t-shirts and coffee cups, etc.
- **Partners:** For a service like event planning, you will do all the work, but the delivery of those planning services will happen at the venue and be executed with other vendors such as caterers and entertainment.
- **Dropshipping:** On the spectrum of complexity, dropshipping a product is the most complex to organize but it is great for a high volume of products. With dropshipping, you sell the product online through your website or an ecommerce market but someone else does the manufacturing, warehousing, and shopping. What's more, you only pay for the product after you've made a sale.

Whether you deliver a product or service, think about how you want to be perceived and how you present yourself. Good customer service makes a huge difference in a saturated field of product and service providers. You can stand out from your competition simply by being present when your customer is in front of you. We heard a story of a hair stylist who kept looking at their watch and the client could see them do this in the mirror. The client thought the stylist must be checking the time, perhaps running late to an appointment. Only in hindsight did the client realize the stylist was receiving messages on their watch. Even when you are on a video call, the people in the "room" see your eyes glance to the corner because a notification has come in. Turn notifications off on your devices and make sure the customer feels seen and heard.

Show Gratitude

Good manners and kindness go a long way in today's rushed world. A follow up email or text message after the product or service has been delivered reminds the customer of their good experience with you. Thank and welcome them as a customer to your business. Show that you're available for any questions or feedback, and perhaps include a special offer in exchange for a review or referral.

Remember, your customer is your best teacher—which leads to the next step.

DISCUSSION GUIDE

- Of the six types of delivery listed previously, which one do you think makes most sense for your product/service and your customer?
- How will you manage inventory?
- How will you deliver your product or services to your customers?
- Does anything about your delivery differentiate you from your competition?
- How can you make the delivery process a positive experience for your customer?

Improve

You don't have to have the perfect offering right off the bat. You will most likely go through lots of iterations and versions of your service before and after your business launches. Aim to talk to your customers as outlined in the previous chapter and test your products and services early so that you can make your first sales. Below are some basic tips to follow.

Product improvement is the process of making meaningful changes that result in new customers or increased benefits realized by existing customers. The two most popular ways to make product improvements are to add new product features or improve existing ones.

Once you have the first version of your business up and running and you are making sales, the next step is to create a plan to understand how your customers feel about your products so that you can improve the quality of what you're providing. No matter how great your idea is, it can always be improved through continuous testing. The best way to test your idea is to get it in front of customers and see what they think.

1. **Get customer feedback.**
   - Prepare a customer survey for users to fill out on their own time.
   - Conduct customer interviews where you ask questions.
   - Conduct a test.
2. **Types of feedback you can collect for your products.**
   - Evaluate what customers say about it.
   - Evaluate how customers use and misuse the product.
   - Evaluate how customers handle and interact with the product.
   - Evaluate the questions customers have.
3. **Types of feedback you can collect for your service.**
   - Evaluate how customers talk about you.
   - Evaluate the questions customers have.
   - Is it easy for the customer to book your services?
   - Do customers say good things about you?
   - Do you have good reviews or at the very least, no bad reviews?
   - Have you listed all services you're providing?

- Are there services you're missing? Should you add them?
- How's your approach? Do you seem likable and kind, are you someone that a stranger would want to do business with?
- Can you demonstrate results? Can you prove that you deliver the result you promise?

4. **Create a way to test your product.**
   - Show the product. Put your product in the user's hands and don't explain everything. Let your customer play around with your product. Then explain the full usability and evaluate the differences.
   - Complete a trial run. Grab a few friends, family members, or customers and give them the full experience, from initial contact to completion of services. But don't explain everything. Let them enjoy the experience and ask that they give you feedback at each critical step in the process, especially when they are dissatisfied or when expectations were not met. Then explain the full experience you design, provide reasoning for any "missed" steps and later analyze the differences.
   - Create experiences. Test your products in a way that feels like an experience that your customer is reacting to, rather than an explanation that your user is evaluating.
   - Compare to competitors. Compare your products to your competitors or a later version to a newer version.

Think of everything you hear as constructive criticism. Be able to understand the difference between what is said vs what is meant—every word of input can positively impact your business. Some people aren't going to like your idea, that doesn't mean your business is not viable. Create a feedback log where you can record all feedback received and who you received it from. Pay attention to trends you hear in the feedback. Do your best to avoid feeling attacked or defensive. Most people are really trying to help!

Getting feedback will also help you maintain a happy and loyal customer base. This is important because your customers will be one of your most important marketing channels, especially when you first start! This is known as the network effect. The network effect comes into play when the first group of users of a product or service rapidly expand its reach by introducing the business or organization to their circle of friends, coworkers, i.e., their "network." As the user base or network of people expands, the product or service grows, the more useful the business becomes to users.

If someone has decided to do business with you, the chances that you can convince them to do more business with you are much more likely than convincing someone brand new. Use tools and technology to create an exceptional experience to motivate them to stay. Exceptional experiences are created when you make improvements on your business based on customer feedback. After all, the most successful service-based businesses are those that are truly customer-centric.

Product improvement is a fundamental step for a successful business. Generally, you should take multiple cycles as you move from working on the initial product design to the nuanced details after launch. Ideally try to use a real, finalized version of the product within a real context of the customer's life. For a physical object, try to get customers to use it within their normal routines. For an experience, try to create a scenario in a location that would capture the real situation.

Continue to improve your service(s). Regardless of how long you've been in the same industry, there's always new technologies and tools you can use to make your business better, grow your customer base and improve your bottom line: profits.

DISCUSSION GUIDE

- What system do you have in place to get constant feedback from your customers?
- How easy is it for your customer to do business with you?
- What feedback have you received that is easy to implement?
- What feedback have you received that will be more challenging to implement?
- Have you received feedback that you don't agree with? Has that feedback made you rethink who your customer is?
- How will you work to maintain and improve this product or service?

You've reached a celebration-worthy milestone. You understand and have defined your customer; you created a product or service that solves their problem; and you have done the work to move your idea further to the right of the Product-Market Fit spectrum. In the next chapter, we dive deep into marketing and selling your product or service to your desired customers.

CHECKLIST

- ✓ Refine the design of your product or service concept.
- ✓ Interview customers about your design.
- ✓ Create your prototype.
- ✓ Interview customers about your prototype.
- ✓ Figure out how to make your product or do your service.
- ✓ Decide on vendors, partners, and/or contractors.
- ✓ Make your first product or deliver your first service.
- ✓ Figure out how you will get your product/service to your customers.
- ✓ Decide on your selling price for your product or service (and make sure you are profitable at that price!)
- ✓ Create a plan to maintain and improve the quality of your product/service.

CHAPTER 5

Marketing and Sales

When Should You Read This Chapter?
Turn to this chapter after you have defined your customer and your product or service. Marketing and sales is a never ending, ongoing process so you may want to revisit this chapter when you want to try a different marketing channel, introduce a new offer, or approach a new customer segment. You may also prefer to read Chapter 6, Branding, before this chapter so you have a clearer idea about how you will represent your business in your marketing and sales efforts.

This chapter may be the most critical of this book. We first present the key concepts of marketing and walk through the phases of the customer journey. We've included a customer journey map that provides the basis for your marketing and sales efforts. The actions of marketing lead into the practical side of sales. By the end of the chapter, you'll have the guidelines and information you need to create and execute a marketing and sales plan that takes your customer on a memorable journey.

Fasten your seatbelt—your business takes off with this chapter!

It All Starts With Awareness

Get the word out! If no one knows that you are open for business, then no customers spend their money at your business, and you can't grow. Many entrepreneurs are afraid about people stealing their ideas, but you really

WANT customers to know about your business. Getting the word out about your business is a big, important job—and it takes time! Start as soon as you can, as soon as you feel comfortable talking to people about your business.

You may find that during your first interviews with customers about their problem, you make a few preliminary sales. If so, celebrate that! Those first sales become treasured memories and you want to add others to the list: biggest sale, hardest sale, most unexpected sale, easiest sale. Sales happen because people know about the product or service you offer, and you keep them informed through marketing.

We present marketing and sales in the same chapter because they are intimately tied together. Marketing is the scientific understanding of the customer before, during, and after sales (also known as pre-, core, and post sales, discussed later in this chapter). Marketing activities include communicating to potential customers that you exist through various digital and traditional marketing channels and advertising. Marketing also communicates with existing customers to keep them coming back to you to make another purchase.

Sales is a process of identifying, documenting, and cultivating leads (leads are potential customers), closing the sale, and then keeping the customer (known as customer retention), which means selling to the same customer again and in the best case making a bigger sale (known as upselling and cross-selling).

Effective marketing informs your potential customer that you understand their problem and shows the value your business offers. The work you did in Chapter 3, Customer Development, developing and refining your customer profile through interviews, surveys, and conversations was useful for developing an appropriate, effective, saleable product/service (the work of Chapter 4, Product and Service Development). Now, you can use that same customer information to develop the messages you'll communicate to reach a wider audience of people who share the same needs, demographics, and mindsets and turn them into customers.

We discussed the idea of customer development fully in Chapter 3, Customer Development, but we can't emphasize enough the importance of investing time to define your target audience. It will determine everything about how you craft your marketing messages, who you decide to sell to, and how you sell to them. Take your time and do your research to create a meaningful customer persona. Look at problems from your client's perspective, and it will be easier to persuade potential clients of your value.

Whether you are a fitness instructor, photographer, personal chef or clothing manufacturer, you need to show that you solve your customer's problem—and your solution is worth their time and money—by showcasing your best qualities, providing real value, and delivering on your every promise.

Marketing Foundations

Marketing is an ever-evolving field with many frameworks and theories about how to best reach and speak to your customer. Richard A. Viguerie, a pioneer in direct mail marketing, specifically in the political arena, coined a concept called the Four Horsemen of Marketing™. These "horsemen" work together to define your business and in turn, inform your marketing message and strategies; they are position, differentiation, benefit, and brand. When you apply these four concepts to your marketing efforts, you stand out in a noisy space and speak directly to your intended customer. Let's look at each one individually and see how they work together.

Position

Position defines where you fit in the marketplace. To find that fit you refer to your customer interviews and their problems. Your position fills the hole of an unsolved problem. Positioning isn't about improving your product or doing something better than the competition, it is about finding a gap in the market and then positioning your product and company as the one to fill it. When you show how you plug that gap, people naturally see the benefit you offer.

A word to the wise: don't try to fill a hole that someone else has already filled. Position is not about being better than the competition but rather is finding a gap, no matter how small or big, that no one else is paying attention to.

Differentiation

Once you've found your position, then you want to differentiate—stand out—from your competition. We talked about differentiation in Chapter 2, Product-Market Fit. Think about the questions you answered then: what makes you exceptional, noticeable in the crowd? In a room full of entrepreneurs offering similar solutions to the same problem, what makes you stand out? Think about a field of daisies with one red rose in the middle; the rose stands out. Standing out gives you the best chance of reaching your goals.

Positioning is a decision you make. It is the hole that no one else fills, it's a place that you choose to be. Differentiation shows up in the public actions that reveal the hole in the market. In other words, differentiation is visual.

Benefit

Identifying the benefit you offer is critical because in understanding the benefit, people see the value in what you do and then are willing to make a purchase. If your benefit is too small, unclear, or not well said, your marketing efforts will fail. The benefit may be the solution to the customer's problem or it may be knowledge that helps your customers get closer to a solution. You'll learn more about identifying the benefit you offer in Chapter 6, Branding.

Brand

Entrepreneurs hear and read so much about brand, and it's hard to sift through the good and the bad information. As we see it, brand pulls together position, differentiation, and benefit. We've dedicated a whole chapter to branding, but for now, know that your brand is how customers perceive and think about your product/service and company. Products/services aren't sold, they are bought, and customers purchase from brands they trust and know. Customers get to know a brand through marketing.

Put together, the four pieces form a sentence or two that describes your business and marketing plan. For example: *Many health-conscious consumers want a snack that's both nutritious and satisfying but often face a market flooded with options high in sugar or artificial ingredients. AwesomeBar positions itself as the better solution, offering a snack that's not only delicious but also made with all-natural, whole-food ingredients. AwesomeBar stands out by focusing on clean nutrition, with clear labeling and a commitment to transparency. Known for its high-quality standards and great taste, AwesomeBar has become a trusted choice for those looking to snack smarter.*

This example illustrates how the Four Horsemen of Marketing™—position, differentiation, benefit, and brand—applied to a fictional product in the health food industry. We'll guide you through how to use this framework in the next section.

DISCUSSION GUIDE

- Think about the customer's problem; what is the position of your product or service in relation to that problem? What hole do you fill in the marketplace?
- How can you differentiate your product from other products that solve the same problem you solve?
- What benefit does the customer gain from your product or service?
- What values does your brand stand for? What words come to mind when a customer thinks of your brand? (We dive deep on these concepts in Chapter 6, Branding.)
- Can you put the four pieces together in a sentence or two that describes your business and marketing?

Customer Journey

The customer journey includes specific phases that begin with the customer learning about your product or service and ultimately reach the point of making a purchase and enthusiastically telling others about your brand. An entrepreneur does marketing and sales activities at each phase. Every task you do at each point on the customer journey should support the statement you created with the concepts from the Four Horsemen.

We address marketing activities here, although marketing and sales are tightly linked. To some degree, you are always marketing and always selling. Later in this chapter when we talk about the three types of selling, you'll see how these eight phases of the customer journey relate to the selling process.

- **Discover:** This is the entry point for the customer, the phase at which they first learn about the existence of your business, product, or service. Discover happens through actions that you take across all your marketing and sales efforts (we outline 15 of them in this chapter) and when other people talk about your business or product/service. Word of mouth—when someone tells someone else about your product or service—is the best way for your customers to learn about you. Think about when your best friend recommends something to you that they know you will like. You quickly move from becoming aware of the product, to looking at it and purchasing it online. The entire customer journey can happen in a couple of minutes!
- **Explore and Connect:** Once a customer is aware of a brand, business, product, or service they begin to explore it by engaging with your marketing efforts, such as social media posts, website, etc. Initially, it's simple: Do I like something about *this thing in front of me?* In time, the more often they are exposed (through any of your active or passive marketing actions), the deeper their engagement becomes. They begin to wonder, *maybe this business could solve my problem.* Or *this company seems like one I can trust.* When they reach

the point of thinking, *I'd like to try, maybe even buy, this,* they move on to the next stage of the journey.

- **Opt-In:** At this phase, the customer is ready to get to know you a bit better. They trust you enough to give you their name, email, and ideally phone number. They look to you for valuable content that addresses their problems; at this point the opt-in happens in exchange for some sort of value-providing freebie, such as a booklet, infographic, or video.
- **Onboard:** Now that you have the customer's contact information, you can promote an easy offer, which proposes a small-value sale or a low-priced webinar or a consultation or discovery meeting where the sales prospect spends time with you. When they make this small investment, you can think of it as the customer coming onboard your company.
- **Inspire:** This is where you make the customer feel special and endear yourself to them. Truth is, this phase never ends. After the customer has accepted your easy offer, you continue to build their trust and the relationships with a nurture sequence—that's a pre-planned series of communications via email, video, or text message—that creates an ongoing conversation to give them confidence that they've made the right decision and keep you top of mind.
- **Grow:** At this point the customer decides to purchase your full product, and you may have an opportunity for upselling (for example, a subscription service) or cross selling (like an accessory that goes well with their purchase). Make this stage as easy and pleasant for the customer as possible: greet them kindly, answer any questions they have, assure them you can solve their problem, confirm their intention, and accept their payment. Providing several options for payment, such as Apple Pay, Venmo, or a credit card, helps make it easy for a customer to pay you.

- **Endorse:** The shift from purchase to delivery is subtle yet critical. The customer's experience continues, and you want to make sure that experience is excellent. Fast delivery is usually better than slow delivery, especially if you keep your quality high. Although purchasing and delivery are later stages on their journey, the customer is constantly gaining new awareness about you and your business and evaluating whether you solve their problem. After they've received your product/service, ask about their experience and request testimonials or user-generated content. At this point, the customer has shown they enjoy spending time with you.
- **Broadcast:** By making a purchase, the customer has demonstrated interest and trust in what you do. At this point, the customer loves you so much they actively promote what you do the value they receive from your product/service. These customers make excellent affiliates or ambassadors, who do your marketing for free.

Marketing doesn't end when the customer makes a purchase; you continue to make them feel special and nurture them. At each phase of the customer journey, you constantly add value and build their trust in you. The time between each phase can be short. For example, if the customer sees a friend using your product, Discover and Explore and Connect may happen simultaneously. The timeline between Grow and Endorse can be less than a second or longer—some people post a purchase on social media immediately. It's critical, however, to go through each step. If you push too fast or skip a step, you lose the trust you've built—it's like asking for marriage and talking about your kids on a first date!

If you think about dating, the customer journey mimics the stages of building human relationships, whether friendships or romantic relationships—from when you first notice someone, all the way through to the wedding day. In the Discover stage, you see someone across a crowded room and walk over to introduce yourself. In Explore and Connect, you begin chatting to garner interest. Ideally, you hit it off and when you ask the person for their contact information, they give it to you, perhaps in exchange for the promise of meeting up later; this is like asking for their email and giving them a freebie. At the Onboard stage, you go out on a date and after that date, you follow up in the Inspire stage with all kinds of different tactics, from fun text messages, flowers, chocolates, to any other things that make the person feel special and think of you fondly. When you move from Inspire to Grow, the person has perhaps agreed to become intimate—they're all in and committed. At the Endorse stage, you're engaged and the person is telling everyone how great you are. The final stage of Broadcast equals marriage. The person has declared you'll be together for the long term, and is willing to publicly proclaim how great you are.

You want to nurture the customer to create a deep, long relationship in which you continue to solve their problems, maybe developing new products/services based on their feedback, and they continue to buy from you. The customer journey forms the foundation of your marketing funnel and campaign. You want as many customers as possible to like your company so much that they start to promote your business to their friends and family. The customer journey provides the process and tactics to move a person from a stranger to a super fan.

As you can see in the diagram that follows, the customer journey is more of a web than a line. It begins with awareness but once a customer is aware of you, they continue to return to points along the journey. For example, a customer who reaches the Opt-In to Onboard stage, may go forward to make a large purchase (sometimes called a core purchase) or may continue to Explore and Connect. All the more reason to remain active and consistent in your actions and messages at every phase of the journey.

Customer Value Journey

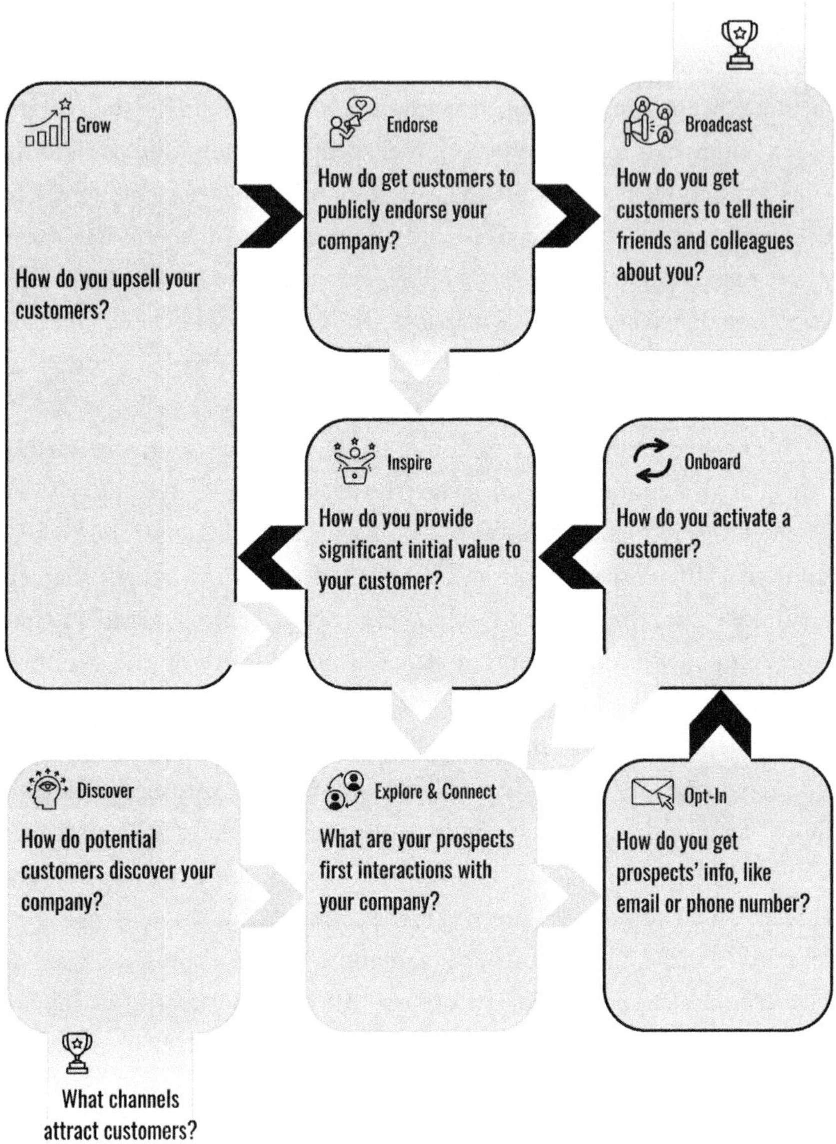

Marketing Funnel

You'll find that not all people who go through the phases of Discover and Explore and Connect move on to make a purchase. This is called a marketing funnel. At the discovery stage, the large pool of target customers come in through the wide end of the funnel; you are marketing to as many people as you can within your target audience. As the customer travels along the journey, the funnel narrows to the point that a fraction of the people who entered the funnel make a purchase and even fewer become return customers and promoters.

When you think about your marketing and sales plans, you assign numbers to the levels of the funnel to determine if your efforts are working. These numbers come from the research you did when creating the Product-Market Fit Plan and were further honed when you worked on the Customer Profile. Later in this chapter in the section Define Your Target Numbers, you'll learn about determining the size of the market and setting your sales goals.

For example, let's say you place a Facebook ad to reach 1,000 impressions (Discover). Of those impressions, perhaps 500 move on to Explore and Connect, then 200 Opt-In. Of those, 50 sign up for your easy offer, 20 make a large purchase, and five purchase a bundle and write a testimonial for you.

When you first start out, the numbers you assign to the levels on the marketing funnel will be your best guess. These numbers will change and become more accurate as you test different marketing tactics and always get to know your customer better.

DISCUSSION GUIDE

- To recap, what problems does your customer have that your product/service can solve?
- What problems is your business solving for your customers? Does the intended customer have the problems you solve? Successful businesses solve clear problems for their customers.
- What product/service are you selling?
- Think about the customer journey, what message will you communicate with the customer at each phase? You'll think about how you'll communicate that message in the next section.
    - Discover
    - Explore and Connect
    - Opt-In
    - Onboard
    - Inspire
    - Grow
    - Endorse
    - Broadcast
- How many customers do you think will pass through each part of the marketing funnel along the customer journey?

Create a Marketing Plan

While large organizations often separate marketing and sales, we believe sales and marketing go together for the early-stage entrepreneur. Marketing is, in part, a one-two punch of creating content—social media posts, blogs, advertising, etc.—that speaks to your ideal customer, and then putting that content in places your customer visits. Sales is an integral part of the marketing process; you are always selling to your customer. While you don't have to continually shout "buy my thing!" you do want your customer to know your solution exists (build awareness) and on occasion specifically ask them to buy from you.

In Chapter 4, Product and Service Development, you defined what you're marketing (your product or service), how much you're selling it for (your price), and how you'll sell and deliver it. In this chapter, you defined your Four Horsemen™ and gained an understanding of the phases of the customer journey. You also did some preliminary work running numbers for your marketing funnel. You're now ready to create your marketing and sales plans.

We've identified 15 channels through which you both market and sell to your customer, and we've explained each of them here. In marketing today, there are two types of marketing: digital and traditional. Few companies can get away with not having an online presence and doing some sort of digital marketing, and sometimes traditional marketing can outperform digital marketing depending on who your customers are. As you read through the descriptions, begin to think about which ones are the best choices for communicating with your customer.

Digital marketing is the act of promoting and selling products and services by leveraging online marketing tactics such as social media marketing, search engine marketing, email marketing, blogging, and others. The number one rule in digital marketing, and marketing in general, is to make the right offer, at the right time, in the right place.

Digital marketing puts you in front of your customers so your best prospects can see you, learn more about you, and even ask questions to learn more about you and your products or services. It also provides a global version of word-of-mouth advertising. Online reviews, testimonials, and stories can show new customers everything they need to know about your brand and product/service before they decide to give it a shot for themselves.

Traditional marketing is a conventional mode of marketing that helps reach a semi-targeted audience with various offline advertising and promotional methods. It's a form of marketing that we have been exposed to at one point or another and includes business cards, fliers, brochures, print ads, media coverage, letters, and call scripts. Some types of traditional marketing, such as trade shows, events, and direct sales, can be more targeted and used to connect directly and in person with your potential customer.

Traditional marketing puts you in front of your customers at a specific location (or through a specific medium), but you won't always have control of when they see it.

The 15 Marketing and Sales Channels

Each of the following channels offers an effective and valid way to reach a specific type of customer. Of course, customers frequent more than one channel, so you want to make sure you have a consistent message in all locations your consumer might interact with your business. When a customer receives an email newsletter from you then sees your post on Instagram, you want them to instantly, unconsciously recognize that the two pieces of content promote the same business.

As you begin to develop content, you'll find you can repurpose content you create for one channel on one or more other channels. For example, the post you create for Facebook could also be a blog post and an email newsletter if you simply adjust the length to fit the medium. A poster-sized ad you create for a local event could also be used as a social media post.

Of course you can create content for all 15 channels, but we recommend that you choose one—and not more than three—to begin with and concentrate your efforts there. You will find that content you create for one channel can be repurposed and used in another channel, and we encourage efficiency in your efforts to save time and energy. As your marketing skills grow and improve, you may decide to add another channel or replace one that isn't performing well for you.

This section is dense with information. We suggest you read through it to familiarize yourself with all the options then choose the one channel that is most appropriate for you to reach your customers.

The key to successful marketing is consistency of your message, your brand, and the actions themselves—posting to social media three times a week, sending an email newsletter twice a month, attending the local community business meeting each month, writing a thank you email after a customer makes a large purchase or posts a glowing review. The goal of marketing is for customers to become familiar with you, your brand, and your product/service. As they get to know you and come to trust you as the expert in the field who can solve their problem—because the quality and consistency of your marketing demonstrates that you understand them—they become more likely to buy from you. The pinnacle of marketing happens when your customers return to buy from you again and recommend your product/service to their friends.

In the next section, we go through the process of creating a marketing plan and a calendar to schedule the marketing activities you'll do.

1. Social media marketing

Social media marketing is the process of creating content that's optimized for each individual social media platform in order to drive user engagement and sharing. You can also buy targeted ads on these platforms to leverage their technology to find your customers at scale. As with any marketing, your goal is to build brand awareness and conversions of different types. You may want to convert an unknown person into a follower or have them sign up for your email newsletter. Often, it takes several conversions before the follower becomes a paying customer.

Use your Facebook, Instagram, and TikTok accounts to engage customers (we talk about setting up business accounts in Chapter 7, Website and Technology). Ask your friends to post about your business. Make interesting, cool, and educational posts to get people to take your business seriously. Let people know what your business is doing, how it can help them solve their problem. Try to post regularly (at least every couple of days). Don't just focus on self promotion, though. Try to find ways to educate, inspire, and elevate your audience as well. While posting provocative messaging or attention seeking content can drive views, you want to get the right views.

Social media is a noisy place and building an audience takes consistent effort over time. Entrepreneurs often get discouraged quickly when they aren't getting as many new followers each day as they hoped. We can offer some suggestions for growing your audience organically, or without paying for ads.

- Create new content regularly. Original photos and videos seem to get more attention.
- Make your content easy for users to discover by using hashtags that relate to your product/service.
- Make content that's easy to share; the more shares, the more people love your content.
- Share blogs or articles that you've written either on your own website or as a guest on someone else's website.
- Share links to any YouTube videos you create or podcasts that you're a guest on.
- Follow and repost content from other people or businesses who reach your audience. When you follow someone, they often will follow back.
- Ask people to comment so you can engage with them; comments are a great way for your customers to get to know you. The quality of comments also factors into how posts get promoted.
- It's okay to repost older posts; not everyone will have seen—or remember—everything you post and it's an easy way to bump up the number of times you post each week.

We think of three phases of engagement between a potential customer and your social media post. The content of your post will vary depending on the goal you have for the post. These are from lowest to highest engagement and impact, but that doesn't mean they aren't equally important.

The customer is on a journey of learning about you and studies show it takes seven hits before they recognize and begin to engage with you. Try to make your social media content a mix of these types of posts:

- **Brand Awareness:** If you're looking to create content that generates awareness for your brand, not for a specific product or service, consider creating videos/blogs that detail stories of and related to your company.
- **Product Awareness:** If you're creating content to build product/service awareness, your content should emphasize the problems that exist and how your product/service solves them.
- **Consideration/Research:** To meet this goal, create actionable content that teaches your target audience how to solve a specific problem.

The trend of social media is heading away from organic engagement and more toward 'pay to play,' so at some point you may want to think about creating ads to target customers. Most social media sites still have very reasonable advertising costs, particularly if you have thought through your advertisements well. Consider the following when planning a paid social media strategy:

1. **Be clear on who your customer is.** You'll be in a better position to take advantage of the paid traffic methods provided by social media platforms. When creating ads, you'll want to choose to target customers based on their demographic, device, age, interests, and a load of other characteristics. The various platforms will often lead you through a process to help you target appropriately.
2. **Decide on your goals.** Get clear on your media campaign goals. Do you want to drive traffic to your website, drive conversions (sales), promote your Facebook Page or business website, get engagement on your post, or something else? The post that you use for an ad should include a clear call to action or CTA, that's the action you want people to take when they see your post. When

you purchase ads, you can then see analytics for how the ad performed. For this type of campaign, you'll be interested in 'website visits and click-through rates.'

3. **Decide on your approach.** Think about the type of content you'll use to achieve your goals, i.e., images, videos, and text posts, etc.
4. **Generate engagement.** Create ads (images, reels, videos, written text, etc.) that inspire action in your customer because the content or message is helpful, funny, inspiring etc.
5. **Set your budget limits.** It is too easy to overspend on ads, so you need to constantly evaluate if the results you're getting are worth the cost of your ads.

Most social media sites have some sort of analytics, or data, that tell you how your posts and ads are performing. You want to see an uptick in visits to your website on the days you run your ads. If you aren't seeing more website traffic, you can adjust the demographics of your ad or adjust the content of the ad itself. Notice if there is any change. Make sure you check the analytics regularly to make the most out of your ad budget!

DISCUSSION GUIDE

- What customer do you want to reach with your social media posts?
- Which social media platforms do your customers use?
- Have you set up your business accounts on those platforms?
- What would you like to achieve with your social media posts?
- Think about the three types of content—Brand Awareness, Product Awareness, Consideration/Research—and list 10 content ideas and types for each category.
- Look at the analytics for each of your posts. Which type of post and content received the most views and engagement?

2. Content Marketing

Everything you create can be considered content, and as we mentioned before, your content should help your customer solve their problem or benefit them in some way. Content marketing specifically involves you becoming a teacher of sorts in your business field. As a sales and marketing channel, content marketing can be everything from creating videos, reels, and images to written posts.

This kind of marketing often means writing articles or blog posts that you share on various platforms, such as LinkedIn, Substack, Medium, your own website, or someone else's website (this is known as guest posting). The thing that sets content marketing apart is that it's not just self-promotional or salesy—it should provide interesting, entertaining, or useful information to the customer even if it doesn't convert them to a sale right away. For that reason, its definition could also be expanded to include podcasts or guest spots on podcasts, a medium where listeners often forge a more intimate connection. In addition, as you build a mailing list by collecting the email addresses of your target customers, you can also send an email newsletter which has a roundup of all the blogs, articles, or content you've published over the last period.

An "article" doesn't have to be overly long or complicated. Many articles are written in the form of lists that provide a roundup of information or how-to instructions, recount an interview with a customer or another expert in your field, or tell an anecdote in an entertaining way. You want your content to be useful and accurate, but it doesn't have to be overwhelming to write.

Content can also be created in the form of videos that teach your customer something that helps them solve their problem. You can then post the video on a video channel like YouTube or Vimeo and/or on your website.

All the content you create can then be mentioned in a social media post or email.

DISCUSSION GUIDE

- What knowledge or skills do you have that your customers would find helpful?
- Make a list of five topics you could write or make a video about that would help your customer solve their problem.
- How can you share your article or video with your customers? Will you post on your website, social media, or both?

3. Viral or Guerrilla Marketing

Guerrilla or viral marketing campaigns aim to strike the consumer at a more personal and memorable level. This technique plays heavily on the element of surprise. It sets out to create highly unconventional campaigns that catch people unexpectedly during their day-to-day routines. Guerrilla marketing tends to be unpredictable and hard to know exactly what the outcome will be. For that reason, they are high stakes and high risk, but if they work out, they make a far more valuable impression with customers in comparison to more traditional forms of advertising and marketing. The goal is to inspire individuals to share the campaign's message to friends, family, and other individuals to create exponential growth.

Think about how you can do something so interesting, crazy, or unique that you attract the attention of newspapers and TV news stations. This could be a marketing scheme, a video you make, a photo, or an article you write. Think about the risks involved in your marketing stunt before you do it! This is a place where your creativity can go a long way to getting your business name out there.

All viral marketing examples—deliberate or accidental—have three things in common: the message, the messenger, and the environment. Each part must be leveraged to create a successful viral marketing campaign. Viral marketing campaigns may be created by any size of business and can stand alone or be a part of a larger traditional campaign. The campaigns themselves may utilize several tools, such as videos, games, images, email and text messaging, free products, appealing to the emotions of users or viewers, raising awareness to a worthy cause, and making such products, ideas, or media easy to consume and share. Viral marketing often relies on the help of an influencer, who has a large network of followers.

Viral marketing can be less expensive than traditional marketing campaigns yet grow faster, especially with the help of social networks. Since it can receive so much traffic in a short time, it can also lead to mainstream media attention. However, keep in mind that social media can also cause viral marketing efforts to misfire, as messages are altered, misconstrued, considered spam, or called out for missing the mark. Viral marketing success can also be hard to execute and measure.

DISCUSSION GUIDE

- What funny or silly trends have you noticed in your field?
- What kind of content are you best at creating that could go viral? Video, images, written, etc.
- Is there an event or holiday you could link to a guerrilla marketing stunt?
- Could you offer an absurd giveaway of your time or product?
- What is a safe guerrilla marketing stunt that you could do?

4. Search Engine Optimization (SEO)

SEO stands for search engine optimization, which is the practice of increasing the quality and quantity of traffic to your website through organic (unpaid) search engine results. This is typically a long-term strategy, so it can be more effective to do after you've launched and are building for the long run. An effective SEO strategy can help you improve the following:

- **Quality of traffic:** You can attract all the visitors in the world, but if they're coming to your site because Google tells them you're a resource for Apple computers when really you're a farmer selling apples, that is not quality traffic. Instead, you want to attract visitors who are genuinely interested in products that you offer.
- **Quantity of traffic:** Once the quality of the search engine results improves, your chances of the right people clicking through from those search engine results pages improves—more traffic means more eyeballs on your website, which gives you an opportunity to create a call to action (buy something, sign up for a newsletter, subscribe to a blog).
- **Organic results:** Ads make up a significant portion of many hits on the Search Engine Results Page (SERPs). Organic traffic is any traffic that you don't pay for.

When a person types a word or phrase into a search engine like Google, Bing, or DuckDuckGo, the search engine—and now Generative AI platforms like ChatGPT—combs the internet for matches. When your website contains words and phrases (known as keywords) someone is looking for, you have optimized your website for that search—and that's Search Engine Optimization. As you create content for your website, you want to include as many relevant keywords as possible to increase the chances of the search engine finding you. The better the match and the more frequently someone clicks on your site, the higher your site ranks in the search engine results, meaning you show up on the first page of the results.

Entrepreneurs spend a lot of time thinking about the keywords their customers use to search for solutions and looking for ways to incorporate them into their website. We'll talk more about identifying and using keywords and other elements that generate SEO in Chapter 7, Website and Technology, about building your website.

DISCUSSION GUIDE

- What keywords do your customers think of when searching for a solution to their problem?
- Make a list of 20 keywords and then search for them yourself to see if those keywords bring up your competition. If so, these are good keywords for you to use, too.
- Search your keywords again and look at the suggested search terms that appear in the list of the Search field. Note any that could be keywords to include on your website.
- What types of content could you put on your website to match the keywords and increase your SEO?

5. Ads: Search Engine Marketing (SEM) and Social Media Marketing (SMM)

Search engine marketing (SEM) is a digital marketing strategy used to increase the visibility of a website in search engine results pages, usually through Google Ads. Similarly, and as discussed earlier in this chapter, social media sites like Facebook and Instagram have a feature that allows you to buy ads for your business, called Social Media Marketing.

You've seen search engine marketing in action if you've noticed the first five to seven results of a search are "Sponsored," which means the company paid to appear at the top of the list. In search engine marketing, advertisers only pay for clicks that result in visitors, making it an efficient way for a company to spend its marketing dollars. As a bonus, each visitor incrementally improves the website's rankings in organic search results. Since consumers enter search queries with the intent of finding information of a commercial nature, they are in an excellent state of mind to receive marketing messages and to be nurtured as prospective customers. Search engine marketing reaches consumers at exactly the right time: when they are open to new information. Unlike most digital advertising, search engine marketing is non-intrusive and does not interrupt their tasks. It is arguably the fastest way to drive traffic to a website, but it is expensive—there is a reason Google is one of the most valuable companies in the world.

Create an ad that helps people understand how your products and services benefit them. Set a spending limit each month so that you don't spend more money than you want to on marketing; consider buying $20 worth of Facebook Ads to market your website or social media pages. Check out Google Ads and see how you can create advertisements on Google for your business.

Combine your paid SEM efforts with search engine optimization (SEO) to improve your chances at driving traffic to your business site. You can also create paid ads to target specific customer types. This way, you can customize your messaging and overall content for the greatest impact.

Look at the analytics for your website traffic after your ad runs; if you see an uptick in website visits, this means your ad is working. Even better, configure your ads to an action that your potential customer takes, whether it is signing up for your list or—best of all—purchasing your product. If you don't see results, it can mean that you targeted the wrong customer, or your message wasn't resonating. If your budget allows, you can try creating a different ad and run it with the same customer demographics or try the same ad with different customer demographics. If you make too many changes at one time, you may not know which change worked (or didn't work), so try to make one change at a time to determine which tactic is most effective.

DISCUSSION GUIDE

- What message could you share in an ad that you place online?
- Which social media platform do your customers use?
- Will you place an ad on social media, i.e., Facebook or Instagram, or a search engine like Google, or both?
- How much can you spend?
- Did your ad drive traffic to your website?

6. Online Platforms

The largest mall in the world is now online, as is the biggest hotel and taxi company. Amazon, Airbnb, and Uber are all examples of e-commerce businesses. The internet is impossible to ignore for entrepreneurs, because consumers have changed how they discover, interact, and shop for products and services. Let's explore the major different types of e-commerce types: business-to-business (B2B), business-to-consumer (B2C), business-to-government (B2G), consumer-to-consumer (C2C), and mobile commerce (m-commerce).

- B2B e-commerce happens when one business buys a product or service from another business. This type of e-commerce deals with relationships between and among businesses and takes up about 80 percent of the e-commerce interactions. Although getting the initial sale can take time, effort, and multiple meetings to demonstrate your capacity, in the long term B2B relationships often develop into repeated, ongoing sales. They have a higher ratio of price to costs (profit margin) and can be more profitable than selling to an individual. To be successful in B2B sales, an entrepreneur needs to:
    - Understand the organization's problems.
    - Help them save money or make more.

  - Help them be better, faster, or cheaper.
  - Build relationships with the customer.
- B2C e-commerce involves individuals purchasing physical goods, information goods such as digitized content like e-books or online courses, or services like booking hotel rooms. Physical goods are purchased online and then delivered; information goods and services are delivered via the internet. B2C is the second largest and the earliest form of e-commerce but is also a tough business model because profit margins are low, even with value-based pricing. To be successful in B2C sales, an entrepreneur needs to:
  - Remove friction along the course of the customer journey—demonstrate that they solve the customer's problem and make it easy for the customer to decide and complete a purchase.
  - In selling to an individual, marketing is often the sale itself, so marketing campaigns need to show they understand the customer and that the product/service meets their needs.
- B2G e-commerce is generally defined as commerce between a company and the public sector. It refers to the use of the internet for public procurement, licensing procedures, and other government-related operations. The government agency at the federal, state, or local level typically issues a Request For Proposal (RFP) for a type of good (from defense airplanes to toilet seats) or service (like cleaning the offices or providing cybersecurity), businesses response with a bid, and then the sale is awarded to the most qualified seller and price.
- C2C e-commerce is simply commerce between private individuals, like online auctions on eBay.
- M-commerce or mobile commerce is the buying and selling of goods and services through wireless technology, such as cell phones.

There are many online marketplaces or e-commerce platforms where you can sell your products and services. Each of them has its own monetization strategy (some offer free plans and others limit you to a free trial), audience, benefits to sellers, and specific products to sell on them. Consider all these factors to choose the best marketplace to sell your product/service and increase profit, as well as promote your brand. You may sell your product/service on one of these platforms alone or use them in addition to other channels, such as your website.

While a site like Amazon.com sells *everything*, a site like Etsy is known for handmade or artisan items. Likewise, Airbnb sells lodging and has branched out to include custom tourist experiences, and a site like Reedsy focuses on editorial services. If you sell services, consider creating postings and profiles on Thumbtack, Freelancer, Craigslist, Postmates, Fiverr, Upwork and others. If you sell products, consider listing your products on Amazon.com, Etsy, and others—don't forget your own website.

When choosing an e-commerce platform, keep in mind the reach and the potential higher costs to reach a larger audience. A platform like Amazon can reach out-of-state and international customers. Consider the fees involved in working with an e-commerce provider and make sure to include them in your pricing analysis.

DISCUSSION GUIDE

- What type of commerce does your business have? You may have more than one.
- What e-commerce platforms are a good fit for your product/service?
- Are you comfortable posting your product on a global platform and shipping internationally?
- What fees does the platform charge and are your prices such that you can be profitable by selling on the platform?

7. Email Marketing

Email is a great way to stay in touch with customers as well as people who support your business efforts, like family and friends who can spread the word about your work. Begin collecting email addresses as soon as you begin thinking about your business idea. Initially, create a list of emails of everyone you know, put their information in a Google Spreadsheet or Excel document, or use a service like Mailchimp or MailerLite (search "free email marketing tools" to find one that works for you). Then, start emailing everyone on the list with updates about your business and photos of your progress on a regular schedule, whether that's once a month or once a week. Reaching out regularly both builds a good habit for you and sets expectations for your future customers.

When you begin creating marketing content, like blog posts or videos, you can repurpose that content and share it with your email list.

Of course, you want to grow your mailing list since, unlike social media platforms that can change or go out of business (meaning you could lose your contacts there), your email list remains yours. When you meet potential customers, ask them for their email address and let them know you'll be sharing useful, helpful information about their problems and your solutions, as well as special offers and promotions. When you post on social media, you can add a link to a signup form and ask people to add their name to your mailing list. If you attend a live event, you can have a paper or digital sign-up sheet to collect names and email addresses from people who are interested in what you do. And, on the emails you send, you can include a sentence that reads, "If you know someone who would enjoy reading this, please forward this email to them."

There are a lot of laws around online privacy and email marketing, and many people don't want to be inundated with email. When you ask someone for their email, let them know in writing that they are agreeing to receive email from you. For example, if someone places an order online, you'll probably need their email to confirm their order, let them know it's shipped, etc., but there should be a separate box they have to check that confirms they allow you to send other types of email to them. Include an unsubscribe button on your email so people can cancel at any time and remove their email from their list.

Every communication you have with your customer is a marketing opportunity, so make it a pleasant experience for them. If you send an order confirmation email or an invoice, take the time to design it to match your brand (all about that in Chapter 6, Branding), personalize it with their name rather than "Dear Customer," and thank them for their business. You want your customer to always think highly of your business.

DISCUSSION GUIDE

- Make a spreadsheet with the email addresses of your friends and family. Think about exporting your contact list from your email and phone.
- What news about your business can you share with your friends and family?
- Have you asked your family and friends to share your email with people they know who may be interested in your business?
- Where and how can you encourage people to add their email to your mailing list?
- Can you list 13 ideas for email content? That gives you an idea to write an email once a week for three months.

8. Speaking Events

Entrepreneurs often love to talk about their business, so signing up to speak in front of potential customers offers a great marketing opportunity. Think about events your customers attend and ask if you could make a presentation at one or more of them. Before you pitch yourself as a speaker, write a few paragraphs about your talk and add a paragraph with your bio that proves you're the best person to give this talk. Remember, your customers want to hear about how you can solve their problem so referring to your customer interviews (Chapter 3, Customer Development) can help you identify the topic of your speech.

If you don't feel ready to pitch a formal speech, you can attend events and participate in discussions with your potential customers. Organizations are more likely to accept speakers who they already know.

Speaking opportunities aren't limited to live, in-person events. You can also pitch yourself as a guest on a podcast or a Facebook or Instagram Live event. Wherever you're speaking, make sure you address the listeners' problem and provide helpful information. You can also host your own webinar. Create an online event, promote it on social media, your website, and to your mailing list, and then run the event on a platform like Zoom or GoogleMeet.

DISCUSSION GUIDE

- What events do your customers attend?
- Make a list of five events where you'd like to speak.
- What topics would be interesting to the audience?
- Why are you the best person to talk about your topic to the audience?
- Have you written a few paragraphs to summarize your speech and a paragraph about you?
- Is hosting a webinar something you could do? If so, when will you create one and what topic will you speak about?

9. Trade Shows

Meeting people face-to-face is a powerful way to communicate the benefits of your business. Most industries have one or more trade shows each year where business owners can meet with peers, suppliers, and customers. You can learn about your industry's trade shows through online searching. Large venues, such as a convention center, will often publish a calendar of events on their website, and these events are typically booked up to five years in advance, so this can be a great way to learn about the trade shows that will be held in your area.

You can attend a trade show as a participant or host a booth. As a participant you have the chance to meet vendors or service providers, compare yourself to the competition, and meet with potential customers. Many trade shows also offer speaker sessions that you can attend to learn more about your industry—or you can pitch yourself as a speaker, if you have experience to share! If you decide to host a booth, you want to evaluate the cost of doing so. It can be a significant investment, but can also be a significant opportunity to meet potential customers and even make sales. Think about splitting costs for a booth or other creative ways to get into the trade show.

DISCUSSION GUIDE

- What trade shows do your customers attend?
- Why do they attend those trade shows?
- Would attending a trade show help you grow your business?
- What trade shows could you attend, or speak or host a booth at?

10. Community

Word-of-mouth marketing—when someone tells someone else about your business or product/service—is the best way to get new customers. When you build a community, you create an enthusiastic group of potential word-of-mouth marketers. Your community can be an informal, highly engaged group of followers on social media or a more organized formal group that meets regularly to talk about topics related to your business, with you leading the conversation.

When you have a handful of people who interact and engage regularly with you on social media, you can reach out to them and create an informal group, perhaps set up a time to meet online and simply chat. This is also a great way to learn more about your customer and their problem so you can improve your product/service.

Most formal communities started as informal encounters. When an entrepreneur saw a need emerging—a like-minded group of people wanting to convene and share experiences—they filled it by formalizing the group. Service-based entrepreneurs often create paid communities where members pay a fee to participate in educational or discussion meetings for a certain amount of time and receive other benefits as well, like workbooks or individualized coaching.

When your customers become part of your community, they demonstrate their loyalty to you and your business. Smart entrepreneurs don't take this loyalty lightly but reward it with appreciation and attention.

DISCUSSION GUIDE

- Do you have engaged customers on your social media accounts?
- How could you build a loyal community for your business?
- Could you schedule a meeting with your most engaged followers?
- What type of activities could you offer to create a formal community?
- Is a paid community something your customers would subscribe to?
- What steps would you need to take to create a paid community?

11. Events

Where are your target customers going to events or meetings? Get out into the community and start speaking at meetings and events. Create an interesting talk to engage these audiences, tell them your story, or educate them on how your business is helping people in the community.

Consider how you can either go to other people's events, or throw your own launch event, to show more people your business and your great products and services. Your local Chamber of Commerce or your town's website may have a list of events in your area, like a neighborhood block party, an arts or food fair, or a holiday extravaganza. Talk to event organizers about how your company could participate. You may be able to speak at the event or sell your products. Community events often look for local sponsors who buy ad space on their promotion materials, and this is another opportunity to build awareness for your business while supporting your local community.

When you launch your business or a new product or service, consider hosting your own event to create awareness and draw people into your space. If you don't have a physical retail space, you can rent a conference room at a hotel, take over a restaurant for an evening, or hold an outdoor event in a local park. With some imagination, you can find low, medium, and high-cost venues. You might also partner with someone who has a complementary business that speaks to the same customers that you do.

DISCUSSION GUIDE

- What kinds of events do your customers like and attend?
- What events in the next year align with your business?
- How can you participate in existing events?
- What kind of event could you host yourself or with a partner?

12. Physical Ads

Think about where you see ads around your community; do businesses like yours advertise on a bus stop? The train? A bench? In the newspaper? We know of a small town with a local, one-screen movie theater that shows ads for local businesses before the film. An ad can be as simple as a flier with tear off tabs that you post in your local school to offer tutoring services or as fancy as a full-color, full-page ad in a glossy magazine. The cost of advertising varies widely depending on where you place the ad, how many people could potentially see the ad, the size, and whether it's in color or black-and-white. For example, a small black-and-white ad in your neighborhood gazette may cost less than $20 a month, while a black-and-white, full-page ad in the national edition of *The New York Times* runs $150,000 for a single day. The key, as with all your sales and marketing activities, is to advertise in places that your customers will see. You want the investment you make in advertising to pay off in sales.

DISCUSSION GUIDE

- Where do your customers see physical ads?
- What type of ad would be most effective for your business—fliers, newspaper ads, bus stop posters?
- How much can you afford to invest in advertising?

13. Public Relations and Publicity

Most of the marketing and sales channels here come with a cost. The only way to get "free" marketing is to convince other people to talk or write about you—and even then, there's the cost of your time to pitch yourself or your story as a topic they want to cover.

As you become known as an expert in your field, people may reach out to interview you. But at the beginning of your entrepreneurial journey, you need to tell them about your business; you can pitch your idea to people in the media. Talk to people who are involved with TV news reporting, popular online blogs, newspapers, or organizations with large communities who would be willing to feature your business or write a story about you. Many local TV stations have a business section that looks for interesting success stories or highlights businesses that are making an impact on the community. Or your trade industry may have a monthly or quarterly magazine that includes articles about members. You need to figure out your edge—why should the media write about you? Often this is about finding a way to fit into what that media person you're pitching wants to write about. Again, talk to them to figure this out!

Write a few paragraphs about the topic you can discuss and one paragraph about why you're the best person to discuss it, then send an email to the contact you've identified to pitch your idea. The overall goal is to make you and your business better-known in the community.

DISCUSSION GUIDE

- What knowledge or skills can you share?
- Does your success story have an interesting angle?
- Is your business having an impact on your local community?
- What media outlets might be interested in your story?
- Identify journalists or reporters at those outlets and pitch your story to them.

14. Direct Sales

Make a list of people and businesses who you think may be interested in purchasing your product or service—start with the ones you know best—and then set up an appointment to sell them on your idea in person or over the phone. You can also look to your community to identify people who can be "brand ambassadors" and will share your social media posts, create their own posts highlighting your product or service, and generally get the word out about your business. You can also identify influencers on social media; if someone has a lot of followers who are your target customer, you can offer them a sample of your product or service—or even cash—in exchange for their honest review or just promoting your company.

Entrepreneurs who are just starting out often recruit college students to conduct direct sales on commission or in exchange for products. While they aren't paying the salesperson a salary, there is the cost of the commission or product to cover. If you decide to enlist someone to help you with sales, consider the cost involved and make sure it's an expense you can afford at this stage of your business.

Lastly, think about other businesses that could sell your products. For example, if an entrepreneur makes hair beads, they may sell them online on their website, through e-commerce at Etsy, and at a local hair salon. If an entrepreneur offers massages, they may work directly with clients and go to their homes, and contract with a chiropractor to offer massages to their patients in their office. In these two examples, the hair salon and the chiropractor are selling the product or service for the entrepreneur.

DISCUSSION GUIDE

- Can you list, and contact, 10 people or businesses who you believe would like to buy your product/service?
- Can you ask five people in your community to be brand ambassadors?
- Can you ask five people to sell your product on commission? Does that fit with your budget?
- Are there any stores or other professionals that could re-sell your product or service?

15. Partners

We identify two kinds of partners who can support your sales and marketing efforts:

- **Individuals**: your personal connections who might be willing to tell their friends and family about your business
- **Organizations**: businesses, clubs, nonprofits, etc. who may be able to partner with you either by promoting your business or directly selling your product/service

Partner, of course, implies that you are doing something for them as well. Your connections help you in exchange for your friendship or relation. An organization will expect mutual support from you toward their success. These types of partnerships often happen when two businesses are complementary.

For example, if you are a caterer, you can partner with an event planner to cater at their events, then you can sell the event planner's services to other customers who come to you for catering.

Influencers—even micro influencers—have the power to drive thousands of dollars in online sales to your online store. Find and partner with influencers across your ideal customer's favorite platform—be that Instagram or TikTok—and leverage their audience loyalty to make sales.

DISCUSSION GUIDE

- Ask 20 people in your personal network to tell one other person about your business, product, or service.
- What organizations reach your target customer?
- What benefit can you bring to those organizations?
- Ask three of those organizations if they will partner with you.

Now that you're familiar with the sales and marketing channels that you can use to reach your customer, it's time to think about the content you will share. Remember, you should NOT attempt all 15 of these channels when you're first starting out—you may never use some of them. We suggest starting with one, but if you're ambitious, we suggest limiting your efforts to three channels.

Putting a Plan in Place

Every entrepreneur is a content creator. From fliers to social media posts to sales contracts to customer service responses, entrepreneurs spend a lot of time thinking about, writing, photographing, and creating content. Effectively communicating benefits to the consumer is a crucial step for all businesses; customers care more about how a product solves their problem or creates value than about how it works. The message you offer your customer should be consistent across all channels, but the type of content you create will depend on the marketing and sales channels you choose to use to reach your customers.

Customers want to know:

- How your business solves their problem
- The benefits of buying from you

The message in any type of marketing content should address at least one if not both of those factors. The language you use in marketing should reflect the tone of your brand (see Chapter 6, Branding) but the goal of your message is to show that you understand your customer and convince them that your business has what they need. To do so:

- Define the techniques (e.g., will your tone be one of teaching, inspiration, or FOMO) you will use to ensure that interest in your product/service translates to a sale.
- Structure messages to inspire your customer (refer to customer profile in Chapter 3, Customer Development) to buy from you.
- Look at the lists of the problems you laid out and make sure messaging responds to those problems. Refer to the work you did in Chapters 3 and 4, Customer Development, and Product and Service Development, specifically the list of problems your customer has and how your product/service solves them.

As you develop content, you want to think beyond simply selling. Engaging customers means sharing something of value to them, which may be an instructional video, something that makes them laugh, or a discount on your product. You want your customer to think of you as an expert and leader in your field. If you offer lawn care services, your customer wants to believe you know what that oddly shaped brown spot under the magnolia tree is or how to get rid of moles. If you offer sustainably produced, organic cotton t-shirts, your customer wants to believe you have done the research and work with ethical partners. Both of those examples are opportunities for creating content. Create a carousel for Instagram or Facebook or send a monthly newsletter to your customers—and potential customers—with quick tips for keeping your lawn green or writing about the difference between organic and non-organic cotton.

As you consider your customer persona, think about which of the sales and marketing channels they see most frequently or that are their favorites. Does your customer hang out on TikTok or LinkedIn? Do they read email or do they respond better to text messages? Do they listen to podcasts or go to tradeshows? Create content that speaks to them and place it where they'll see it. This accomplishes several marketing goals:

1. You put yourself in front of your customer, creating awareness and potential for engagement.
2. You demonstrate your knowledge and are generous in sharing it.
3. You can prompt your customer to visit your website to see your latest offers.

The successful entrepreneur is intentional and consistent in whatever channel they choose to use. Building awareness and recognition and keeping customers on the journey with you takes time and effort. You can use the customer journey map as the starting point of your marketing plan. What type of content will you create at each phrase of the journey? In the next section, you'll choose the specific channel(s) you'll use and create a calendar for your marketing and sales tasks.

This kind of content marketing plan increases customer engagement and loyalty, leading to more repeat business and referrals. For many entrepreneurs, marketing efforts start as small as posting a flier on the school bulletin board or setting up a social media business profile. Starting small is a step in the right direction but thinking about a larger, long-term marketing plan goes a long way to finding customers sooner rather than later.

DISCUSSION GUIDE

- Who is your customer?
- Why are they your customer—why is your business important and relevant to them?
- How are you going to get their attention?
- What key words or phrases will you use to describe your business? Refer to the Four Horsemen Marketing™ work you did earlier.
- What message will you use to convince your customer they need your product/service?
- What knowledge can you share with your customer that gives value and demonstrates your expertise to solve their problem?
- Create the content you plan to use and show it to a few trusted friends or customers to see if it appeals to them.

The easiest and cheapest way to begin marketing your business is through word of mouth and through social media. So, create a business social media site (see Chapter 7, Website and Technology), post content regularly, and ask your friends and family to share it!

Create a Sales Plan

While effective marketing will build awareness and drive customers to your website, it's only half of the marketing and sales equation. On the marketing side, entrepreneurs build a marketing plan that identifies the channels they'll use to communicate with their potential customers and a calendar that defines when specific marketing activities will happen. The sales plan provides the other half of the equation—the half that's concerned with how you'll earn money. Your business needs to make money to pay its bills—and you—and sales bring in the dough.

A sales plan outlines all activities that lead to selling your products or services to new customers as well as growing your business with existing customers. It sets sales targets and marketing tactics for your business and defines the steps you will take to meet sales goals for the year.

While a great product or service is the core of any business, many still fail because of poor sales. It is vital for your growth and success that you create a strong marketing and sales plan. Here are some key steps you should be thinking about to create a great sales plan. Yes, this will take some time and work, but it will save time in the long run because you'll be focused on a clear goal—remember the entrepreneurial principles from Chapter 1, Entrepreneurial Foundations.

We suggest creating a preliminary sales plan to test three sales tactics, and then going full force with the one tactic that is most successful.

Version 1: Preliminary Sales Plan

1. **Think about each of the 15 sales methods discussed.** Look at the Traditional and Digital Marketing and Sales Channels list, and write how you would use EACH of these sales tactics.
2. **Choose three to test.** Look at your brainstorm and decide which three make the most sense for you. Think about the resources you have, the skills/experience you have with each, and the estimated impact that route would have on your customers and business. Now, pick three that you are going to test.
3. **Design experiments to find the best one.** Create a quick plan outline for each of the three:
    - Who are you trying to reach? Remember your ideal customer profile and everything you learned about your customer. When you reach out, be sure to include the people on your customer interviews list.
    - What are you going to do?
    - Will you promote a special offer?

- How frequently will you do the sales activity?
- What does success look like? For example, let's say you choose social media and post a special offer five times a week on three platforms. If 25 people buy your special offer, is that success or do you want 250 or even two? Would having 100 new followers be success for you?
- Answer those questions for three channels.

4. **Run your experiments.** How long will your experiment last? Set deadlines for yourself.
5. **Evaluate your experiment**. Which channel brought the best results? Pick the best one to keep going with.

When you begin to think about sales projections, you assign a percentage of your predicted sales to each customer segment, if you have multiple segments. Many entrepreneurs use the Pareto Optimum or the 80/20 rule mentioned in Chapter 1, Entrepreneurial Foundations. That means 80 percent of their sales come from one customer and the remaining 20 percent come from other customers.

DISCUSSION GUIDE

- How might you use each of the marketing and sales channels to reach your customer?
- Which three channels will you test?
- When will you reach out? Are there certain days of the week or times of day they're more active or likely to engage?
- What does success look like for your marketing efforts?
- Which of the three channels you tested gave the best results?

Version 2: Integrating Marketing and Sales

Now that you've chosen one channel to focus your efforts, you're ready to level-up the process by creating three different stages of selling: pre-, core, and post sales.

Breaking up selling into three stages creates a constant flow of leads. You're focusing on different customers in different places along the customer journey. With these three stages, you have a higher conversion rate because the barriers and objections to a purchase are easier to overcome at each stage. A customer who has engaged at the pre-sales stage has an easier time saying yes at the core sales stage, and likewise a customer who has purchased your core product is more likely to make additional post-sales purchases. What's more, the sales process is easier because you're only selling one thing. Let's look closely at what happens at each stage.

Pre-sales is more about serving than selling. This stage is all about adding value to the customer, it should be 90 percent about service and value and only 10 percent about selling. You want to focus on *their* problem and offer a solution. When a customer first learns about you—awareness—you ask them to do one thing, and it should be appropriate to that phase of the customer journey. Your 10 percent sale would be a free or low-priced version of the product or service you sell. This level of selling is sometimes called the *easy offer* because it's hard for the customer to refuse. For example, you may offer a free, downloadable booklet or infographic with information that addresses their problem in exchange for signing up for your mailing list. If you typically offer high-priced services, your easy offer may be a $75 consult.

The next stage is core sales, and here the ratio of service to sales is 50:50. This level of sales is your main source of revenue. Here you demonstrate your value and capability by providing an excellent product or service that fully solves the customer's problem. You're selling your main product or service, perhaps even upselling to include an accessory or add-on. You continue to add value while you deliver on your promise—you want to make the entire customer journey a good experience.

Post sales return to the pre-sales ratio of 90 percent value and service to 10 percent selling. Having made a core purchase, your customer is familiar with your product or service—and should be thrilled because you've solved their problem! Continue to provide value to turn those customers into raving fans who will tell their friends about your business. Ask them for reviews and referrals, perhaps in exchange for a valuable perk. Look for ways to encourage them to be a long-term customer, perhaps with a subscription service. It takes three times as much effort to convert a new customer than to keep an existing one; make them feel special by asking for their feedback about products in development or upcoming launches.

For example, an entrepreneur who offers interior design services may have an easy offer that's an infographic with tips for creating a new home look with items you already have. Or the easy offer could be a video consultation for a low-fee. The core service would be redecorating the client's home. The post sale could be a bundle package of four rooms in a year or a holiday decorations subscription. The service is always interior design but sold at different phases on the customer journey. Of course, the entrepreneur nurtures the customer with valuable social media posts, perhaps a newsletter or ask-me-anything events, and any number of other ways to offer value and stay front of mind for the customer.

Marketing experts typically create a calendar that lists each activity and the date they'll do it. Rather than creating a social media post or sending a newsletter when the mood strikes, taking the time to think about and list your activities and when you'll do them presents an image of a solid, professional business to your customers. Define your marketing tactics, create a marketing calendar, and then do the tasks as planned!

Define Your Target Numbers

Working with pre, core, and post sales helps you create sales targets or milestones. If your goal is to sell 100 easy offers, perhaps your goal is for 60 of those customers to purchase your core offer, and 15 of those to purchase your post sale offer. As your sales skills improve, those numbers may change.

But how do you determine the size of the market and define those goal numbers initially so you can measure your success? Let's look at each part of that question.

How Big is the Market?

In Chapter 2, Product-Market Fit, we talked about matching your product or service to the problem your customer has; the whole of your customers and their needs is called the market. Although you'll get the best information about market viability from your customer interviews, it can be helpful for your sales projections to have a rough idea of the size of the market.

That said, sizing your market requires lots of research online and often the answer you seek is proprietary data that you won't have easy access to; you may need to purchase it from business intelligence/analysis/research firms. You can do some sleuthing on social media by looking at the number of followers your competition has but those numbers often provide a false picture of true buyers—think about how many companies or people you follow but have no intention of ever buying from them. Better yet would be conducting Google or AI-assisted searches with long-tail search terms, such as *how many people bought "your product or service type" in 2023?* Or *how many single-family homeowners with an income higher than $50K live in Milwaukee?* Go back to the demographics you defined for your customer and use those terms to search for the number of people who meet those demographics.

There are three levels of market sizing that are important to be familiar with and they have a catchy acronym, TAM SAM SOM. Businesses use this framework to estimate the number of potential buyers for their product or service.

- **TAM** means Total Addressable Market and reflects 100 percent of the available revenue in the market. TAM is calculated by multiplying the number of potential customers in the market by the average amount each customer spends. If everyone in the market bought your product or service, you would capture the TAM.

- **SAM** means Serviceable Addressable Market and counts the portion of TAM that you can reach. SAM considers limits such as price, location, and distribution. SAM is a better reflection of the *potential* market.
- **SOM** means Serviceable Obtainable Market and reflects the *probable* number of customers a business can capture within a market. SOM considers the business' offer, strategy and tactics, and focus.

Once you've given some thought to TAM SAM SOM, you can more accurately set your sales goals.

Setting Your Sales Goals

Set the number of sales (e.g., 10? 100?) you want to make and a deadline date (three months from now) that you want to make them by. How many products or service appointments do you need to sell to cover your expenses (the sum of your COGS, your marketing costs, any business costs such as insurance, rent, car, any contractors or employees you pay, and yourself—more about this in Chapter 10, Accounting and Bookkeeping) and make the profit you desire. Make sure to include any expenses related to sales such as commissions and travel.

Align your marketing plan with your sales plan. Do the marketing activities you've established help you reach your sales goals? When will you do those activities? Think about the channel you chose. For example, if you're using social media, your marketing posts will be about building brand and product awareness or providing expertise about your field; you may also post specific promotions or calls-to-action that drive the follower beyond awareness to making a purchase.

Setting a goal allows you to measure your efforts and compare different tactics when you try more than one. In the beginning, when you're getting to know your customers' true behaviors—observing how they actually engage with your business along the customer journey, not just listening to their answers in an interview—you'll make an informed guess about how many people will respond to your ads, share their email for product updates, and become repeat purchasers. As your customer following grows, you can make better predictions about the number of people who engage at each step of the customer journey and how many reach the Broadcast phase.

DISCUSSION GUIDE

- How might you use each of the marketing and sales channels to reach your customer?
- Which three channels will you test?
- When will you reach out? Are there certain days of the week or times of day they're more active or likely to engage?
- What will you do at each stage of sales:
  - Pre-sale?
  - Core sale?
  - Post sale?
- What are your target numbers for each stage of sales?
- Does your marketing plan align with your sales goals?

The Cost of Marketing and Sales

Marketing can quickly become the biggest expense in an entrepreneur's budget. Entrepreneurs justify marketing expenses; it's how they let potential customers know they exist. In the early stages of your business—especially if you're a bootstrapper—you will invest a lot of your own sweat equity, rather than paying someone else to do it. Think of this work not as work for free, but as an investment. It's called sweat equity because you earn equity, or value, in your business but pay for it with your sweat rather than money.

Track details of your marketing plan like the goal, budget, channel, and customer you want to reach. Remember to include expenses like website design and maintenance and operations costs when calculating the costs and budget. The investment in these initial efforts leads to future revenue, which will then support your budget for future efforts and that ongoing cycle of investment, revenue, reinvestment creates a map of how you run your business. We'll talk more about business operations in Chapter 9, Operations.

New entrepreneurs need to look for creative ways to keep their expenses low. With the advent of online marketing channels, there are many opportunities for (almost) free marketing. Almost because you'll be using personal items that you already pay for, along with your time, which does have value, yet free in the sense that you're not taking money out of your pocket. Here are a few ideas to get you started:

- You can talk to people about their problems and get feedback on your business idea—that's free! Many community events are open to the public and are a great opportunity to meet potential customers and spread the word about your business.
- You can use your personal phone (that you're already paying for anyway) to take photos, make videos, or create graphics and post them on social media to let existing followers know you're starting a business and begin to gain more followers.
- You can set up a free website (see Chapter 7, Website and Technology), although you may have to pay a small fee to register the name of your website (the domain). If you don't have a computer, ask around and borrow one. Some local libraries or community centers have computers you can use.

Earlier in the section about Search Engine Marketing and Physical Ads, we discussed the costs of advertising. If you have a little bit of money to invest in marketing, you can try running ads on a search engine like Google or a social media platform, like Facebook or Instagram. Start small and see if the effort pays off in more followers or new customers. As you make sales and begin to see some revenue, you can re-invest a portion of that revenue in more marketing efforts.

However, if you don't have the money, you don't need to use paid advertising. When we've mentored or spoken to entrepreneurs, many early stage entrepreneurs *think* they must have an advertising budget. This almost never works in and of itself. Having good product-market fit is a far more important requirement. Earlier we talked about how your customer is your best teacher; your customer is also your best marketer and best brand ambassador. And if you're doing a good job, they'll help you increase awareness, therefore sales, creating a fly-wheel. Your goal, then, is to move as many customers as possible to the Broadcast phase of the customer journey.

Marketing supports sales and customer retention. The sheer number of vendors and service providers customers can choose from makes it imperative that you maintain a presence, constantly working to keep your business top of mind for customers, and that happens through consistent marketing efforts.

The Spending Trap

Establish a marketing budget as soon as you begin thinking about your marketing plan. You may be using your personal phone or computer and internet service, but the time you spend taking photos or creating social media posts has value. If you're designing and printing fliers, there's the cost of making the photocopies. You might also decide that you want to invest in paid advertising on Facebook or Instagram. We suggest you set financial triggers to help you decide to grow or stop a specific marketing strategy. For example, if you notice that a lot of customers are coming to your website after seeing an Instagram paid ad, perhaps it will be worthwhile to increase your Instagram budget. If you don't see any movement, you want to consider changing the demographics for the ad, redesigning the ad itself, or investing in ads on a different platform. These decisions come down to knowing your customer; you can spend a lot of money on ads but quality trumps quantity in social media advertising. If your ad doesn't pass in front of your customers' eyes, the money is ill spent.

DISCUSSION GUIDE

- How much money can you spend on marketing and advertising?
- What triggers will help you decide to stop or spend more on a specific strategy?

Ready, Set, Launch!

One of the first marketing campaigns you'll do will likely be launching your product or service—that first big announcement that your business is, well, open for business. The Go-to-Market or Launch Plan leads up to the day your product or service is available. We find a calendar is the best representation of the plan to track all the marketing content and sales activities you'll do to support product or service releases. We recommend starting with the launch date and working backward to the current date to schedule the activities that support the launch.

For example, your first marketing campaign leads up to the date when you release your first product or service. After you release your product, another marketing campaign will support ongoing sales of the product/service and carry through until you're generating consistent revenue. At that point, another marketing campaign may reveal new features. In between, you may have smaller marketing campaigns that demonstrate your expertise or announce a special event that you're hosting.

Getting Commitments that Matter from Customers

If your marketing is successful, customers will begin to place orders on your website or schedule appointments with you for the service you offer. Selling the product/service isn't the end of the process for an entrepreneur. With each new customer, you begin a relationship that ideally will be long and fruitful for you and for the customer. The customer evolution has three steps:

1. The customer buys your product/service as a pre-sale, on the spot, or with a letter of intent.

2. They buy it again—and maybe they buy more, also known as an upselling.
3. They tell other people to buy it.

That first sale is sweet. When your customer says "yes," you want to confirm their agreement to pay for your product or service. Sometimes a verbal confirmation is all you need. If you're cutting someone's hair, you don't need a formal contract—they make the appointment, come in for the service, pay you, and come back six weeks later.

If you sell a higher-priced product or service or do any kind of custom work, a letter of intent confirms the sale. A letter of intent states quite simply the customer's intention to buy from you. It details the object of the sale, the price, and any time constraints for delivery. For high-priced products or services, the customer may also pay a deposit up front.

Pre-sales, Subscriptions, and Repeat Business

We also like pre-sales where the customer pays you before you deliver the product or service, often before the product is available. You see this a lot in the publishing industry, authors pre-sell their book before the publishing date by promoting it online and asking potential readers to buy their book before it's available, and then the physical or digital book is delivered on the publishing date. On a site like Amazon, pre-sales help push a book up the sales ranking list and help publishers see there's a demand for the book. Pre-sales gives customers a sense of anticipation and excitement about the product.

Pre-sales help you predict the amount of income you'll receive in a set time period and give you funds to cover business expenses or invest in new features of your product or service. Pre-sales also occur when you sell subscriptions to your product or service. Subscriptions can be applied to many more businesses than magazines and ad-free apps. A hair salon could pre-sell a year's worth of haircuts, and perhaps make an enticing offer of nine cuts for the price of eight. That small town movie theater we mentioned earlier offers 10 tickets for $50, a big savings over the regular $7.50 full-ticket price.

If pre-sales are gold, return customers are platinum. A customer who comes back to buy from you again tells you they like your product and your business. Treat them with utmost care and they'll continue to return. Retaining a customer is far better, faster, and cheaper (yes it hits all the notes) than getting a new customer. You don't have to spend marketing dollars to build awareness because the customer already knows you and knows your products. When you have a new offer, you want to tell your existing customers about it first, and they'll be the ones to give you valuable feedback.

Upselling

Upselling happens when a returning customer spends more by buying more than one product from you or buying a version of your product with more features than their previous purchase. "Do you want fries with that?" is the classic upsell. The customer came in for a burger but left with fries and a drink—upselling is convincing the customer to buy more than they intended when they walked in.

Referrals

When your customer begins to tell other people about your product or service, you have developed a loyal customer. This customer is an excellent source of feedback for future iterations of your idea or ways to expand your business.

The more effort and sacrifice a customer makes—typically in terms of money they spend on your product/service—the more they are your customer. In turn, the more you can trust their feedback, which you should ask for often.

As you're selling, you'll want to stay in touch with your early customers. Reach out to them via email or phone to ask how they're enjoying their purchases or services. Or use a site like SurveyMonkey to build customer satisfaction surveys and track customer feedback that you can use to further promote your business. Even short, one-sentence testimonials go a long way in convincing other potential customers, and you can use those testimonials on your social media posts, your website, and blog posts.

Closing the Sale

The most trying moment can be when you have a customer on the brink of saying yes. You want to be your most helpful and charming at this moment. The human brain responds well to storytelling so describe the customer's future with their problem solved, help them see that you can solve their problem. If the customer is still unsure about committing, ask them what they need to say yes. If you can satisfy their request, by all means do. If not, present an alternative that still offers a win-win situation.

In the early stages of one of his startups, Nic had a request from a customer for a special feature that would benefit only that customer. Making that change would mean shifting resources from other types of development to making a custom product that couldn't be sold to anyone else. However, the sale to that customer would cover 90 percent of the sales goal at the time. They decided to say yes to this customer and the influx of funding kept the company going while other customers were acquired. In hindsight, was it the right thing to do? Probably.

The Sunk Cost Trap

Sooner or later, you'll have a bad customer—you'll know what we mean when you see it! You dread answering the phone or opening the email every time you see their name, they make unreasonable requests, they neither respect nor value your time, they may even be passive-aggressive or narcissistic. And yet, you keep them as a customer perhaps because you invested a lot of resources to acquire them (that's the sunk cost), they were one of your first customers, they pay you on time, or fill in the blank with whatever excuse you make for them. In your heart of hearts, however, you know it's time to break up. Indeed, sometimes you must fire your customer. Of course, you want to honor the contracts you've signed with them and be kind about it, but when you know, you know. Practice how you'll tell them it's time to part ways, maybe offer alternative solutions (send them to your competition) but cut your losses sooner rather than later.

Sales is a Process

All of the above begs an important question: What if sales aren't coming in? As outlined in the sales plan, selling today is all about providing value and service. Before you blame your customer or product, look at *how* you are selling. Are you offering service? Does your customer have a chance to get to know you and the value you bring? Do you have a customer journey and marketing funnel that allows them to build trust and believe you can solve their problem?

If you can answer yes to those questions then you get an A+ for selling, but something is still not working. Go back to the three levels of interviews you did with potential customers. Think through what you learned from those conversations: what problems do they have, why isn't their current solution satisfactory? When you talked with them about your idea, what did they like about it, what would they want to be different, did they say they would actually buy the product?

Sales can be slow in the beginning. If your product/service solves the problem your potential customers said they have and they liked your idea, make sure you're marketing to those types of customers. Are your social media posts on the right channels? Are you running ads targeted to the appropriate customer? Have you tried direct selling?

As a sales channel, direct selling is the original sales tactic. Picture Ray Kroc selling milkshake machines before he took over the McDonald's burger shack and turned it into a franchise. Entrepreneurs may no longer knock on doors and display their wares but sending a direct, personalized email or better yet, calling a potential customer on the phone can be the best tactic for making sales.

As you interviewed potential customers, you've been keeping a list of their names, email addresses, and their problems. We suggest you contact the first 10 people on that list and ask them if they've solved the problem they said they had. If not, are they willing to talk with you about your product and consider buying it to solve their problem. Remember to make your communication about them and how you can help them, demonstrate the benefits of buying from you. The worst answer they can give you is no. Rejection is part of your life as an entrepreneur. Don't take their "no" personally, thank them for their time and move on to the next potential customer. And remember that not all rejection is final. Sometimes "no" really means "not right now."

When you've exhausted the list of customers you spoke with during the interview process, look to your social media followers. One of the goals of your marketing efforts is to generate leads, i.e., potential customers. Who is most engaged in the comments? Who asks questions? Send a DM to these followers and see if they're interested in setting up a short call to talk about their problem (and your solution).

If you have an email list, send an email to everyone on your list asking them for their help. You can also reach out to people in your network to ask them if they know anyone who has the problem you can solve. Even though your friends and family know about your business, they may not think to tell others about it. Entrepreneurs often must make an explicit request for referrals; don't be shy about asking for help.

Four Sales Traps to Avoid

Remember to avoid the four traps of selling by building the right product or service from the beginning. A customer-centric company rarely fails!

Trap 1: You build something people want, but people won't pay you for it.

Trap 2: You build something people want, but there just aren't enough customers to be profitable.

Trap 3: You build something people want, but to get them your product or service costs you too much money.

Trap 4: You build something people want, but you there are too many competitors doing what you're doing so it is hard to become profitable.

Now that you have your marketing and your sales plans in place, you're ready to home in on the vision and messaging you communicate with your brand.

CHECKLIST

- ✓ Write a sentence or two to reflect your marketing plan using the Four Horsemen Marketing™ concept: position, differentiation, benefit, brand.
- ✓ Create a customer journey map with the marketing tasks you'll do at each of the eight phases.
- ✓ Establish marketing and sales goals.
- ✓ Choose three of the 15 channels to test to promote and sell your products or services.
- ✓ Choose the one channel that brought the best results to focus your marketing and sales efforts.
- ✓ Create what you need to promote your business and make sales (i.e., website, email marketing campaign, fliers, business cards, payment processor, etc.)
- ✓ Go out and get your first paying customer!
- ✓ Get your 10th paying customer!
- ✓ Get some testimonials from your early customers as you go (i.e., ask them for a sentence describing why they like your products or services or business). Don't forget to send regular updates to your customers as your business grows!
- ✓ Consider creating a video about your business and products/services to engage your customers.

CHAPTER 6

Branding

When Should You Read This Chapter?
When you have your product or service idea and customer defined, you can begin thinking about how you want to present yourself to the world. Branding can be fun but also takes deep thought to do well. Read this chapter before you begin creating your website and marketing campaigns so that you develop a cohesive brand across all your communications.

If you talk to a dozen branding professionals, you'll hear a dozen different ideas about what it is. When most people think of a brand or branding, they may limit their definition to a company's logo, tagline, and color palette. But in reality branding is so much more.

Branding informs people about your company. Done well and properly, branding communicates your values, helps people decide if they align with your ideas, your products, services, and business, and over time becomes immediately recognizable. People also tend to identify with the brands—and the people behind them—they know and love. If you think about big brands you know, ideas about them immediately come to mind. Are you a Coke or Pepsi drinker? Do you have an iPhone or a Samsung? Do you prefer Toyota or BMW? People make assumptions about other people based on the brands they use.

The same thing will happen for your business. When you interviewed and defined your ideal customer, you began to see how that customer aligns with your values, how that customer can see themselves as someone who supports your business. Your brand makes a promise, and a consistent brand presence sets expectations for your customers; they know what they'll get when they interact with your brand, your business, and your product/service.

The feelings customers have about a brand don't happen overnight or with a single social media post. They develop over time as the customer experiences the brand in a consistent, constant way along their customer journey. The visual elements and language that customers see and hear make the first impression. Repeated exposure to those along the customer journey reinforces or evolves that impression. Every interaction with a customer is an opportunity to create and grow brand awareness, recognition, and trust.

Your brand also influences how you—and eventual employees—feel about your business. You, too, want to be excited about your brand and feel that it stands for values you believe in. You transmit your excitement and belief to your customers and employees whenever you talk about your business.

At the beginning of your entrepreneurial journey, you don't have a brand history so you must make sure the first impression represents what you and your business stand for and offer. Thinking through your brand before you make that first social media post or create your website goes a long way toward creating good first impressions. In this chapter, we go through the thought process and steps for creating a brand you love, from writing a mission and vision statement, to defining your core values and brand promise, to creating your name, logo, and color palette. At the end of this chapter, you'll have everything you need to convey and communicate your brand to your customers and the world, and you'll be able to fill out one of these charts.

Creating an Effective Brand

Before taking you through the steps to create all the pieces, we want to review some rules of branding. Keep these rules in mind as you think about and define the words and phrases, look and feel of your brand.

- **The riches are in the niches.** Your brand should be narrowly focused. Often this is referred to as having a niche product or selling to a niche market. A niche—pronounced as either "neesh" or "nitch"—means a specialized segment. Having a niche for your business and for each product you sell helps you reach your target customer. If you know your niche, you know who your customer is. When products or businesses fail, it can often be traced back to going outside of the brand's defined niche—it's not surprising that the Apple car hasn't made it to market.
- **Publicity vs. advertising:** Your brand grows fastest and farthest when people talk about you (known as publicity), which is far more powerful than what you say about yourself (known as advertising). And advertising, while necessary to keep your product/service front of mind, is expensive. The clearer your niche, the easier it is for people, including journalists, influencers, and customers, to talk about your product/service.
- **Own a word.** When a brand becomes known as the leader in the field, the name often comes to replace the thing itself. For example, Kleenex, Band-Aid, and Jell-O are product names for facial tissues, bandages, and gelatin desserts. If you can create a category and you do it first, your brand becomes associated with that category, and in the mind of the consumer, your essence is reduced to a single thought or attribute.
- **Credentials:** Claim your authenticity and promote yourself as the leader in your category. In the beginning of your entrepreneurial journey, that category may be quite small and yet this is a way to distinguish your product. Look at how many sub-sub-sub-categories

exist on Amazon. Many products become the number one item in sales in miniscule categories, but they can still put that orange "bestseller" flag on their listing. Also, you may not be the leader in sales, but you can be the leader in customer service, or on-time delivery, etc. For example, while Hertz claims to be number 1 in rental cars, Avis claims they try harder (the alternative is to say, "We're number 2" and it's obvious why that tagline doesn't work). Make your unique leadership position part of your message.

- **Quality:** No doubt you want to create the highest quality product or service possible within your means and skills, but quality is often more about perception than truth. A higher price can play into the psychology of the customer about the product/service being worth more. This all goes back to value pricing, as explained in Chapter 4, Product Development. Your branding conveys the perceived value of your offer.
- **Choose a name.** Don't be generic. Intelligent Chip Company is awful, but Intel Corp. is catchy. The brand name is more important than the company name. People buy brands. Band-Aids are a brand of Johnson & Johnson; Kleenex is a brand of Kimberly-Clark.
- **Essential characteristics:** Once defined, your message, logo, font, and colors should be consistent and constant across all your communications and over time. Think long and hard about this so you don't end up rebranding in a year.

The Brand Consultant Trap

You can pay someone a lot of money unnecessarily to make you look cool, but that may not actually make you money. We believe you can do a lot of the initial brand work yourself—who knows your business better than you do? Take the time to be thoughtful and sincere. Some day in the future you can hire an expensive consultant to revamp your brand as your company evolves (and can afford it) but for now, trust your instinct and abilities and invest your money in the most crucial areas of the business.

Your Values

Most entrepreneurs start a business because they believe their way to solve a problem is better than the solution anyone else offers. They stand for something. We describe what they stand for through values. Defining those values provides words that can be used to market brands, products, and services; talking about your values shows the world who you are.

Values are things you believe in. They dictate how you behave toward others and in the world and reflect your sense of right and wrong. If you search for "values list" online, you'll find lots of choices to prompt your thinking. Here are some to get you started:

Acceptance	Creativity	Knowledge
Accountability	Excellence	Leadership
Adventure	Freedom	Loyalty
Autonomy	Friendship	Poise
Beauty	Fun	Pleasure
Boldness	Generosity	Responsibility
Commitment	Growth	Safety
Community	Influence	Service
Competency	Integrity	Stability
Courage	Justice	Trust

Think about why your business' product or service is valuable to your customer. What are your customers really paying for? Is your design or service something they can't get anywhere else? Do they trust you as a person? Do you cost less than your competitors, for the same quality of service? Are you conveniently located or do you go to the customer's home? Do you offer high quality? The words in those questions help you identify your values: exclusive, trust, low-cost, convenience, quality.

Some businesses will say honesty is one of their values; we like to believe that honesty is a given value for everyone. Customers tend to believe this too—they will pick up on hypocrisy. Actions do speak louder than words.

Think about a company like Ikea. Their values are cost-consciousness, simplicity, and togetherness. You can see it in incredibly affordable furniture, family-oriented stores, and approachable visual design. Everything about the Ikea brand is cohesive; their values infuse their product, the shopping experience, and their service.

Identifying your values can be harder than it sounds. We find it helpful to do it with another person, whether that's a mentor, a partner, or a friend who's interested in helping you with your business. Sometimes it's helpful to talk with someone with a similar business but a slightly different audience. Entrepreneurs who approach this process with an open, nonjudgmental mind often come up with the most authentic and resonant values for their brand. The steps that most branding and marketing experts take clients through to identify values are similar to the following:

1. Write a sentence or two that describes your target audience and then write four phrases that describe how you uniquely solve their problem. In the example, we've put our values in parentheses:

   Skysthelimit.org is a unique entrepreneur development organization because it targets earliest-stage, underrepresented entrepreneurs who want to start a business. We understand the challenges of starting a business when you're doing it for the first time and with few resources!

   - Combines training, coaching, startup grants, advisors and mentors all in one place (competent)
   - Uses technology smartly, i.e., mobile apps + online platforms (innovative)
   - Provides one-on-one support to entrepreneurs to make sure they get what they need (personalized attention)

2. Write out adjectives or expressions that describe what you stand for. Be specific and think about opposites—what you aren't—to generate ideas about what you are. Write each word or phrase on a single sticky note, so you can move ideas around and group them in the next step. If you're struggling:

- Think about your personality (childlike, expert, old soul) and define the values that reflect that.
- Think about two opposing brands and choose values you believe they have that are similar to yours. For example, more like Google than Apple, or more like Ford than Audi.

3. Take a break and then look at all your sticky notes again. Remove any that don't belong.
4. Look for connections between the values and group them by the ideas those connections represent. For example, competency, knowledge, and excellence may all represent leadership.
5. Look for words that relate to how you communicate, such as authoritative, friendly, funny, conversational, or snarky.
6. Keep grouping and narrowing your choices until you have three values. You want to have no more than a list you can remember. Words that don't make the final cut but resonate can be noted as attributes; these ideas will still inform how you present your brand in images and words.

Values influence everything an entrepreneur does in their business from how they respond to customers, to how they negotiate with partners or vendors, to the words, images, and colors they use for brand imagery. Their values go hand in hand with the mission statement of the business. Writing that will be your next step.

DISCUSSION GUIDE

- Why is your brand, product, or service valuable to your customers?
- What three words best describe your values?
- What message do you want your brand to tell your customers?
- What words do you want your customers to think of when they see your brand?

- How do you want customers to feel about your brand?
- What does your business have that other or more established companies do not?
- What do you want your brand reputation to be?
- Who can help you build your brand and make it visually seen?
- What core values will your business operate by and define your future business decisions?

You're on a Mission

A mission statement states the purpose of your business. When thinking about your mission, ask yourself why you started this venture in the first place. Like thinking about why you want to be an entrepreneur, your mission statement explains your business aspirations in a concise manner and helps you stay focused on the important decisions and tasks of running your business. When you feel overwhelmed, indecisive, or doubtful about your business, reading your mission statement reminds you why you began your entrepreneurial journey.

Mission statements can also serve to inform employees, friends, neighbors, and other entrepreneurs about why your business is important, the problems you want to solve, and the goals you want to accomplish. As with your values, however, you need to walk the talk and totally commit to your mission yourself before anyone else will believe you're really serious.

A mission is a broad statement of personal or business scope, purpose, and operation that distinguishes you and your business from others. There are no quick and easy tips to writing a great mission statement, but it should be an accurate reflection and useful summary of your business. The mission statement answers questions like, Why are we here? Why do we exist? Why do we get up each day and do what we do? What is it that we get paid for? And what function does this business perform? For whom? How? Below, we've created a list that you can use as a general guideline to help you as you create your mission statement.

- **Make it short and snappy**. The mission statement sums up your business and you want to be able to remember and repeat this sentence with confidence and conviction.
- **Make it memorable**. Try to make it something that people will be able to remember the key elements of, even if not the exact wording.
- **Make it unique to you.** Focus on what you strive to do differently: how you achieve excellence or what quality of your business sets you apart from the rest.
- **Make it realistic**. Your mission statement is a summary of why you exist and what you do now—not a vision for the future.
- **Make sure it's current**. Though it is not something which should be changed regularly, neither should it be set in stone.

Here are some examples of mission statements for brands you probably know. Think about whether the mission statement aligns with your thoughts and beliefs about the brand:

- **Skysthelimit.org:** "To build a global community where all entrepreneurs and their allies can build meaningful relationships and grow together."
- **Coca Cola:** "To refresh the world, to inspire moments of optimism and happiness, and to create value and make a difference."
- **Google:** "To organize the world's information and make it universally accessible and useful."
- **Walmart:** "To give ordinary folk the chance to buy the same things as rich people."

- **University of Cambridge:** "To contribute to society through the pursuit of education, learning, and research at the highest international levels of excellence."

Your mission statement provides a basis for developing other aspects of your strategic plan and can help guide strategic, operational, and tactical decision making.

DISCUSSION GUIDE

- Why did you start your business?
- Why do you get up every day and do what you do?
- What do you get paid for?
- What function does your business perform? For whom? How?
- What is your mission statement that states the purpose of your company?

See Your Vision

A vision statement paints a picture of the future you're working to create, what you want to be when you grow up, what you aspire your business to become. Your vision statement shows what you believe about yourself, what you're capable of achieving, and how you can change the future. It presents a possible future you see, the value you create in it, and the actions you'll take to get there.

Your vision represents an ideal goal that you deeply care about. Ask yourself what benefits your company or organization provides that change the world or marketplace. The vision statement answers questions like "Where are we going?" "How do we want to be seen by others?" "How will we know we are successful?"

Like a mission statement, there is no one formula to develop a vision as long as the result is a statement that sets the direction or tone for your business. Below, we've created a list that you can use as general guidelines to help you create your vision statement.

- **Be inspirational.** Use powerful words and vivid phrases to articulate the kind of business you are trying to become. This is your chance to focus attention on the bigger picture and the potential rewards that await.
- **Be ambitious.** The targets you set and how high you aim will, in themselves, also say something about you as a business. So create the impression of a business that is going places, that aims high, and demands high standards.
- **Be realistic.** People need to believe that what is envisaged is actually achievable; otherwise, there is no reason for them to buy in to it.
- **Be creative.** Think imaginatively about what your vision is and how you describe it to help stand out from the crowd. Perform a quick search on your vision to see how many other businesses are saying the same thing.
- **Be descriptive and clear.** Take as much space as you need to get your vision across but keep sentences short and to the point. Use precise, uncluttered language.
- **Be consistent.** There should still be an element of continuity between your mission and vision statements, or at least some careful thought and discussion given as to why this is not the case.
- **Be aligned.** Make sure your business's vision reflects core values you can uphold.

Consider the following vision statements and think about whether they reflect the values you believe these organizations represent:

- **Skysthelimit.org:** "A world where every entrepreneur achieves their full potential."
- **United Nations:** "Peace."

- **Microsoft:** "There will be a personal computer on every desk running Microsoft software."
- **Amazon Kindle:** "Our vision is every book ever printed in any language all available in 60 seconds."
- **McDonald's:** "To be the best quick service restaurant experience. Being the best means providing outstanding quality, service, cleanliness, and value, so that we make every customer in every restaurant smile."

As your business and capabilities grow and the world and your customer changes, you may revise your vision statement. A dynamic vision statement encourages creativity and a growth mindset, which enable you to adapt to changing needs of your customers. Like the other aspects of your business, your vision is part of a loop of sharing something, getting feedback, improving what you shared.

A vision provides the map for the future and defines the destination. Nothing was ever created without a vision. It guides your business, gives you direction and purpose, and serves as a powerful motivator for your employees, competitors, and yourself.

DISCUSSION GUIDE

- What is the future you see for your business?
- How does that future create value and make your customer's situation better?
- What unique capabilities do you have that make that vision possible?
- What actions will you take to make that vision come true?
- How will you know you are moving toward your vision?
- What is your vision statement that states what you aspire your company to become?
- Does your vision statement inspire you?

What's Your Name?

Maybe you've had a name in mind for your company or product since the day you conceived of the idea. We saved naming your product or service to this point because the name holds such an important place in branding that you want to make sure it reflects your values, mission, and vision. Large corporations and organizations can and do spend millions on branding consultants to name new products. You probably don't have that kind of money to invest but you can take a cue from the processes they use to come up with a name on your own.

For many entrepreneurs, particularly service providers and restaurants, their personal name is part of their business name, for example William Green Real Estate or Joe's Pizza. Using your name has positive and negative aspects. On the upside, people often relate to a name and quickly associate a name and a face, and if you live in a small town, many people may already know you. On the downside, your name by itself doesn't reveal what you do—unless your name is Flora Grubb, and you own a garden store or Les Plack, and you're a dentist; sometimes your name is your destiny. There's no one formula for coming up with a name. You'll want to spend some time brainstorming, so we've listed some general guidelines to keep in mind. Many entrepreneurs are also turning to online name generators or ChatGPT to come up with business and product names.

- **Easy to say, easy to spell, easy to remember:** Like naming a dog, you'll be repeating your name a lot, so choose something that's easy for you to say and easy for others to remember. Be wary of words that are more than a dozen letters, have unusual spellings, double letters, or can easily be confused with a different word that sounds the same. You'll probably use your name for your website domain, and you want people to be able to type it in correctly when searching.
- **Representative of your business:** You can use your product type or the service you offer as part of your name along with your personal name. For example, Johnson's Electric or Johnson's Popcorn

(two real businesses in the same town that are differentiated by stating what they do in their name). A descriptive name helps people immediately know what you offer—you know what to expect when you go to the Dollar Store.

- **Resonant with your brand:** Think about the feeling you want to convey; are you evocative, whimsical, professional? Look at your list of values and attributes. If one of your values is quality and your attributes are luxury and comfort, you don't want to name your hair salon Cheap Waves.

You can probably think of many businesses that have names completely unrelated to their product or service or are made up names, like Apple or Google. While other names use clever word or letter combinations, or alliteration, such as IBM, KFC, Hobby Lobby, or Knick Knack Shack. The possibilities are truly endless.

Make a list of different ideas, sleep on it, look at it again and delete names you don't like. Share your list with your family and friends and get their input.

When you've narrowed your list down to a few favorites, you want to make sure they're available, that is, no one else has already trademarked the name. You can investigate trademarks through the US Patent and Trade Office's Trademark Search site (https://tmsearch.uspto.gov/search/search-information). If someone else has already trademarked the name you want, you're better off to choose a different name or you risk being sued.

Keep the internet in mind as well when you're choosing a name. Check domain availability before you make the final decision on a name. You could do this by simply searching for the name you chose online and see if someone else has that website, but someone may own the domain and not have created a website yet. A better option is to use a site like domain.com or bluehost.com, which will show you if your name is being used and offer alternative suffixes. If your name is used by someone in a completely different industry, you may still want to use it with a different suffix. For example, our website is *skysthelimit.org* but *skysthelimit.com* is available. If someone were running a travel agency, they might think Sky's the Limit is a great name and decide to use the .com suffix.

If your favorite name is unavailable, keep working on it. Choose a name you love because you'll be using it for a long time.

DISCUSSION GUIDE

- What values do you want your name to communicate?
- What do you want people to think of when they hear or read your name?
- What business are you in? Can that be part of your name?
- Do you want to use your personal name as part of your business name?
- What are five different names you could use?
- Does anyone else use the name you like best either online or as a trademark?
- What name did you choose?

Tagline and Slogans

An average customer doesn't spend much time deciding whether they care about a new brand or not. More often than not, you must grab their attention while they're scrolling and stand out from Aunt Bobbi's cute puppy video and an ad for face yoga. A good tagline combined with an eye-catching logo illustrates both your brand and the benefits you're promising.

A tagline is a short, powerful phrase that is permanently associated with your business. It's always better to be concise rather than try too hard to be clever. The tagline represents the tone and feeling you want for your products or services and focuses on the solutions your brand offers as a whole. Ideally, you want to create a tagline that becomes so well known that it is instantly recognizable.

Another type of catchy line is the slogan, which differs slightly from a tagline. A slogan serves the purpose of advertising and is associated with a brand's marketing campaigns. Marketers use a slogan while promoting a product on social media, in print ads, or at sponsored events focused on pushing sales. The main difference between a tagline and a slogan is that a slogan can change. For example, Nike's tagline is "Just Do It" but one of their recent campaign slogans is "No Guts, No Gold."

As you craft your tagline, work to capture the essence of your brand and business in three elements:

- **Your mission:** Clarity wins over cleverness. Start building a tagline with your mission in mind. Remember what you have to offer as well as the focus of your business.
- **Your promise:** Your promise identifies the "So what?" factor of your brand. Think about the benefits a potential customer receives from your business. People come to your brand because they want something. By adding benefits to a tagline, you're telling people what they get from you and how their life will be better.
- **Your brand:** Your tagline reflects your business image and differentiates your brand from the competition. Your business has a personality, so show it. Give people a little taste of your business's brand in your tagline.

As you create your tagline, refer back to the sentences you wrote following the Four Horsemen Marketing™ process (Chapter 5, Marketing and Sales). Your tagline must be precise and hit all four horsemen. A short snappy tagline that is fun to say but has no meaning is useless. Your tagline supports the functions of your brand as discussed earlier, and a tagline:

- gives you ownership of your category.
- differentiates you from other businesses.

- clearly communicates your value proposition.
- includes one or more key parts of your brand.

Coming up with a tagline takes time. Make a list of 10 or 15 and then sleep on it. Use ChatGPT or another generative AI tool to brainstorm. Come back the next day and cross out any you don't like; add new ones you thought of. If you're feeling stumped, sites like Shopify and Canva offer tagline generators, or you can search for others online. Type in a few details of your business and see what comes out. Share them with friends or family who know your brand and ask for their feedback. You could even run a survey on social media to get input from your followers.

Consider some of the following examples of great taglines to get your creative juices flowing. These taglines are great because they're so memorable you don't need anyone to tell you the brands which they represent.

- "Just Do It" (Nike)—perhaps the best tagline of all time!
- "15 minutes could save you 15 percent" (Geico)
- "We have the meats" (Arby's)
- "The happiest place on Earth" (Disney)
- "I'm Lovin' It" (McDonald's)

Remember, taglines are permanently associated with your business. A good tagline has the potential to build value over time. When you use a tagline for long enough, it can become one of the most memorable parts of your identity.

The Tagline Trap

Audiences may even become more likely to remember your tagline than your company name. This can backfire, however, if your tagline is particularly dated or if it is less believable. If your tagline calls your company "the best" when you clearly aren't, you'll be breaking your customers' trust before you've even had a chance to disappoint them. Be honest and authentic in the promise your tagline makes.

DISCUSSION GUIDE

- What problem does your brand solve?
- What promise does your brand make to your customer?
- How can you convey the solution and promise in a few short words?
- What's your tagline?

Your Story

Humans tell stories through art, music, inscriptions, photos, and words. Our brains are wired to learn and remember through story. Entrepreneurs use stories to portray their brand's values as well as their mission and vision statements. They use stories to connect with their audience at an emotional level. And when an emotional connection is made, the customer is hooked, because it's at the emotional level we understand and feel understood—we connect. It's time for you to write your story.

Ed Catmull wrote a wonderful book titled *Creativity, Inc.* that recounts the story of Pixar, during the many years it took to bring *Toy Story* to the screen. As a film production company, Pixar wanted to make something old, new again. They applied sophisticated storytelling to full-length animated features, which hadn't been popular since Disney's animated versions of *Snow White, Sleeping Beauty,* and *101 Dalmatians.* Early in the book, Catmull outlines Pixar's template for storytelling, which you'll use to write your story. Fill in the following blanks:

1. Once upon a time there was _____.
   Refer to your why to answer this question.
2. Every day, _____. One day _____.
   What did you used to do until one day you did something different?
3. Because of that, _____.
   What changed when you did the new and different thing?

4. Because of that, _____.
   And what changed again?
5. Until finally_____.
   What transformation took place?
6. And ever since that day_____.
   What do you offer now?

Some brand and marketing experts call this story your origin story. You can make it part of your website, share it when people ask what you do, and use it in speeches and presentations you give. Even if you never tell this story, however, doing the exercise shows you how far you've come from where you were when your business was a glimmer of an idea. It informs the way you think and talk about your brand.

DISCUSSION GUIDE

- Who were you before you started your business?
- What problems did you see every day?
- What ideas did you have about solving those problems?
- What steps did you take to solve them?
- What changed when you took those steps?
- What further steps and changes happened?
- What is the happy ending that occurred because of those changes?
- What is your origin story when you put those answers together?

The Short, 10th Floor Elevator Pitch

Your story serves as the basis for your elevator pitch—a 20 to 30 second introduction to your brand that you could say within the time it takes an elevator to go from the ground to the 10th floor. An elevator pitch uses the art of persuasion to create interest in your brand, idea, or product.

When you meet someone you never know if they're a potential customer or may be able to connect you to a potential customer. If they ask what you do, you have an opportunity to generate a sales lead, or expand your network. In its simplest form, an elevator pitch follows this template:

My business (or nonprofit or social enterprise) [insert name]

helps [your main customer group]

with [describe your customers' problems]

by [describe your unique solution/ product/ service]

so that they can [how customers' lives are changed for the better, accomplish goals, etc.]

This template immediately tells listeners who you are, what you do for whom and how you do it. Think about the top three valuable things your business does for customers and conclude with a sentence of evidence, such as a customer testimonial, sales statistics, or an award you've won.

For example, Skysthelimit.org helps underrepresented earliest-stage entrepreneurs by providing one-on-one mentoring support, resources, and access to funding so that they can build their business dreams together.

The Long, 40th Floor Elevator Pitch

When your business is more established—or if you're headed to the 40th floor to meet with an investor—you can have a slightly longer version of your pitch. Ideally, you'll have time to present this to a potential investor or partner in a meeting room or over coffee, not in an elevator. This elevator pitch is a preview of the Pitch Deck that we discuss in Chapter 13, Funding and Finance. It paints a picture of your current and future business and serves to convince listeners of the validity of your business. The pitch includes the following:

- **Problem:** Describe the problem you solve or pleasure you provide to customers.

- **Solution:** Explain the value of the pain you solve or pleasure you provide.
- **Unique Value Proposition:** Describe the magic behind your business.
- **Business Model:** Briefly define your business model—this is how you make money.
- **Competition:** Offer a detailed picture of your competition.
- **Team:** Introduce your management team and advisors or Board of Directors.
- **Progress to-Date:** Describe your current business and any progress you've made to-date.
- **Launch Plan:** Describe how you'll launch your business.
- **Forecast:** Provide a three-year forecast of your financial projections and performance.

The short elevator pitch stays with you during the life of your business. You'll pull out the long elevator pitch when the stakes are higher. The short pitch is really about the customer, while the long pitch is about your business.

DISCUSSION GUIDE

- Who does your business help?
- What problems does your business solve for those customers?
- How does your business do that?
- What benefit does the customer receive?
- What is your elevator pitch?

Brand Imagery

When you think of your brand, what's the look and feel you want to convey? Is your brand warm and inviting, trendy and edgy, stable and professional, cool yet trustworthy? The look and feel of your brand should both reflect your products and appeal to your target customer. Does your customer want a quick fix to their problem, or have they been burned in the past and want to buy from a brand that's thorough and reliable?

When we have a problem and are looking for a solution, we make judgments about brands in just a few seconds based first on what we see—the colors, the logo, the imagery. If we're drawn in, then we go on to read the written words or watch the video. If the brand is still meeting our needs and expectations, then we may begin to investigate and evaluate the brand to see if it offers the solution we need.

It's amazing to think how much influence the combination of a squiggly graphic, a name, and specific colors can have on the decisions a human makes about where to spend their money. But there we are: branding.

You've done the work of thinking about the values you want to demonstrate. You've written your mission and vision statement. You've chosen a name for your brand. Now, you're ready to match the imagery with the idea. Let's begin by thinking about color, then we'll discuss your logo, your fonts, and photos and video, leading up to the creation of a brand style guide.

Color Palette

Color psychology is the idea that colors evoke feelings, and that's a powerful tool for you to harness in the logo and color palette of your brand. Notice how colors make you feel—what memories and dreams they elicit, both negative and positive. Think about some of your favorite brands. What colors do they use? Now, think about the audience for your brand. What colors might they respond to and why? You may also want to choose the opposite color of your competitor as a way to differentiate your brand.

Whole books have been written about color psychology. Here we've summarized the ideas primary colors represent and mentioned a few examples of companies that use those colors in their branding.

- Red is the color of energy, youth, and excitement. It's a sexy, "in-your-face" color. Red attracts attention and is popular for retailers who want to create urgency. Coca-cola, CNN, Netflix, Lego, Target, and KFC have red logos.
- Orange conveys the idea of youth and enthusiasm. Orange is popular for kid-related brands and is friendly, confident, and optimistic. Brands like Nickelodeon, Fanta, Harley-Davidson, Payless Shoesource, and Amazon use orange.
- Yellow suggests optimism, clarity, and warmth—think Subway, McDonalds, Ikea, Best Buy. But it can also indicate safety (think of a yellow yield or caution sign) so be mindful of how you use it. An advantage of yellow is that its brightness helps it stand out among all the other colors.
- Green represents health, growth, peace, and the environment. Whole Foods, Land Rover, Starbucks, and Holiday Inn have green logos.
- Blue conveys trust, stability, strength, dependability, and leadership. It's not surprising companies like Dell, HP, IBM, and Walmart use blue.
- Purple and pink represent creativity, imagination, mysticism, and wisdom. Purple has traditionally been associated with royalty and can reflect a business that makes things happen. T-Mobile, Hallmark, Barbie, and TacoBell use these colors.
- Black, gray or silver communicate balance, calm, neutrality, and luxury. Brands like Apple, Puma, Honda, and Mercedes use this palette.

- White signifies purity but is always in contrast with another color, so its influence is never absolutely pure.

Look back at your list of values and match up colors that reflect or convey those adjectives.

The colors associated with a brand communicate the specific vibe of that business. Picking a few colors for your business will give it an overall look that is cohesive and recognizable. Keep your logo in mind as you choose colors, although these colors will have a presence beyond the logo. Even if your logo is only one or two colors, you'll most likely need others to use for your website, product packaging, and all the materials that will be associated with your business.

If you search "color palette" you'll find online apps that create groups of four or five colors that go well together. If you know your main color, you can then search for complementary colors to use with it. The color palette may be different shades of the same color, three colors that are similar and one contrast color, or four very different yet complementary colors.

Every color has a HEX code associated with it that allows you to recreate the exact same color in different places. When you make your final selections, note the HEX code so you're always using the same colors.

As you choose your color palette, think about the meaning of each color and how they work together to reinforce the values of your brand.

DISCUSSION GUIDE

- What values does your brand stand for?
- What colors most relate to your values and your industry?
- What colors does your competition use?
- What four or five colors will you use for your brand?

Your Logo

A logo is a visual element that represents your business. It's often the first image of your business that people see. Along with the colors you choose, the logo will provide the foundation for the way your brand will look and, ultimately, feel. A good logo can help attract the right audience, while a bad logo—one that sends the wrong message—can turn off potential clients or customers.

A logo often combines both words and images into a single visual item, which can be tricky to achieve. As you design a logo—or provide guidelines for someone to design it for you—keep in mind the shape, legibility, and simplicity. That is, you want to be able to use it in different formats, so consider how the shape will occupy space on a package, a social media post, your website, business cards, etc. You want it to be legible, even at small sizes since people are often looking at things on their phone screens. Lastly, although logos are the product of many thoughtful decisions, often the strongest ones are quite simple.

Elements of Your Logo

You'll want to choose your logo color based on the information we shared previously. Here are other elements to consider:

- **Typography:** You may want the entire name of your business on the logo but remember that you have options. Sometimes an abbreviation or just an initial is enough. Some companies also include their tagline in certain versions of their logo, but very large, recognizable brands like Facebook can get away with just a single letter in their logo.
- **Imagery:** The graphic element of your logo can be abstract or concrete. That means, it can be a seemingly random shape or a specific symbol like a cat or a moon. Or maybe all you need is simple lines or dots around the typography you've chosen. The iconic sphere that comprises the Pepsi logo is a recognizable shape used in a somewhat abstract way.

- **Context:** Lastly, think about where your logo will appear. Your website is a likely spot but it may also show up on product packaging or business cards, stickers, and other items that accompany the process of building brand awareness. Where your logo will live affects the shapes and colors you choose. For example, if you are only using it on a website, you might opt to use complicated color combinations, like gradients. But, if you plan to print it or use it on merchandise, printers may charge by the color, so using one color or only black and white may be more cost-efficient.

You may need more than one version of your logo, such as a full-color logo, black and white versions, a square version that's easier to read on a social media profile image. For example, Eventbrite inverses its color (and of course uses a square shape) for its smartphone app so that it stands out among the other apps. Skysthelimit.org uses full-color, black, white, or square versions of our logo depending on the context.

Designing Your Logo

We recommend starting with generative AI tools to create a logo for your company, essentially for free. You can always go back and improve your logo later, even change it entirely, as logos evolve over time for most companies. If you're creative and comfortable using online tools, create your own logo in Canva (they have great templates to get you started) or Squarespace. If you prefer to have someone else make a logo for you, try Fiverr or Upwork for a less expensive version or 99Designs for a more expensive version.

As we mentioned earlier, your logo is often a potential client, customer, or partner's first look at your business. It establishes the attitude you want your business to project. A good logo gives a business an easily recognizable symbol, provides a way for your business to stand out, and can even work as a signal to your potential clients and customers that this product or service is for them.

Differentiating your brand from others is critical to business survival. So is communicating the benefits of your brand. Research from MIT's management school[2] suggests that logos can help brand managers create a cohesive, compelling brand. They found that a brand's logo works to integrate all the different marketing efforts of a given company, and that it serves as an icon of what the brand means to customers. In short, good logos act as a synthesizer. They help customers identify, differentiate, and create a positive association with your brand.

DISCUSSION GUIDE

- What values does your logo represent? For example, Nike started out selling running shoes and the "swish" conveys movement, speed, and agility.
- What types of images come to mind when you think about your brand and its values?
- How could those images become a logo?
- What is your logo? Share the final (for now…) design.
- What colors did you choose for your company? Include the HEX codes.
- Which color from your color palette will your logo use?
- Will you include your tagline on your logo? Maybe one version of your logo has it and one does not.
- Do you need multiple versions of your logo, i.e., color, black, white, square?

---

2 https://sloanreview.mit.edu/article/the-power-of-a-good-logo/

Typefaces and Fonts

You may have never taken notice of the fonts or typeface of various brands, but just like color, fonts can set the tone for your brand and influence the perception people have of you. Take a look at websites you like and don't like and notice the types of fonts they use. How do they make you feel? Are they easy to read? Do they jump off the page? Have they used color and fonts together to make an impact?

Like color, fonts convey different meanings and moods. Fonts that look like someone wrote them by hand with a marker can be fun, bold, or soften the digital environment, while fonts that look like an old typewriter (Courier) or an old newspaper (Times) lend a classic, traditional feeling. Simple fonts can look modern or futuristic.

If we want to be picky about it, there's a slight distinction between typeface and font. A typeface is a collection of fonts. For example, Arial is the typeface, and each version is a font, i.e., Arial Bold, Arial Italic, Arial Condensed, etc. Three typefaces and their associated fonts give you plenty of options for all the places you write about your brand. Readability is key; some elaborate or fun fonts can be hard to read so think about using those as accents or headings and use highly readable fonts for longer text. You'll use each of them as follows:

- **A heading typeface:** Something that looks good in a large size and grabs viewers' attention. This can be more playful like those script or handwriting typefaces or stylized letters, such as **Bauhaus 93**, HERCULANUM, or **Marker Felt**.
- **A serif typeface for longer text:** These typefaces are easier on the eyes for reading long pieces of text, so how much you use them depends on the type of product or service you offer. You might use them for the About page of your website or for blog posts. Serif typefaces have small lines or squiggles attached at the ends of the main letter. Typefaces like Times, Garamond, or Palatino are serif typefaces.

- **A sans serif typeface:** This works well for captions, subheadings, or short descriptions. Sans serif are clean and easy to read for short pieces of text. Typefaces like Avenir, Helvetica, and Skia are sans serif.

You can select from thousands of typefaces and spend a lot of time finding the right ones. We suggest listening to your gut reaction and choosing typefaces that give you an immediate positive reaction. As with the color palette generators, there are typeface combination generators that put together two or three typefaces that complement each other.

The Font Trap

When looking for a typeface, scroll through the selection of the apps that you use, whether that's your website host, Word, or Canva and choose ones that are available for free. If you find a typeface you like and discover you have to pay for it—and that is only available on certain platforms but not others—that's an added expense that you probably don't need to take on right now. With some searching, you can find a similar typeface that's free and widely available across platforms.

DISCUSSION GUIDE

- What feeling does your brand represent? For example, friendly, professional, authoritative, silly, fun, nurturing.
- What typefaces do you like for headings?
- What serif typefaces do you like?
- What sans serif typefaces do you like?
- Which typefaces best match your brand values?
- What typefaces did you choose?

Photos and Video

People respond to photos and video more quickly than to text. Entrepreneurs think about the look and feel they want their brand to convey and use photos and videos that are consistent with the brand's look and feel and resonate with their target audience's expectations. Let's say a brand's values are all about comfort and nurture and it uses neutral colors like rose gold, beige, and cream. But then that same brand's photos show gothic punk rockers in heavy jewelry and dark colors; customers will be confused and scroll on by.

The search engine and social media algorithms reward original photos and video, as opposed to stock photos that you get from sites like Unsplash or Canva. Authentic, original photos of you and your products are worth having. People want to know the person behind the brand, so don't be shy about standing in front of the camera. You don't have to pay for professional photos; the quality of images you capture on your phone will be fine for most of your purposes. If you have a friend who takes good pictures, spend an afternoon doing a photo shoot so you have lots of photos to choose from to use on your website and across your marketing channels, such as social media, advertising, or fliers.

You want to have a headshot, which is a closeup that shows your head and shoulders and comes in handy for your social media profile. It's also a good idea to take photos showing you in the environment of your business or using your product. Walking, standing, sitting, maybe talking with other people. Find photos of others that you like and recreate the pose.

If you sell a product, you want photos of your product as well. Again, the quality of photos taken with your phone will probably be fine. With bright, natural lighting and a clean background, you can showcase your product. If you offer clothing or accessories, show people wearing them. If you offer a service, take some candid shots of you and your customers—make sure to ask their permission to use their image!

Brands use video in multiple ways. Video offers an opportunity for entrepreneurs to talk directly to their customer and tell stories that show they understand the customer's problem. Video can feel more personal, making it easier for a customer to connect emotionally to the brand and entrepreneur. Think about ways you can use video—you can talk about your origin story, maybe interview customers to showcase testimonials that demonstrate the value of your product/service, and sometimes, add a personal video about who you are and how you spend your day. Again, people want to know the person behind the brand. Again, we recommend you try using generative AI tools to create photos and videos for your business—but remember the power of authenticity and "realness" in creating photos and video.

Having a selection of photos ready to go saves you time when you're preparing your various marketing campaigns.

DISCUSSION GUIDE

- What kinds of photos will you need for your website, social media posts, or advertising?
- What kinds of videos can you make to show your customer you understand them?
- Do you have photos or videos of your product or service?
- Are there any customers who would make a short testimonial video or a photo of them with their written testimonial?

Create a Brand Style Cheat Sheet

Large corporations with big brand and marketing budgets create a document called a brand style guide—but we recommend making sure it's worth your time before you invest in this. A style guide keeps the brand collateral—the pieces that support the look and feel of your brand—in one place. In the beginning, most entrepreneurs are creating their website and marketing material themselves, so having the materials in one place saves time. Small businesses, even solopreneurs, can benefit from creating a min brand style guide or cheat sheet—a one page document that includes the basic brand collateral. Then, when revenue permits hiring some help, it's easy to teach others how to represent the brand.

This mini style guide is a simple document that includes the values, mission, and vision statements and your origin story. It includes the logo in various formats (color, black, white, square) and the tagline. It shows the color palette and the HEX codes to recreate the colors online. It lists the typefaces and describes where and how each one is used. It describes the types of images the brand uses. It's helpful to put the style guide doc in a folder on your computer or GoogleDrive and store the files for the logo variations as well as photos and videos. This keeps all your brand collateral—all the pieces that support your brand—in one place.

The Brand Perfection Trap

All this branding preparation may seem like a lot of work. Although many entrepreneurs enjoy this creative phase, others allow themselves to get stuck in it, and become obsessed with finding the perfect name, tagline, logo, colors, and fonts rather than moving on to focus on their product and selling to customers. Done is better than perfect. Set a specific amount of time you'll spend on brand development and then move on to marketing and selling your product or service.

DISCUSSION GUIDE

- Do you have all the pieces of your brand: values, mission, and vision statements, origin story, logo and tagline, color palette, typefaces, photos and video?
- Do all the pieces seem to go together and support each other?
- Does your brand stand out among the competition?
- How do friends and family react to your brand?
- Are you ready to put your brand out in the world?

Now that you have defined your brand, you can create your website to reflect the choices you've made. We've got you covered with steps to do that in the next chapter.

CHECKLIST

- ✓ Define your values.
- ✓ Craft your mission and vision statements.
- ✓ Choose a name for your business. Check that no other business has that name copyrighted or trademarked.
- ✓ Write your origin story.
- ✓ Write your short elevator pitch.
- ✓ Create a pitch outline (long elevator pitch) for your business.
- ✓ Create a tagline for your brand.
- ✓ Test your name, tagline, and pitch with all of your friends and family.
- ✓ Choose the colors for your business.
- ✓ Create a logo for your business.
- ✓ Choose the fonts you'll use in your communications.
- ✓ Take photos and videos of you, your product, your clients.
- ✓ Create a mini brand style guide or cheat sheet.

CHAPTER 7

Website and Technology

> **When Should You Read This Chapter?**
> Once you've defined your product or service and developed your brand's message and imagery, you have the material you need to build your website. Read this chapter after you've spent time thinking about your customer, your product or service, and your brand.

The internet has made it so easy, and relatively inexpensive, to start a business. Today's entrepreneur no longer fronts the expense of a brick and mortar location nor limits their customers to people within driving distance. The internet offers a world wide web of opportunity for an entrepreneur, limited only by time and imagination. As we discussed in Chapter 5, Marketing and Sales, an entrepreneur can market and sell their product or service in many places—online and off—but having their own website is mandatory. You must have a website, even if it's a single page with a description of your product or service and your contact details.

It's not hard to create a website, but if you've never done it before, understanding the basic steps first goes a long way toward doing it well. We walk you through the steps of creating a website from obtaining a domain to building a landing page. We'll also give you insights to the tech that can assist you in your business activities.

Create Your Website

Many entrepreneurs hesitate to publish their website because they think it needs to be perfect before making it available to the public. The great thing about websites, and anything online, is how easy it is to make improvements. Much like you develop an MVP for your product or service, start with an MVW—a Minimal Viable Website. Put essential information and a simple design in the beginning then add information and improve the design as you move forward in your business.

Of course, if you have the funds to do so, you can hire someone else to design your website, but when you are getting started, it's best to try and tackle this stuff on your own or get help only for the skills you lack.

For example, if you like to write and do it well but struggle with design, you could do the writing and hire a freelancer to do the design. Or vice versa, if you're adept at design and online tools but struggle with writing, you could hire a copywriter. You can hire an agency to do everything, although at the early stages of the business, most entrepreneurs don't have the money to pay an agency. They have only their elbow grease and spare time, so building their website is paid for in sweat equity. There are many platforms that make building a website from a template really easy—which will discuss more below. Most earliest-stage entrepreneurs have more sweat equity than cold hard cash, and to that end, we've detailed the steps, in plain English, to build your website.

Select a Website Platform and Domain Name for your Website

We highly recommend you use a website builder platform to create your first website. Some good platforms we've used are Squarespace, Shopify, or Wix. We also like Carrd.co for single-page websites.

These platforms offer easy-to-use templates and instructions to design your own website. And when you need to design an image or graphic for your website, there are easy-to-use platforms like Canva.

You can buy your domain name directly through these platforms. Your domain name is the address for the website. It should reflect your products or services so that your customers can easily find your business through a search engine. Your customers also expect your domain name to be similar or the same as your business name. For example, our domain name is skysthelimit.org.

We talked a bit about your domain in Chapter 6, Branding, reminding you to make sure the name you give your business and product is available as a domain. Use the website builder platforms or a site like www.godaddy.com to check availability. If your name is fairly common, say Joe Smith, and you want the domain www.joesmith.com, you may find it's not available (in fact, it's not). You can consider other suffixes, such as .org, .net, or .shop. Or you can add a middle initial or some other variation like www.josephsmith.com or www.joesmithshoes.com.

Keep in mind that pricing for domain names is all over the map, from a few bucks to thousands. You pay a certain price to buy the domain name the first year, but you must pay to renew your domain every year. Fortunately, renewal fees are very low.

Spend some time comparing the platforms' services and deciding which features you need. Some features you should be thinking about are:

- An eCommerce feature that allows customers to buy your products/services and allows you to link your website to a payment acceptance service like Stripe or your bank
- Calendar for scheduling appointments with you
- Customer review or customer feedback forms
- Chatbot or capacity to contact you via text or WhatsApp
- Storage capacity—the more images or video you have, the more storage you'll need
- Analytics to see where site traffic comes from and whether people are spending time on specific pages
- Marketing integration such as keeping a list of email addresses (how many addresses are included?) or creating email campaigns (how many campaigns and how many total emails each month?)

DISCUSSION GUIDE

- What domain name would you like to use? Is it available? Have you registered it?
- What kind of hosting services and features do you need for your website?
- Which website builder did you choose?
- How will you design your website? Choose one:
  - Do it yourself.
  - Hire a freelance developer and designer. Expensive.
  - Hire an agency. Very expensive.
  - Hire someone to write and structure your content. Expensive.

Plan Your Website Content

Your website is the digital storefront for your business, a reflection of your brand, your product/service, and you. The work you did to define the look and feel, the voice and tone of your brand will help with the design of your website. As we've said before, think about your customer first; your website should welcome your customer, and make them feel they've found the right place and that you understand their problems. It should be easy to get around, easy to read, and make them want to stay.

Before you begin the actual task of designing your website, we suggest making a plan. Determine what you want to publish and how it will be organized. Think carefully about the purpose of your business and how your website can communicate that purpose, consider how you can differentiate your project or business, and put your ideas in one document.

Think about what you want your customers to be able to do via your website. This will help you work out the sections or pages you want to include. A website that is well designed and easy for customers to use will help your business stand out. Having relevant and appropriate content and images will help customers understand your products and services and will make them feel comfortable with buying from your business.

Look at other websites in your industry, noting the design elements you like and why. Put yourself in your customer's shoes and think about the experience you want them to have.

Some web designers find it helpful to sketch out the pages and the information that will go on each one before putting the content into the website itself. You can find website planning tools and templates online in design apps like Canva. Keep the following elements in mind as you plan the content:

- **Write easy-to-follow content**. Write for your target customers. Don't make customers use a dictionary to understand what you're trying to say. Break things down into short paragraphs, with headers if necessary. Use bullet points. Remember to clearly communicate benefits and features. In the design, you can highlight important words or phrases by using a different color or typeface. (Refer back to the choices you made for your brand style guide.) You'll need content that describes your product/service, the benefits to the customer, and information for an about page. You'll also write more content as you build the actual website pages.
- **Define a call to action**. Be clear about the action you want your customer to take when they visit your website. Use special buttons or highlight text to encourage customers to sign up to receive your exclusively online coupons, or add products to the online shopping cart, etc. The main call to action should be above the fold, which means it doesn't require any scrolling, and be the main thing you want someone to do when they visit your page. If you're building a mailing list, it should be a subscribe button; if you run a wedding planning company, it can be an interest form; if you sell cakes, an order form.

- **Choose representative images.** You don't need professional photos to make an inviting, impactful website. Most smartphones today take high-resolution photos that look great on a website and are easy to upload. (Some website hosts have apps that allow you to build your website on your smartphone—look for that feature if you'll be using your phone instead of a computer to build your website.) Take multiple photos of your product or service so you have an assortment to choose from and can use them in different places on your website. That said, don't go overboard with too many pictures or designs and make sure the character of your brand shines through. If you don't have the types of photos you need, you can find free photos online at sites like www.unsplash.com or use a generative AI tool to create exactly the type of photo you want.
- **Less is more.** Try to condense information into as few pages as possible to avoid overcrowding your website. Don't make visitors dig too far to find what they are looking for. When your content is written and images selected, you're ready to design your website.

DISCUSSION GUIDE

- What is the main message you want to convey to your customer on your website?
- What information will support that message?
- What does the customer need to know about you and your product?
- What action do you want the customer to take?

Design Your Website

Most web hosts offer different types of pages and layouts in each template. The pages you will find most useful depends on the business you're in. For example, a photographer would likely look for a template that has a layout with placeholders for images and a little text, an about page, a contact page, and perhaps a scheduling page. An entrepreneur who sells products online will need a product display page, a shopping cart and checkout, but probably won't need a scheduling page.

Look for a template that works well with your brand. You can usually change the color scheme of a template so you can keep your brand theme and color scheme consistent. (Refer to the work you did in Chapter 6, Branding.)

Once you choose a template, you'll want to begin filling it in with the text and photos you assembled previously.

A typical web page layout has several components:

- **Business name and logo**
- **Navigation bar:** The links here may go to other pages on your website or link to different sections on the home page itself. The navigation bar is often a header that's repeated on every page within your website. Your navigation should be easy to understand and use for a first-time visitor. You want someone to arrive on your website and know exactly where they can find the information they want and need without being confused.
- **Search field:** Make it easy for your customers to find exactly what they're looking for. (You may not need a search field in the early stages of your website.)
- **Content:** this will vary depending on your business. You may have several sections of different types of content such as featured products with photos that link to the product page, or article teasers that link to the full article or blog post, or a video.
- **Testimonials:** honest words from others help make your products or services more tangible to customers who are visiting you online. As you work with customers, ask them to write a testimonial for you and place those testimonials throughout the different pages of your website.

- **Footer navigation:** Make it easy for your customers to find additional information on your business like contact information, location, and terms and conditions. You may include the navigation links to other pages on the site, repeating the navigation bar at the top. Social media links are often found here. The footer navigation is typically a fixed section that's repeated on every page within your website.

When you're first starting out, you may well get by with a single page for a website that includes all the information about you, your product/service, and how to work with you. However, usually a website will have multiple pages including the ones below. Within the navigation menu, you don't have to use these names but can be creative. For example, you can name the About Page, "Get to Know Me" or the Contact Page, "Get in Touch."

- **Homepage:** this is the first page visitors see. Include a short description of who you are and what you do, a brief explanation of your services and products, and perhaps some bullet points on how you can help your potential customer or client. This page would be a great place to add newsworthy mentions and awards and let customers know if you have great reviews on Google or Yelp.
- **About page:** people like to know the person behind the product or service. Write your story and the story of your business, any special achievements you attained, and the ways you differ from others that provide the same product or service. Include a photo of yourself and any team members. You'll want a clear, professional picture where you look sharp and aim for 500x500 pixels to get the best resolution. Customers want to see your face more than your logo. Make sure you convey your enthusiasm, show them that you love what you do!

- **Contact page:** Make sure your contact details are correct and easy for your customers to find. This page may include a form that allows people to send an email directly to you to ask a question or make a request—or to discuss purchasing your services.
- **Products/services:** Include pictures of the products or services you're selling along with bullet points of features with short explanations, the benefits you offer, and/or how you differ from your competition. There may be a click-through for expanded information about the product or service with the option to put the item in the shopping cart or to schedule an appointment. You can also add facts and metrics of your business so far, like the number of customers who keep coming back or the numbers of products you've already sold.
- **Checkout page:** If you sell something from your website, the checkout page will enable the customer to share their name, address, payment, and shipping information. Make checkout easy. The more steps customers have to go through to buy something from your website, the more often they'll abandon their carts. Don't make them jump through hoops for an online purchase.
- **Scheduling page:** If you offer a service, your customers may want to schedule appointments with you. A scheduling page allows them to do so.
- **Opt-in page:** This is the place where people who visit your website can share their email (and perhaps their phone number), allowing you to send them email or text messages with offers, updates, or other information. Email or cell phone are the only direct lines of communication you have with your customers. Encourage people to share their email or cell number and send them regular content, such as educational videos, or cart abandonment notifications. Unlike social media platforms that can restrict your content

at any time, email marketing means you'll always reach your customers' most sacred virtual place: their inbox and chat.

- **Resources page:** Visitors can find videos, blog posts, links to podcasts you've been on or articles you've written for publications or blogs here.
- **FAQ page:** Include answers to the most frequent questions you are asked. The frequently asked questions (FAQ) page will tell everyone what they need to know. This will save you time answering those same questions on an individual basis.
- **Privacy policy page:** Define the data you collect, how it is collected, how visitors can obtain a copy of the information you save, if such content will be shared, and if so, with whom. When you're getting started, don't worry about having perfect legalese, find a comparable organization, and copy what they have, but be sure to change out names, locations, before publishing on your own website.
- **Terms and conditions page:** This is a link to the legal disclosures that a business should make about how their website is used. Similar to the above mentioned privacy policy, a terms and conditions page is usually a must for most websites. This is a page that outlines the "rules" a visitor to your site must agree to abide by in order to use your website. You can search for standard website terms and conditions for your business online. We discuss legal topics in Chapter 11, Legal and Regulatory.

As you're fleshing out your website with content and media, it's important to keep some key tips in mind:

- **Ask for input.** Find out what your friends or even customers think about your website to get fresh perspectives on what works and what needs tweaking.

- **Know your flow.** Understand data such as how many people are visiting your site and what pages people spend the most time on so you can focus your energy wisely. Most website building platforms will include analytics so you can see where your visitors are clicking and how long they are spending on certain pages. You can use this information as evidence for what to spend more or less time on.
- **Keep your website updated.** Update prices, tell your customers about discontinued products/services.
- **Test your site.** Test the page across different devices to make sure your website works properly on mobile devices and tablets. This is really important! Make sure your website looks good on Android and iPhones. In the US, the iPhone has a 58.81 percent market share. As of 2024, Android has a 70.93 percent global market share.
- **Search engine optimization (SEO).** Make your website easy for search engines, such as Google, to find. This is called search engine optimization (SEO). We discuss SEO in depth in the next section.
- **Consult your web builder's tools and resources.** An unprofessional website can potentially put customers off. Most web builders offer a ton of resources to make your website as polished as possible, some will recommend website designers who specialize in their platform. If you don't feel confident to do it on your own, you can seek help from a website designer; the cost of a few hours for someone to polish your site can be helpful. But it's probably easier in the beginning to keep it simple, and when you start to see a profit, invest some of that profit in a professional designer to upgrade your website.

When customers are unfamiliar with a brand, most will search the internet for a product or service review before making the purchase to check the credibility first. Your website gives your business credibility—would you trust a business you can't find online? Your website is your opportunity to tell consumers why they should trust you and share the testimonials and facts to back up those opportunities. When you provide a good service or product, positive word-of-mouth about your business is likely to spread, which in turn, delivers more repeat and new business. Not only that, but it will provide customers 24/7 access to search and shop!

DISCUSSION GUIDE

- What types of pages do you need for your website?
- Which template did you choose?
- How does your website design support your brand, i.e., colors, fonts, messaging, taglines, etc.?
- What feedback have you received about your website?
- Are there any changes you want to make to improve your website?

Optimize for SEO

Search engine optimization (SEO) is a long-term marketing strategy that increases your chances of appearing in the search results of your target audience. You can do this directly through the website builder you choose, like Squarespace. You may want to wait to invest deeply in SEO when your business has a thriving customer base. From keyword research to building backlinks, following SEO best practices helps potential customers who are already looking for the products you sell find you online.

First, you want to include keywords—the same words that your customers use to search for your type of solution—in all of your content, such as headings, narrative copy, product descriptions, and metadata for photos and images. When a person types a search term into a search engine, like Google, the search engine scans the internet and displays a list of websites that match the search criteria. The algorithm rewards headings over copy, original photos over stock photos, and—here's the tricky part—the more people who visit your website, the higher your ranking on the results list. Sort of like being popular helps you become more popular. The goal of any business is to show up on page one of the Search Engine Results Page (SERP), but don't be discouraged if you don't start ranking well right away, it takes time to build a digital reputation.

Keywords

But how do you identify those keywords? You want to think about the words you want to rank for in correlation to the words your customer uses to find the type of solution you offer. And, you want to be specific. For example, if you sell hair products, you'll be competing with Sephora and Sally's Beauty in the search engine results if you choose a broad generic keyword. If you can niche down to something more specific, your chances of rising in the search results increases. You can start with a simple search yourself. When you type a keyword into Google's search field, a list of suggested keywords appears; look through that list to find a more specific keyword relevant to your product/service. This keyword is the starting point for other keywords you want to include on your website.

Once again, AI is your friend. Google itself has a keyword assistant, and searching "keyword research app" brings up many other options, like MOZ, Wordstream, and Ahrefs. The keyword tools will show you how often a term has been searched in the past month and the web pages that get the most results. They will also reveal other keywords that people searched related to your keyword. Your web host may also have resources to show you how to take advantage of SEO in the planning of your website.

In addition to specific words that define your product, the algorithm looks at long-tail keywords, which are search terms with three or more words. Google's search engine, with the advancements of AI, becomes more sophisticated each day and people who are searching can type in full sentences or questions to get better, more focused, and relevant results. Think about questions your customer has related to the problem you solve. (This is also a great way to come up with blog posts, where you can incorporate keywords and improve your SEO.) For example, if you offer haircare products, your customer might search, "easy hairstyles for a bride" or "how to braid your daughter's hair when she won't sit still." If you have blog posts that directly address those questions, the customer visits your website to get the answer and then also sees that you have a product that helps them do the thing they want to do. The great thing about hosting a blog or your own website, is that you get to promote yourself, and each time you create a piece of content, you can share that page on your social media channels, email the content to your subscribers, and reconnect with your previous customers.

As you add new material to your website, make sure to incorporate the keywords you want to rank for. You may also want to create specific content to address the keywords your customers use to find solutions.

Backlinks

Another element that influences your SEO and high ranking on the search engine results is backlinks. Think of backlinks like word-of-mouth marketing. When someone links from their website to your website, that's a backlink, and the search engine algorithm rewards websites with a higher number of backlinks. As you work on your marketing and sales plan, think about public relations; how can you get people to write about you and include a backlink to your website? Here are a few ideas to get you started.

- **Position yourself as an expert.** Apply to be a guest on podcasts your customers listen to, write guest posts for blogs that your customers read, and make yourself available to journalists through services like Help A Reporter Out (HARO), which is part of Connectively. Make your products available to influencers for review or pitch your services as part of a resource roundup. You can and also should rate, like, subscribe, and comment on other online posts that give you an opportunity to share your point of view. The more thoughtful and personalized your comment, the more weight the social media platform gives it, so don't just comment, "cool"—add more value than that.

- **Create link-worthy content.** On your website, include blog posts, FAQs, and guides that provide answers to your customers' problems. Conduct a survey or research that interests your customer and publish original results of the findings. Develop free tools such as templates or checklists. Most people love a roundup of information or a tool that makes their lives easier or is simply entertaining.
- **Search mentions and ask for backlinks.** With so much information and reposting, someone may mention you and you don't even know it. Google your product or business name regularly and see where it's been mentioned. You can also set up a Google Alert for your company name. If you find a mention but there's no backlink, send a quick note to the site that mentioned you and ask them to add a link. We recently saw a post by author and *Wild Kingdom* host Dr. Rae Wynn-Grant who—totally by chance—saw that her book was mentioned on people.com! Now that's the kind of backlink you want to request. Don't be shy about asking for these. The more links on the web to your website, the more connected it is to search engines.
- **Be a good community citizen.** Everyone is trying to improve their search engine ranking so offer reciprocal backlinks to people you want to support. Look to your business network or any associations you're part of. Sign up for groups on sites like Facebook, LinkedIn, Reddit, and Discord and contribute to the conversation. You'll expand your network, have the opportunity to engage with customers, and establish yourself as an expert in the field.

The algorithm also counts backlinks you create between pages on your website, so make sure you cross-reference and link pages there, too.

Use Google Analytics and your web builder's analytics to determine the success of your keywords. You can test different headlines and see if the ranking improves and you get more visits.

DISCUSSION GUIDE

- Are you going to invest in SEO now or later?
- What keywords, short and long-tail, will have an impact on SEO for your business?
- How will you use those keywords throughout your website and social media content?
- What new content will you develop to include keywords you want to rank for?
- What activities can you do to encourage backlinks?
- What community will you join to enhance your online networking?
- Three months after you first launch your website, check your analytics; which pages are getting the most traffic? Where is that traffic coming from?

Social Media

Social media can be one of the best ways to reach your customer, especially at the awareness stage of the customer journey. When you're just beginning to build your brand presence, social media provides a low- to no-cost opportunity to reach a large number of your customers. As people get to know you on social media, their trust in you and your ability to solve their problem increases. Some of those people on social media will begin to follow you, like what you do, and ideally visit your website, share their email and phone number with you, and become buying customers, repeat customers, or avid fans. You know you've arrived when a customer reposts your posts or talks positively about your product/service on their *social* media.

Which social media channel should you use? There are many to choose from and the best suggestion we can make is, once again, know your customer. Where do your customers hang out? Are they on TikTok?

Get comfortable making videos because that's where you want to be. Are they on LinkedIn? Go there. Do they use Pinterest? Start pinning.

If you don't know, spend some time on each platform. Search for products/services similar to yours and see where there's active engagement. Do a bit of sleuthing and look at the profiles of people who follow your competitors; are they your customers? Look back at your customer profile research; what parallel products/services do your customers use? Do some detective work on those profiles too. Look for the platform that seems to get the most engagement. Last but not least, go back to the customers you interviewed and ask them specifically which social media platform they use to get information about products/services similar to yours.

If you chose social media as the channel you'll use for marketing (in Chapter 6), then you've probably done some of this work already. If you chose a different marketing and sales channel to focus on, choosing one social media platform in addition to that channel can be a good idea.

The primary social media channels—Facebook, YouTube, Instagram, X (formerly known as Twitter), LinkedIn, Pinterest, and TikTok—all offer the option to create a specific business profile. The line between your business brand and your personal brand may be blurry, but we recommend having a separate profile for each. You probably have a lot of family and friend followers on your personal profile and post things that are, well, personal. Your business profile has a different purpose: you want to reach customers. You want to show you understand them and their problems. Your posts should reflect the look and feel of your brand and most of all, add value to the customers' lives and provide solutions. And, you want to invite them to take the customer journey with you (see Chapter 6, Branding).

Social media channels can be used alongside your website to distribute information and create extra buzz or user engagement. Use tools like LinkTree or LinkInBio to draw people to your website from your social media posts.

The Too Many Channels Trap

Just because a competitor has an account on LinkedIn doesn't mean that's where your customers are. Many entrepreneurs create a profile on every social media channel but then don't use them effectively. The algorithm (the program that decides which profiles get more air time) rewards consistent relevant content and activity. It may be worse to have an unused profile on a platform than to have no profile at all.

DISCUSSION GUIDE

- Which social media channel best aligns with your business?
- Look back at your marketing plan; what types of posts will be most helpful to promote your business?
- Have you set up a LinkTree or LinkInBio to connect your social media profile to your website?
- Are there groups on your chosen social media platform that you can participate in to establish yourself as an expert and encourage backlinks?

Applied Technology

Small business owners spend hours working on their business every week. Technology—in the form of apps, automations, and AI—can take on some of the repetitive tasks you spend the most time on. You can then use the time you freed up on higher-impact activities that will help your business scale. We've put together a list of the nuts and bolts technology that can help your business almost run itself. We encourage you to try free versions in the beginning and then switch to paid versions when you outgrow the free version. The cost of subscriptions can add up quickly and hurt your budget more than they help your business.

You probably already have some of the items listed below. Consider whether any others can help you save time and effort, making it worth the cost of the subscription. Keep in mind, most online apps offer a free trial period, so try before you buy.

- **Website domain address and landing page:** If you have a website, you already have a domain and landing page. It's hard to be in business without the bare minimum of a landing page for your domain but many entrepreneurs build their whole business on platforms like Etsy or Pinterest.
- **Personal email address (linked to your domain):** Yes, you can create an @gmail or @iCloud email address but it's far more professional—and easier for your customers to remember—to have an email with your domain address, i.e., [name]@skysthelimit.org. Your web host very likely includes a domain-linked email address, perhaps the possibility of creating more than one so you can have admin@, or contact@, etc. We like Google Workspace for this, and it includes a bunch of other useful apps, like Drive for storage and Docs, Spreadsheets, and Slides.
- **Email capture and management:** Begin collecting email addresses of potential customers (and partners) as early as possible in your entrepreneurial journey. Many website platforms will include this feature. You can have an opt-in section on your landing page, a separate opt-in page on your website, a pop-up opt-in that people see when they visit your website, or you can use Google Forms. Ideally, you'll make it as easy as possible for a potential customer to share their email. You should have a link to that opt-in on your social media as well. Building your email list is a little like collecting a new kind of currency, it's basically direct access to a potential customer's inbox. Many email management apps also include email marketing functions to send newsletters, promotions, or information to customers via email during the customer journey. Your website platform

may include or have an add-on for an email marketing function, or you can consider a service like ConvertKit, HubSpot, or FloDesk—though when you're just starting out, you likely don't need these paid services. You can send emails to your list manually in the beginning.

- **Email marketing:** So, what do you do with the email you collect? The goal of email marketing is usually to inspire an action for your potential customer. You should send valuable content via email to your potential customers, either as a group or individually when you think the opportunity to make sales is worth it.
- **Customer Relationship Management (CRM):** While lead generation focuses on sales, CRM considers the whole customer journey. Customer data (i.e., name, contact info, purchase history, birthday, preferences, etc.) is stored on the CRM, and entrepreneurs use it to—as the name implies—manage the relationship with the customer. Think about the best customer service experience you've recently had, did they remember your name, your favorite order, your size? By collecting information about your customers, you can reference it later. At first you might think you can do this all in your head, but that won't scale. A CRM not only stores information but often allows you to automate tasks such as sending reminder emails. This software also usually organizes the sales process and helps you define the tasks that happen when you have a contact with a potential customer and what you need to do to move the customer forward on the customer journey—the goal is usually to get the customer to purchase again and again.
- **Scheduling software:** If people frequently schedule appointments or sessions with you, you probably want to have a way for them to schedule time on your calendar without making a phone call or embarking on a lengthy email exchange. We like Calendly for this.

- **Video calls:** At some point you will want to speak to a customer or client on a video call. The Google Suite offers great features and is free. Zoom is free for calls up to 40 minutes long. Think about the type of service you need for your business and consider the ease of use for your customer.
- **Basic Software:** You can do a lot with a few basic apps for word processing, crunching numbers, and making slide decks. You can opt for Google's free version (Google Docs, Google Sheets, Google Slides, etc.) or Microsoft 365 (Word, Excel, PowerPoint, etc.), both of which create documents that are easy to share with other people. If you have a Mac, it comes with Apple's version of those apps (Pages, Numbers, Keynote) but those can be harder for everyone else to access.
- **File Storage:** It's surprising how quickly you generate a ton of documents and images for your business, and you want to keep them in a safe place. While you may store some of those docs on your computer locally, we suggest you keep everything online in cloud storage so you never lose it and can access it from any device. Sites like Google Drive, Dropbox, OneDrive (if you're a Microsoft 365 subscriber), and iCloud (if you're an Apple user) are some of the bigger names in online storage. Some have a special feature for photo management, which can be helpful if you have a lot of product photos to organize.
- **Payment management:** Even if you have a brick-and-mortar store or offer services in person, most people will pay with their credit card or phone. As discussed in previous chapters, it's crucial to make it easy for your customer to pay you, so it's important to set up a service to accept non-cash payments. Entrepreneurs often choose services like Square, PayPal, Venmo, Stripe, Zelle, and Wise. You sign up for the service and then link it to your bank account; a customer pays you with their credit card and the service

transfers that money to your bank account. Many offer invoicing within their apps, if that's a feature you need.

- **Online banking:** Likewise, managing your own money online is both efficient and cost-effective. With online banking you can transfer funds, pay your own bills, check balances, etc. Open a business bank account if it's free, or just open a second personal account, so that you can keep all your business expenses and revenues in one place that's separate from your personal bank account.
- **Bookkeeping:** We talk more about banking and bookkeeping in Chapter 10, Accounting and Bookkeeping. Using an online app to manage your income and expenses helps you quickly see your budget and allows you to automate ongoing payments. We like apps like Quickbooks or Xero.
- **Project management:** As a bookkeeping app helps you manage your money, a project management app helps you manage your time. We discuss project management in Chapter 9, Operations. These apps help you create a process for your tasks, whether they are ongoing, like customer management, or project specific, like a marketing campaign or product development. We like ClickUp and Notion for this. Related to project management are time management apps, like Toggl, that enable you to track your time by task or project so you can see how long it takes you to do tasks and manage your time more effectively. It doesn't matter which one of these you use, it's just important to have some discipline around it.
- **Social media scheduler:** Most social media marketing experts recommend batching the creation of your posts—that is setting aside a few hours to create posts for a week or more—and then scheduling when they'll be posted using an app. Some social media scheduling apps include content calendar templates with suggestions for the type of content to share, others have stock or

suggested imagery as well. These apps can be a huge time saver in your marketing efforts. We like Hootsuite for this.

- **AI:** Sites like ChatGPT, Claude, and Venice.ai provide interactive artificial intelligence. While we love the direction this technology is going, it's changing all the time, and you'll need to practice using it to get better results for your business. Use AI to augment your ideas or facilitate your tasks, not replace your imagination, creativity, or decision-making. Also, double check the results from these platforms because AI has no judgment so it doesn't know if it learns something that's wrong, and it repeats it anyway.
- **The list of apps for business is endless:** There are so many apps out there to help you solve your problems, some of which you didn't even know you had. For example, an online app like Loom lets you record videos, demos, and personalized messages to share with people. It saves time for you and the recipient—they can watch when they want—and increases clarity. CareCart automatically sends an email to a customer who has abandoned the purchase process at checkout. Apps exist to virtually manage inventory and shipments. Finding apps that solve your business problems is a great task for AI. Ask ChatGPT for recommendations for apps that do the task you would like to offload and then try its suggestions.

While online apps and services can save you time, make sure you're subscribing to a service that truly serves your needs. For example, in the beginning you probably don't need an email management app, a lead gen app, and a CRM. One full-featured website building platform will satisfy your needs: create an opt-in page to capture email, store the email, send an automated email sequence that guides your customer through their journey (also known as a nurture sequence), offer analytics for open rates and click-through.

The App Trap

All too quickly you can find yourself signing up or subscribing to a dozen or more services that seem cool, necessary, and efficient. We heard of one entrepreneur who had 37 (!) subscriptions for various online apps and services. Some were two different apps that did the same thing, a few weren't even being used, but they'd never taken the time to cancel the subscription or the automatic payment. When the entrepreneur did an app audit they wound up saving more than $1,000 a month on subscriptions by canceling those that were unnecessary. We might recommend taking some time to learn how to use Google Sheets or Excel, you can build your own mini CRM, accounting, forecasting, task lists, and more with just that from the get go.

DISCUSSION GUIDE

- Which types of apps do you currently use?
- How do people schedule appointments with you?
- Where do you store your documents and photos?
- How do you bill people?
- How do you get paid by your customers? What are the options?
- How do you access your bank account for your business?
- How do you record the processes or repeating tasks you do?
- How do you post to social media?
- Which apps would help you save time?
- Have you tried some of the apps suggested?

You've accomplished the steps to create a foundation for your business. It's time to think about the future by setting goals and developing a strategy and the tactics to reach them.

CHECKLIST

- ✓ Select a website building platform.
- ✓ Purchase a domain name.
- ✓ Create a content plan for your website. Write descriptions of your company's origin and "why," the benefits and features of your product or services, etc. Take photos.
- ✓ If you choose to invest in SEO, identify and incorporate keywords to improve search engine ranking. Create a backlinks strategy.
- ✓ Build your first version of your website.
- ✓ Create a business email address, even if it's a free one [business name]@gmail.com.
- ✓ Choose a system for your docs, spreadsheets, and presentations.
- ✓ Sign up for multiple ways to get paid, i.e., Paypal, Stripe, etc.

CHAPTER 8

Strategy

When Should You Read This Chapter?
When first starting out, most entrepreneurs fly by the seat of their pants—and learn by trial and error, a lot of errors due to lack of planning. Setting goals can help you prioritize and be efficient in how you spend your time, so this chapter (especially the work on SMART goals) can help you from the very early stages of starting your business. As your business grows and you want to make good decisions, the ideas and tools in the second half of the chapter can be helpful.

Being an entrepreneur requires making decision after decision—deciding who your customer is, deciding what product to make, deciding where to market and sell your product, deciding to hire an employee, the list goes on. You learned about making initial decisions for your business using effectuation (Chapter 1, Entrepreneurial Foundations). But once you've decided what to do, how do you make it happen?

Your business strategy is the plan for the continued and future success of your company or organization. Formulating and executing a strategy includes a range of activities that ultimately should help your business grow and meet your goals. In this chapter, we present a series of frameworks to help you set business goals, create a strategy and tactics to reach them, and measure whether the strategy and tactics are leading to your success.

We'll admit that when presented one after the other, these frameworks—which take the form of acronyms—can seem a little overwhelming, and perhaps be hard to differentiate from one another. But keep in mind you don't have to use them all at once. Different frameworks may be helpful at different points in your business journey. As you review this chapter, know that you can choose the tools and frameworks that feel the most relevant to the challenges that you're facing now, and return to the others later.

Setting and Achieving Goals

Goals are part of every aspect of business and life. They provide a sense of direction, motivation, focus, and priority. By setting goals, you are providing yourself with a target to aim for. We like the framework of SMART goals, presented below. A SMART goal incorporates all of the criteria needed to clarify your ideas, focus your efforts, use your time and resources productively, and increase your chances of achieving your goals.

SMART Goals

The idea behind SMART goals is relatively simple. When you set a goal it should be: Specific, Measurable, Attainable, Relevant, and Time-bound.

- **Specific** meaning the goal is clearly defined and detailed. This point may seem obvious; however, not creating a specific goal is one of the most common missteps in goal setting.
- **Measurable** goals should include an outcome that can be measured. If you can't measure whether or not you have accomplished your goals, then it will be very difficult to determine if you are making progress towards them.
- **Attainable** forces you to think about any obstacles that might stand in the way of achieving a goal and to think about any resources that can be leveraged to help you achieve your goals.

- **Relevant** and appropriate goals for your business will make you more motivated to accomplish them and prevent you from doing tasks that don't lead to the success you want.
- **Time-bound** goals have a set deadline, so that the tasks won't go on endlessly. Having a time-bound goal can help you define the strategy and tactics you'll apply to reach the goal. Also, almost everyone in the world has a tendency to procrastinate. That's ok, so do we sometimes, but by setting a time-bound date, you can create what's called a forcing function, that can motivate you to complete the goal.

For example, your business goal is to "make more money so I can quit my day job," but this goal is not a SMART goal. Applying the SMART framework:

- **Specific:** I want to increase revenue and profit.
- **Measurable:** I want to increase profit by 20 percent.
- **Attainable:** I can increase new sales by 10 percent and upsell half of my existing customers by 25 percent; the additional revenue from these increases will result in 20 percent more overall profit.
- **Relevant:** My long-term goal is to quit my day job; increasing profit allows me to pay myself a salary and quit my job.
- **Time-bound**: I'd like to increase profits by the end of the current year.

Your goal becomes, "I want to increase profit by 20 percent. I will do this by increasing new sales revenue by 10 percent and upselling half of my existing customers by 25 percent. My aim is to do this by the end of the current year so I can quit my day job."

GSTM

Goals are useless without the strategies and tactics to reach them. With your understanding of setting SMART goals, you can now place goal-setting in the context of achieving them, and that requires defining your strategies, tactics, and specific measurements you'll use to determine if you've achieved your goal. We call it GSTM. There's some overlap between the ideas of SMART and GSTM, but we believe it's important you understand and implement both.

- **Goals:** Set your goals, using the SMART format.
- **Strategy:** Assess the strategic options you have and decide on one.
- **Tactics:** Assess the tactical options you have for that strategy, and decide on one or a few.
- **Measurements:** Define how you measure success and when, track your progress to your goal.

Goals: Ambitious goals fuel an entrepreneur's dreams; you can set a hundred goals but don't try to attain them all at once. We suggest setting no more than three goals for each area of your business, i.e., sales, product development, operations, etc. You can begin by creating a list of all your goals, big and small, and then prioritizing the list to determine which goals you'll work on first. Create short- and long-term goals as well as subgoals that help you reach your long-term goals. When you set a goal, make each goal SMART. Share your goals with others to create accountability and get feedback on them.

Strategy: Two things happen during the planning stage: you create a strategy and the tactics to bring it to life. For example, if your goal is to increase profit by 20 percent, your strategy could be to raise your prices (with the risk that you sell fewer products and actually earn less rather than more), reduce your production costs (with the risk of reducing the quality your customers expect), or sell to more customers. The tactics are the active steps you take to support the strategy.

Think about different strategies for your goal and choose one, then break your plan down into small achievable steps based on sub-goals. Breaking down a big goal into subgoals and the tactics to achieve it into single steps allows you to make progress without becoming overwhelmed by trying to tackle a goal that is too complex or hard to achieve. Identify resources (including people), and tools needed to achieve your sub-goals. Consider possible barriers or obstacles that may impede achieving your sub-goals and think about how you'll react if that challenge occurs. Write down the steps in a logical order—we talk about project management later in this chapter.

Tactics: Just creating a goal and plan, but not taking the steps to achieve it, will not magically make it happen. The steps to implement your strategy are known as tactics. Take the first step. Follow your plan and follow through. Don't get discouraged if everything doesn't go as planned. Persevere and remember your actions are critical to realizing your goals. Do more than what is required, if you can, to achieve competence, mastery, or excellence. Share your actions with others who can provide you with praise and encouragement to help you stay motivated. We know it's not going to be easy, but we've got your back. This is another reminder to find a peer, mentor, partner, or sponsor to help you stay the course.

Measurements: The measurement of your SMART goal happens when you reflect on the process and outcomes. Evaluate what worked. Think about what didn't work and what was challenging to do. Recognize your mistakes and think about what you would do differently in the future. Reflection is not a weakness; the ability to self-correct is an asset and a strength. Sometimes things just don't work out. When a patient has an adverse outcome at a hospital, doctors and nurses conduct a post-mortem or review of what happened, so they can learn from it. Baking time into your work to go back and review will help you to avoid repeating mistakes or thought patterns.

Revise your plan, if needed. Get feedback from relevant stakeholders, and take pride in your accomplishments. Many people leave out reflection from their goal-setting process, but it is a critical step for correcting your course of action and learning for the future. In many businesses, a quarterly review is sufficient; consider starting with that and adjusting as necessary.

DISCUSSION GUIDE

- What are your top five SMART goals?
- What strategy do you have for each goal?
- What will you do?
- What obstacles or challenges might you face in trying to achieve this goal?
- What can you do to overcome this obstacle or challenge?
- Who can provide you with support when I need it?
- What's the first step you'll take toward your goal?
- What's the timeline for your goal?
- What is your plan for reflection and measurement?
- When will you review your progress toward this goal and maybe even revise your plan?

Understanding your Strengths, Weaknesses, Opportunities, and Threats

When you begin to see results from the strategy and tactics you applied to reach your goal, you want to periodically review the state of your business to better understand how to improve.

A SWOT analysis identifies a business's internal strengths and weaknesses, as well as its external opportunities and threats. Whenever you do a SWOT analysis on your business, make it two dimensional and look from both a product and a brand point of view. Then and only then will you have a well-rounded and actionable look at your entire business.

SWOT helps you define and choose the strategies that will help you reach your goals. By analyzing the strengths, weaknesses, opportunities, and threats of your business, you can think about whether you need to take a defensive or proactive approach to growth. SWOT analysis enables you to see clearly the goals with the highest probability of attainment and the challenges you need to plan for.

SWOT Analysis

SWOT stands for the four elements of your business that you'll analyze: Strengths, Weaknesses, Opportunities, and Threats.

- **Strengths** looks at all the strong points of your business. You can think of Strengths as what your company is capable of doing well, or capabilities. Strengths reflect the unique competitive advantages of your business and your products or services. Some examples of strengths include:
    - You: As the founder, you are the biggest asset your company has. Your personal strengths matter a lot, like being great at sales, or having excellent design skills.
    - Your company's products and services:
        - Better: How are you better than your competitors?
        - Faster: How can you deliver value faster?
        - Cheaper: How can you beat the competition on price?
- **Weaknesses** focus on the factors that weaken your competitive stance. If you're thinking of strengths as what you and your company are good at, weaknesses are what you and your company aren't good at. For example, if you are planning to start a business, you may not have previous experience in the industry you are considering. You may lack required credentials or may be trying to compete against very entrenched competition. You may struggle with focus and follow-through on your ideas. Knowing your weaknesses is as important as knowing your strengths.
- **Opportunities** are considered mostly external to you and your business. Opportunities are changing all the time. Has there been a recent change in your local or regional market? For example, did a competitor go out of business leaving a gap? Is there a new

partner out there for you and your company? Is there a new way to cut costs? Can you offer a new value proposition that you couldn't before?

- **Threats** are from outside of the business and will directly impact you. While you can't usually control the threat, you can control how you prepare and react to it. Most threats are universal to all businesses in a given category, which is why you should look at the potential threats to the brand along with more obvious product threats. If you are planning to start a business, you may have the threat of local regulations negatively impacting your business. Unforeseen competition (local or foreign), dissolution of markets, and adverse weather may also have a negative effect on your new business.

A Skysthelimit.org member wanted to expand her business, a swim school in Ohio. She had seven specific goals to reach and with the help of a SWOT analysis she was able to define the strategies to reach them. Her strengths were her experience as a swimmer, lifeguard, teacher, and lifeguard instructor. Her weaknesses were limited knowledge and skills in technology and fundraising. She had the opportunity to work with mentors to learn about growth marketing and development through social media platforms. The external threats were potential competitors. Guided by a mentor, she also raised money for her business through crowdfunding.

Competitive Risk Analysis

The weaknesses and threats of your SWOT analysis often reflect your position in relation to your competition. Any way the customer is solving their problem right now is your competition. To beat your competitors, you first have to know them. Understanding your competitors is not as important as understanding your customers, but it will allow you to understand why customers use products or services offered by existing providers.

Competitive analysis is the act of analyzing your competitors' product offering, and doing it enables you to better position your business to your customers. What makes a customer choose you instead of your competition: Is your product or service better? faster? cheaper? You thought about this when developing your unique selling proposition in Chapter 2, Product-Market Fit. To reiterate, you can be two of the three—better and faster, but not cheaper; faster and cheaper, but not better; or better and cheaper, but not faster. By looking at how you differ from your competition—in a good way—you can see the advantage you bring to your customer with regard to your competition.

While the landscape of competitors may seem endless at first, there are probably only a handful of main competitors if you are a small business owner who is just starting out. It will be less overwhelming for you to identify several competitors who sell similar products as yourself and highlight their strengths and weaknesses. A competitive strategy highlights your strengths, which means you have to understand your competitors' weaknesses. Doing your research and having all of your information in one place will give you a high-level view of your business' position in the market.

The first step is to identify your competition. Finding your competitors doesn't have to be taxing or complicated. The first step to finding your competitors is to differentiate between two major categories of competitors that should be on your radar, and you'll approach the analysis of them in different ways.

- **Direct competitors** are the companies that first come to mind when you think about competition. They're in your sector or neighborhood, marketing products and services that do the same like-for-like job as yours. Your customer is the same as theirs. For example, you're a local business selling garden supplies, and so your direct competitors are all the local garden supplies stores.
- **Indirect competitors** are trickier to spot. They address the same customer needs as you, but they do it in a different way or with a

different product. Your customer will overlap with theirs but won't be an exact match. So an indirect competitor to your garden supply business might be a large chain of supermarkets. Gardens aren't their core business, but if they offer gardening products, they may use their economies of scale to undercut your prices or offer convenience to consumers as a one-stop-shop.

Once you understand the different types of competitors out there, use the following steps to find your competitors. Get into the shoes of your target customer and think like them to find your competitors.

1. Run a Google search with keywords associated with your business like "printed t-shirt" or "website design services." Write down the name of businesses that show up on the first and second page of the search results in the "Competitive Landscape" template.
2. Refer to the customer interviews you conducted (or conduct new interviews) to learn how customers are solving the problem you're trying to solve.
3. Find your competitors through advertising. This can be through social media, physical ads, events, conferences, etc. How do you want to promote your business? Are your competitors promoting their business in the same ways?
4. Once you've listed your competitors, complete a competitive analysis for the first five.
    - Analyze their offerings. Include features like:
        - Price
        - Benefits
        - Quality
        - Durability
        - Image/style
        - Service

    - Warranties: lifetime vs. limited time
    - Ease of use and convenience
    - Ease of return
    - Free shipping
    - Number and type of features
    - Location(s)
    - Distribution/Sales
    - Certifications: LEED, Green Manufacturing
    - Endorsements
- Analyze their websites.
- Analyze their social media presence.
- Identify their strengths and weaknesses. You can refer to SWOT to guide your thinking.

Remember to keep tabs on your competition, but don't completely obsess over them! You can stay updated by simply setting up a Google Alert that will notify you for updates on keywords, like your competitors' names, industry events, or market developments. Another way to keep up with your competition is to sign up for their newsletters or to follow them on social media so you'll receive notifications as their customers do.

Benefits of SWOT Analysis

Focus is the key to making your two-dimensional SWOT analysis really actionable. The study isn't about making lists, but rather about thinking critically about your product and your brand and identifying the two or three factors in each section that will drive your business forward. Focus on a short list of truly actionable items. By looking at your SWOT analysis from both a product and a brand perspective, you'll be able to bring a renewed focus and action plan to your business. A great SWOT analysis can also help you:

- Explore possibilities for new efforts or solutions to problems.
- Make decisions about the best path for your business. Identifying your opportunities for success in the context of threats to success can clarify directions and choices.
- Determine where change is possible. If you are at a turning point, an inventory of your strengths and weaknesses can reveal priorities as well as possibilities.
- Adjust and refine plans mid-course. A new opportunity might open wider avenues, while a new threat could close a path that once existed.
- SWOT also offers a simple way of communicating about your initiative or program and an excellent way to organize information you've gathered from studies or surveys.

When conducting your SWOT analysis, keep in mind that one item can offset another. For example, your strengths may combat your weaknesses and your opportunities can offset your threats.

DISCUSSION GUIDE

- What are the strengths of your business, product/service, and brand?
- What are the weaknesses of your business, product/service, and brand?
- What opportunities do you foresee to expand your business?
- What threats present a risk to your business?
- Who is your direct and indirect competition?
- Why are they a threat? What advantages do they have over you? Where do you bring more benefit to the customer than the competition?

Decision-Making Framework (DMF)

Being an entrepreneur means making one decision after another, and then taking action. You are constantly bombarded with problems. A big part of being a successful entrepreneur is figuring out which problems to work on now and which to ignore. You'll need to brutally prioritize your time and investments. This is why our 40/40/20 Rule is so helpful—it helps you focus your priorities on making sales and improving your products or services. When thinking about your goals, strategies, and tactics, you're often faced with choosing between two or more ideas, solutions, or steps. Use the knowledge you have to consider outcomes, evaluate risk, and choose the best path forward. For big decisions, it can be important and helpful to write down your thinking—use these questions to help you make the best decision:

1. What's the expected value in time and money? Why do you need to make this decision, what do you expect to happen?
2. What will it cost in terms of time and money?
3. What are the risks? How much can you afford to lose?
4. What are the alternatives?

The Delayed Decision Trap

Use no more steps or complexity than is necessary to make a sound decision. Needless complexity not only wastes the time of those involved, it also places unproductive obstacles in the way of profitable decisions, discouraging initiative and innovation. Slowing down the decision and making it more burdensome can cause opportunities to be lost.

DISCUSSION GUIDE

- What's the most important decision you have to make today?
- Use the DMF to make a decision:
- What's the expected value in time and money? Why do you need to make this decision, what do you expect to happen?
- What will it cost in terms of time and money?
- What are the risks? How much can you afford to lose?
- What are the alternatives?

Day in and day out, you work on your business, often doing the same tasks over and over. Those tasks support your goals, strategies, and tactics. The processes you use to run your business fall under the category of Operations. Read on to understand the importance of defining and recording your operations.

CHECKLIST

- ✓ Set your goals, using the SMART format.
- ✓ Use GSTM to create your strategies, tactics, and measurements.
- ✓ Assess the strategic options you have and decide on one.
- ✓ Assess the tactical options you have for that strategy, and decide on one or a few.
- ✓ Define how you measure success and when, track your progress to your goal.
- ✓ Conduct a SWOT analysis of your business.
- ✓ Prioritize your goals for the next six months.
- ✓ Research your competitors and analyze your competition.
- ✓ Use the DMF to decide your next strategies to grow your business.

CHAPTER 9

Operations

When Should You Read This Chapter?
In the beginning, you may be making things up as you go along, reacting to situations rather than proactively planning for the future. It can be helpful to be aware and think about operations at the beginning of your entrepreneurial journey, but you probably won't be able to define your operations until you've worked on your business for a while. The tips on project and time management may be helpful to you from the very beginning but mapping your operations and creating playbooks will happen after your initial efforts.

Operations is how you and your business deliver your product or service—essentially how you create value for your customer. Operations processes include design, production, and delivery of your product/service and the efficient use of time and resources to meet customer needs. Operations is how you get things done. Operations can also include parts of the business that don't directly affect the customer but are required to keep the company alive, like taxes. The goal of investing in your business operations is to increase efficiency and effectiveness so that you can be better, faster, cheaper—repeatedly and consistently.

To understand how operations relates to everything else in your business, we've matched operations to the customer journey map. We then review processes for project and time management.

Playbooks

Operations thinks about the activities and processes that need to happen across your company, looking for time and labor efficiencies, cost effectiveness, and how the different components of your work interact to delight your customers. While large companies often have a Director of Operations or Chief Operations Officer who is an expert in processes, when you're a new entrepreneur just starting your business, you likely have to think about and manage operations as a whole and a great way to do that is to create playbooks. Coaches in the NFL drill their teams with specific plays that everyone needs to memorize, so they can run predictable plays with a high degree of accuracy. Playbooks do the same for your business—establish predictable processes (plays) with a high potential for accuracy.

Creating playbooks for your most essential operations is a good idea, and it can be easy to do quickly with ChatGPT. These playbooks include the steps you take to create, deliver, etc. your products and services, checklists to help you remember the most important steps to take, and anything else needed to be efficient and effective. Playbooks are also known as Standard Operating Procedures or SOPs. Creating playbooks doesn't need to take a lot of time in the beginning, and can save you time and money later. As your business evolves, so will these playbooks.

You may have playbooks that you create for many parts of your business including:

- Customer development
- Product/service development
- Marketing and sales
- Branding
- Website and technology
- Strategy
- Operations—yes operations is a category of operations!

- Accounting and financials
- Legal and regulatory
- Building the team
- Funding

If you've read other sections like Marketing and Sales or Product Development, you've already begun to do activities in some of the categories. You're already managing operations and didn't know it!

A playbook codifies the standard procedures you follow to run your business. There are two types of information a playbook can communicate:

- **Standards of Procedure (SOP):** These high-level playbooks outline your strategies, processes, procedures, and decision-making trees for the categories of your business, i.e., sales, operations, finance, human resources, etc.
- **Task:** These instructions often fall within an SOP playbook. They convey a how-to list of specific steps to do a repetitive task.

Many solopreneurs we know keep all their operations processes in their heads. They know how they get things done and just do it. And, if that works for you, go for it. However, if you ever want feedback on your systems and processes, writing down how you do things can be good use of your time. And, if you ever plan to hire someone to take over some of your tasks, use a robust project management app (which requires step-by-step task definition so you can check items off a list and the app can list your tasks for the day and display progress). Hey, you could block a half hour a week to document one process, and in a few months, you'll have a full playbook of how you run your business.

A hidden bonus that happens when you create a playbook: when you write down all the steps, you begin to see ways that you could improve your strategy or boost efficiency, or where there's overlap and you can combine tasks. For example with sales, you'll describe the overarching strategy and approach you take with sales, and then the process for lead generation, prospecting, qualifying, selling, and closing. Within each of those processes the customer's response triggers specific actions. If a customer wants more information, then this happens; if the customer is ready to buy, then this other thing happens. The if-then instructions are particularly helpful when you hire someone and want to guide them to make decisions as you would make them. The playbook offers a glimpse into how you think about projects and processes.

The task-specific documents should list every step—you'd be surprised how many steps occur for some of your tasks when you record each movement. Think about how you manage your billing: open and sign-in to Stripe, click Create Invoice, select the client name, item, and price from the menus, add a Thank You memo, review the invoice, click send.

That's an easy process with not too many steps, but if you decide to hire a student to send your invoices each month, having a list of instructions will keep them from asking you how to do it each time. In the not too distant future, there will probably be an AI assistant to which you can give simple instructions for repetitive tasks. If you were to talk to a Stripe expert, they probably have ways to automate the process or reduce the number of steps.

As stated earlier, operations is about getting things done. You learned about setting SMART goals and creating strategy and tactics in Chapter 8, Strategy, now you need to choose the activities—or operations—to do and the order to do them. We like to map the operations categories to the customer journey, because all your operations should work toward the goal of moving the customer further along the journey, in turn contributing to the success of your business.

DISCUSSION GUIDE

- When you think about how you conduct the different parts of your business, do you have standard procedures that you repeat?
- Do you have guidelines to make decisions?
- Have you ever written down your guidelines or procedures? Why not?
- Which parts of your business could benefit from having a playbook?
- Which tasks do you repeat each month, week, or day?
- What specific steps do you take to do these tasks?
- Bonus question: Could any of those steps be automated? If so, do it.

Map Operations to Customer Journey

An entrepreneur can set many goals and plan many projects but if the outcome doesn't improve their relationship to the customer, the work they've done is worthless. Matching goals and the projects to meet them to the stages of the customer journey provides a waypoint to make sure those goals and projects keep the business moving forward and focused on customer outcomes. We've listed the stages of the customer journey below; write your goals and projects associated with each one.

Customer Journey Stage	Your Goals and Projects
Discover	
Explore and Connect	
Opt-In	
Onboard	
Inspire	
Grow	
Endorse	
Broadcast	

At each stage, ask: what does your business need to DO? Look at the customer journey map you created for your marketing plan and think about the goal you need to reach in each category to support those marketing efforts; not every stage will have every category. Then, on the Operations Priority Template shown below (available on Skysthelimit.org in the Business Resources/Operations/Time Management section), write the goal under each category (some of the categories are discussed in upcoming chapters so you can come back to those priorities). The next section discusses project management and how to identify the tasks necessary to reach each goal.

Operational Priorities

What is the most important thing to focus on in each cost center category right now?

Cost Center	Priority
Business Plan	
Customer Development	
Product/Service Development	
Marketing and Sales	
Branding	
Website and Technology	
Strategy	
Operations	
Accounting and Financials	
Legal and Regulatory	
Building the Team	
Funding	

DISCUSSION GUIDE

- What processes have you developed so far for the various categories of your business?
- How do those processes support your efforts to guide your customer through a journey with your business, leading them from awareness through promotion?
- What goals do you have for each stage of the customer journey?
    - Discover
    - Explore and Connect
    - Opt-In
    - Onboard
    - Inspire
    - Grow
    - Endorse
    - Broadcast
- Which operations will support you reaching those goals?
    - Business plan
    - Customer development
    - Product/service development
    - Marketing and sales
    - Branding
    - Website and technology
    - Strategy
    - Operations
    - Accounting and financials
    - Legal & regulatory
    - Building the team
    - Funding

Project Management

Project management applies knowledge, skills, tools, and techniques to plan activities to meet the requirements of a project. Think about the goals you set in Chapter 8, Strategy; each goal is a mini project that requires planning—the strategies and tactics discussed previously. A project plan has six major components: defining goals, developing scope, estimating, planning, executing, and reviewing.

1. **Define SMART goals**: Think about and write down what you want to achieve at the conclusion of this project. This is the basic foundation of your project that will guide you along the way.
2. **Develop scope:** With your goals in mind it's time to think about what has to be done to achieve the defined goal. Look at the list of goals you created in the last chapter and define all activities and tasks you need to complete them. For example, if your goal is to start your business, your list might look like this:
    - Activity 1: Create your website.
    - Sub task 1: Plan your user experience, how do you want customers to navigate your site?
    - Sub task 2: Hire a website designer/developer.

    Prioritize your activities and list how you will complete them in a logical order. Start prioritizing your business activities with our operational priorities template.
3. **Estimate:** Consider how long each of the defined activities will take to be completed. Then, block time to do this work in a calendar or time management plan (we offer specific time management tips in the next section).
4. **Plan:** Identify how long it will take to complete the full project depending on the resources you have available. Put it on a timeline so you will have a visual of the total time it will take to achieve your

goals and complete your project. Check out some of our favorites, like Asana and Trello. AI can also help with calendar planning, online apps like Motion and Trevor build schedules for you. As mentioned in Chapter 7, Website and Technology, in the Applied Technology section, look for an app that matches your needs and take advantage of the free trial period to test it—test more than one. Choose the app that you need today and for a short time in the future; when your business grows, you can upgrade to a more robust app.

5. **Execute:** Do the work. Check your plan daily and follow the tasks you have identified. Tracking the time you spend for each task can be helpful for future planning. Problems can appear, so update your plan as you go to keep everything on track. Most important in the execution phase is not straying from your plan.
6. **Track and review:** As with any SMART goal, you want to measure productivity and track progress. Reviewing the project is part of the process to ensure you stay on track. You'll want to do this periodically as you progress through your project and at the end when the project is complete. Reviewing will help you understand what worked, what didn't work, and will provide you with valuable insight for the next project.

Most small businesses can't afford to waste time and effort spinning their wheels to accomplish work. Using a project management approach in your business can minimize confusion, rework, errors and best of all, it can help you delight your customers.

DISCUSSION GUIDE

- What is the top goal that you'll develop a plan for?
- What is the scope of your project? What steps do you need to take to reach your goal?
- How much time do you need for each task?
- How long will the entire project take? What is your completion deadline?
- When will you do the tasks?
- Will other people help you do the tasks?
- How will you track your time and your accomplishments?
- What will success look like?
- What are the consequences of not meeting your goal?

Time Management

Time management dictates how you spend your time and make progress on project tasks and activities. The goal of time management is to reduce the distractions so you can focus on what's most important to the business.

As an entrepreneur, you probably have a creative streak and maybe prefer to do tasks when you feel inspired to do so. Truth is, if you only work when inspired, you could soon be out of business! Contrary to what you might think, time management allows you to be more creative because you focus on key tasks, are more organized, have less stress, and have more time for family, friends, and other hobbies. Keep these guidelines in mind as you schedule your project tasks in your calendar.

- **Plan ahead.** Assign a time estimate to complete each task from your project plan. There are two parts to this: First, how much total time will the task take? Second, what is your deadline? For example, if you have to write website copy for 15 new products, you may estimate that it will take eight hours to write but you probably won't spend eight hours at one time to complete that task. You may spend an hour a day for the next week or so. This calculation shows that you need to block an hour of time each day on your calendar for the next two weeks to write website copy. Most time management gurus suggest that tasks tend to take longer than we estimate, so add a bit more time than you believe the task will take. Ensuring that you have enough time to deliver a high-quality product or service should always be a top priority.

- **Build in flexibility.** Avoid filling every hour of the day with tasks. Leave plenty of unscheduled time for flexibility. One time management expert suggests leaving one day a week as a spillover day (her choice is Friday). So, if your car breaks down on Tuesday and you spend the day waiting for the tow truck, you have time on Friday to catch up on the work that didn't happen on Tuesday.
- **Select a tool for planning your daily and weekly time.** Example tools include organizers, day planners, software applications (with mobile apps), AI assistants, and spreadsheets.
  - Create a schedule and implement the 40/40/20 Time Management Rule: 40 percent on your product/service, 40 percent on selling and marketing, and 20 percent on internal operations.
  - **Daily:** Each day you will be working toward accomplishing a list of tasks. Don't forget about ongoing business functions that are not directly related to a goal, like meetings and social media management. Many entrepreneurs find time-blocking to be an effective time management system. Put everything on your calendar, not just meetings or appointments but also the time you plan to spend on social media, on writing, on sales calls, on research or personal development.
  - **Weekly:** List the tasks that need to be completed each day to create a five-day time management plan. List the tasks in

priority order for each day. These tasks will give you the greatest return toward your goals.

- **Plan to plan.** Set aside time in your schedule to work on planning your schedule. Allow 15 minutes each day to review, and schedule a two-hour time block each month or quarter to plan the month(s) ahead, and consider scheduling a full day toward the end of the year to plan for the year to come.
    - **Daily:** At the end of the day, take 15 minutes to clear your work space, update your daily task list—and cross off what you accomplished. Celebrate everything you have done, little victories matter! Then, prepare the list for the next day. The next morning, arrive a few minutes early and assemble your prioritized to-do list. This may prove to be the most productive part of your day.
    - **Monthly:** At the end of the third week of the month, assess your progress toward your monthly and quarterly goals. Ask yourself if you need to make adjustments to meet your monthly and quarterly goals.
    - **Yearly:** As you enter the last quarter of the year, use all of your weekly time management plans to start reviewing your overall progress toward your annual goals. Assess yourself and start identifying your quarterly and annual goals for the next year.

Time management tips abound, and we've added a roundup of our own suggestions:

- Automate parts of your business, for example automatically send emails, book meetings, or send invoices (see the Applied Technology section in Chapter 7, Website and Technology).
- Minimize distractions and limit access to time wasters. Use apps like Focus Booster or Rescue Time to help you concentrate to stay on task.

- Utilize software such as Paymo and Toggl to track time usage, time spent on different types of work activities or projects, and billable hours.
- Avoid multitasking. Recent psychological studies have shown that multi-tasking does not actually save time. In fact, the opposite is often true.
- Take care of yourself. The care and attention you give yourself is an important investment of time. Scheduling time to relax, or do nothing, can help you rejuvenate both physically and mentally, enabling you to accomplish tasks more quickly and easily.
- Say no often. You're the boss—remember? If you have to decline a request in order to attend to what's truly important and urgent, do not hesitate to do so.

DISCUSSION GUIDE

- What kind of time management tool do you use?
- What does a typical day's schedule look like for you? A typical week?
- What monthly goals do you have?
- What yearly goals have you set?
- What's the most challenging part about time management for you?
- How could you address that challenge?
- How could you better manage your time?
- What benefit would you see if you improved your time management?

Customer Service

Customer service is essential. Customer service can be a huge advantage—or disadvantage—for your business. It can be reactive to your customers or proactive. Customer service often looks different for a product business than a services business.

Customers turn to customer service when a problem arises: a product arrives broken, a salesperson is rude, the color or size they want is unavailable. For an entrepreneur, customer service can happen at every stage of the customer journey and indirectly happens during customer development—because you are always responding to your customers' needs. Customer service should be the mindset an entrepreneur brings to every working minute of the day and should infuse a company's culture. Great customer service is a competitive advantage you shouldn't ignore, particularly for services businesses where the line between customer service and delivering your service is blurry.

As a part of operations, however, customer service requires both a strategy and tactics to become part of your competitive advantage. If your strategy is to respond to a customer within an hour, what tactics will you take to make sure that happens? If your strategy promises to always have a live person available (instead of a bot), what tactics allow you to enable that?

Customer service automation continually improves. Many websites offer live chat that allows customers to talk to someone. The initial conversation is usually conducted with an AI bot and when the questions become too complex, the conversation switches over to a live person. Think about the questions or problems your customers might have and set up a process to address them before they happen. Of course, you want to do what you can to avoid the problem in the first place.

Good communication between various parts of your business enables customer service to do a better job. If the salesperson on the frontline repeatedly hears about the same problem or objection to a product, customer service can develop strategies to address the problem—until product development updates the product to eliminate the problem altogether. Don't let customer service be the last to know when there's a problem.

DISCUSSION GUIDE

- What's the best customer service experience you've recently had? What was memorable about it? How did it make you feel and what can you apply from that experience to your own business?
- What's your customer service strategy, i.e., what kind of customer service do you want to be known for?
- How will other areas of your business communicate with customer service?
- What technology and automation can help you offer better customer service?
- Which parts of customer service will you automate and when will a live person intervene?

Efficiencies in your processes and operations keep your business flowing smoothly, but you also want to manage your income and expenses as part of that flow. The next chapter presents the basics of accounting and bookkeeping.

CHECKLIST

- ✓ Make a project plan for each of your goals.
- ✓ Choose and use a scheduling tool.
- ✓ Align your business operations to your customer journey map.
- ✓ Create a customer service process.
- ✓ Start creating a playbook for each operations category.

CHAPTER 10

Accounting and Bookkeeping

> **When Should You Read This Chapter?**
> Early on, you want to open a separate bank account for your business and keep track of your expenses and revenue. This chapter can be read at the beginning of your entrepreneurial journey and referred to as your business grows.

Making a lot of money may or may not rank highly on your list of reasons for becoming an entrepreneur—either way, it is the lifeblood of a business. Money requires tracking, thought, structure, and management, and those tasks fall under the title of accounting and bookkeeping. While the tasks in this cost center—we'll explain what that means in this chapter—are related, they have distinct responsibilities:

- Accounting refers to the analysis of your business income and expenses and contributes to strategic decisions to best manage your funds. Taxes fall under the accounting umbrella.
- Bookkeeping tracks the incoming and outgoing transactions, and passes that information on to accounting for their analysis and management.

In the beginning of your business, the line between bookkeeping and accounting can be blurry; a part-time bookkeeper or accounting software may be all you need to manage your income and expenses, including taxes. As your business grows and you face complex spending decisions, the difference between bookkeeping and accounting becomes clearer.

The Bookkeeper Trap

You need to right-size your investment in this cost center at each stage of your business. We've seen far too many businesses struggle because as the company grew, the founder relied on the original bookkeeper to make accounting decisions. A bookkeeper is not an accountant. That's not a slam against bookkeepers; they have their role, but typically don't have the business acumen to advise you as your business grows. The investment of a few hours with an accountant to help you analyze and strategize your income and expenses can pay for itself by lowering the risk of poor money management.

Your Bank Account

As an entrepreneur, you should keep your personal money and expenses separate from your business' or organization's money and expenses. So, one of the first steps with regard to your business's money is opening a bank account. With all the online banking options, this can be really easy to do, and it's never too early to start a business banking account. A lot of banks offer free business checking accounts and debit and/or credit cards—and if you can't get a business account, you can just open a separate personal account that you use for your business. All of your business transactions—revenue and expenses—should run through this account so you can easily see how much you're spending. Consider using a credit union for your banking needs; their fees tend to be lower than a traditional bank, and they often offer free educational tools for their members like webinars about budgeting or consultants to help with investment decisions.

Think about how you will receive and make payments. If all of your transactions happen online, you may not need a local branch that you can visit, but rather just a bank account where you can deposit funds from online payments. You can then make online payments with direct pay, a service that enables you to make payments from your bank account to a creditor, or a debit/credit card linked to your account. If you plan to collect cash payments, look for a bank that allows you to make daily deposits (most do) to minimize the risk of having high cash amounts in store.

To get started, put some money in your business checking account, and only use the debit card or credit card associated with the account to pay for your business expenses. Then, every time you get money from the sale of your products or services, put that money into your business checking account to replenish your debit card or to pay off your business credit card.

Keeping track of your expenses and financials is an important part of running a business. It will help you file your taxes effectively and save you the stress and heartache that comes with poor management of finances.

You need to track your revenue and your expenses to know:

- Whether you can pay yourself more or not
- Whether you are profitable or not
- Whether to pay or not pay taxes

At the end of each month, your banking statements will give you a quick snapshot of how much you spent and made—in the beginning, this may be the only bookkeeping and accounting system you need. Some online banking apps have a feature that lets you categorize your income and expenses and create a budget directly in the app. You can also set up a spreadsheet in Excel or GoogleSheets, or use an app like QuickBooks or Xero. We'll talk about setting that up in the later section on Budgeting.

If you're using the money you earn to pay off business-related expenses on your credit card and debit card charges and you still have money left over, that's a very good sign! That means that you're bringing in more than you're spending.

The Credit Trap

There are business credit cards that offer special rewards for spending a certain amount of money and give you access to more credit to make big purchases. Put on your accounting hat—or consult with an accounting expert or mentor—and analyze these decisions before making a commitment. Be very cautious to not rack up spending you can't pay off.

DISCUSSION GUIDE

- Have you opened a separate bank account for your business?
- Can you manage the bookkeeping and accounting tasks yourself or will you hire/contract someone to help you?
- How will you track your income and expenses?

Invoices and Receipts

When a customer decides to purchase an item from you, they will pay you. If you have a retail store, the transactions are typically immediate: the customer puts an item in their real or virtual shopping cart, goes to the checkout, and pays for the items. You, the seller, issue a receipt to the buyer. If you sell business-to-business, create products made to order, or offer a service, you will probably use an invoice, perhaps a purchase order, or both. The type of business you own will dictate how you issue requests for payments.

Invoices and receipts act as official sales records for your business. Maintaining accurate records of all transactions will help you track your sales numbers and the income generated. As a business, you're also legally required to record your sales and the tax you charge your customers. The information you collect on your sales receipts will help you file and pay your taxes accurately. You can use an app like QuickBooks or Xero or a simple spreadsheet to track sales, income, and expenses, including tax.

Invoices and Purchase Orders

The main difference between an invoice and a purchase order (PO) is that an invoice is generated by you, the seller, while a purchase order is generated by the buyer. A PO confirms that a customer or client is placing an order. The invoice or bill is how you request payment for the order. Not all customers will issue a PO, but if they do, they'll usually want you to reference their PO number on your invoice to help them keep track of the sale in their own accounts payable system—that's the way they track invoices they need to pay. POs can also help you keep track of the orders you have and still need to fulfill.

Once an order has been filled, you should send your customer an invoice or bill that includes the PO number in the description. You should also make sure to include payment terms that define how you want to be paid by a specified date. Search online to get templates you can use for invoices and POs—you don't need to pay for this until it's becoming too time consuming for you to manage individually, and if that's happening, you're making revenue.

Payment Terms

Payment terms are the conditions under which you (the seller or vendor) expect to be paid. This includes:

- **When payment is expected.** Standard due dates are typically expressed as follows:
    - PIA: Payment in advance
    - Net 10: Payment 10 days after invoice date
    - Net 30: Payment 30 days after invoice date
    - Net 60: Payment 60 days after invoice date
    - EOM: End of month
    - COD: Cash on delivery

- **Any conditions on that payment.** Examples of conditions include:
    - Cash account: Account conducted on a cash basis, no credit
    - Stage payment: Payment of agreed amounts at specific dates over time
- **Any discounts the buyer will receive.** For example, "1 percent 10 Net 30" means the customer will receive a 1 percent discount if payment is received within 10 days, otherwise full payment is due 30 days after invoice date.

As you can see, there are many different ways you can accept payment, and how you do so is up to you and your customers. For products, you'll usually get paid at the time of the order. For services, you'll usually get paid within a certain time frame after you deliver your services, although it is not unusual to ask for a certain amount in advance, or to ask for stage payments. This might look like 25 percent upon signing the contract, 25 percent at the first and second milestones, and the final 25 percent upon completion of the project.

Whatever your terms, just make sure that they are clearly communicated to your customers as early as possible, and preferably in writing, to avoid any issues down the road. (Read about contracts in Chapter 11, Legal and Regulatory.)

Creating an Invoice

Invoices come in many different forms and businesses can design their template in a way that works for their specific business needs. To be useful, your invoices should contain specific information about the transaction. The most common components include:

- **Your business information:** Include name, phone number, email address, and business address.
- **Customer information:** Include name, phone number, email address, billing and shipping address if needed.

- **Important dates:** Include the date the receipt/invoice is created and provide a due date if applicable.
- **Invoice number:** Payment management apps like Stripe will create sequential invoice numbers. If you have a lot of invoices, you may want to start with the year or month number so you can find or sort a specific set of invoices easily.
- **Product/service details:** Include item name or identifier for each product or service, quantity of items purchased, and cost per unit (sale price).
- **Taxes:** Retail sites and payment management apps will calculate the tax for you based on information you provide, such as where your business is located and where your customers are.
- **Total amount of the sale:** Include all taxes, fees and shipping.
- **Payment terms:** As defined above, be sure to include your return policy and/or available discounts.

Your invoice is another stop on the customer journey and an opportunity to reinforce brand recognition and create a smooth process. You always want to make it easy for the customer to pay you. If you have a subscription service or any sort of repeat payments, you can set up automatic invoicing to save you time and effort.

Receipts

A sales receipt is the customer's proof that a purchase was made, and it acknowledges that the seller has been paid for goods or services. The receipt is always issued by the seller and given to the buyer. If you use an e-commerce site like Shopify or Squarespace or accounting software like QuickBooks, you can automate receipts to be generated upon payment.

Detailed receipts have similar information to an invoice but declare the debt paid. Customers often use receipts to claim deductible expenses on their taxes, track business costs, and record taxes paid. This can help them at tax time, as well.

We recommend keeping digital copies of all your receipts to make it easier to file your taxes when the time comes. Think about naming the files with the tax year and any other type of category that will help you sort your receipts easily at tax time. Storing a digital copy in a cloud-based service like Google Drive or Dropbox will also allow you to easily copy your business information and document comments while keeping your data safe and virtually impossible to lose. These virtual filing cabinets can be set up like their physical counterparts with separate folders for Income (customer invoices and receipts issued) and Expenses (the invoices and receipts for business expenses you pay). There are also receipt-tracking apps that may be worth getting.

DISCUSSION GUIDE

- Will your customers use purchase orders to place orders with you?
- Do you have a template for invoices with all the required information?
- How will you send invoices to your customers?
- How will you send receipts to your customers?
- How will you make sure you get paid? What system will you use to track invoices and payments?

Budgeting

You may or may not have a household budget to track and manage your income and living expenses. If you do, that serves as good practice, because your business is going to be even more complicated and you need to have a plan. The numbers don't lie and seeing your income and expenses in black and white helps you make decisions about how much to pay yourself, when to hire someone, when to expand, when you need to cut expenses, or when you need to think about raising or lowering your prices. The data you input as part of your bookkeeping tasks will allow you to do the analysis of accounting and budgeting.

The first budget you need to create is your startup and launch budget. For a first-time entrepreneur, the number of items to consider, track, and budget for can be surprising. To begin, make a list of the products and services you need to purchase to start your business and how much each item costs. If you're not sure how much something will cost, do a search and make sure the costs reflect your location—an hourly wage in California will be higher than Iowa.

Expense Categories

Expenses here are divided by category, but each business has different types of expenses within the categories. For example, if you're a solopreneur who provides in-home manicures, you may contract with a website designer, but you probably won't have a sales team or a physical retail space. An entrepreneur who plans to open a coffee shop will need a physical space, equipment, and probably at least one employee.

There are three types of expenses to consider:

- **Startup expenses:** These are initial purchases that you need to get your business off the ground; things like furniture, a computer, or a vehicle, that you won't need to replace in the near future.
- **Fixed expenses**: Your regularly scheduled bills fall into this category. They include yearly insurance premiums, quarterly taxes, and monthly utilities, as well as any supplies that you replace on a regular basis.
- **Variable expenses**: Unplanned or irregular expenses are as the name implies, variable. These include entertainment, like taking a client out to lunch or buying coffee for your team. You want to budget a fixed amount for variable expenses and keep your spending within your budget.

Create a spreadsheet and use a separate line for each type of expense. The total startup and ongoing budget costs add up quickly. When you have all the estimated expenses in the spreadsheet, look closely at each one to identify places where you can trim costs, be more efficient, or delay a purchase until a later date. This list can help you think about your specific startup and ongoing business expenses. To make sure you don't overlook an expense, it can be helpful to think about the cost centers—the different parts of your business that require spending such as sales and marketing, finance, legal, human resources, product development, etc.—and the expenses associated with each.

- **Startup assets**
    - Materials to create your product
    - Cost to manufacture
    - Costs to distribute/deliver (how you'll get your products to your customers)
    - Site furniture
    - Promotional materials
    - Business laptop
- **Legal**
    - Seller's permit
    - Logo Trademark/Copyright
- **Sales and Marketing**
    - Website designer
    - Sales associates
    - Promotion team
    - Website hosting
- **Operations**
    - Business site rental
    - Business phone
    - Business insurance
    - Business utilities (internet, lighting, water etc)

- Payroll
- Supplies such as paper, ink/toner, pens, napkins, toilet paper, etc.—consider the quantity you need and the costs.

Knowing how much your business will cost can help you plan how much funding you'll need in order to start your new business. It can also help you visualize what you'll need including stuff you haven't planned for, like an emergency cash fund in case you need to buy stock to fill last minute orders.

Cost Management

Small businesses are being constantly squeezed by increases in expenses, so controlling costs is more important than ever. Cost management is the process of planning and controlling the business budget. This accounting practice allows a business to predict impending expenditures to reduce the chance of going over budget. It includes managing the costs of goods sold and overhead costs.

Use your startup budget as your baseline. As you incur expenses, compare your estimate to the actual cost; this will help you better predict future expenses. If an item costs considerably less or more, note that and evaluate if you need to adjust the allotted amount for other expenses to compensate.

Even the smallest reduction in expenses can have an impact on profitability. Reducing your costs improves your chances to succeed and become a successful entrepreneur. Simple, common sense activities often improve the bottom line. We've used the following practices at Skysthelimit.org:

- **Avoid debt.** And only take it on if it will help you make more profit. And be sure you can pay it back.
- **Lower your overhead costs.** Overhead means the operating expenses you have to run your business that aren't directly linked to income. Ways to do this include:

- Use technology for meetings. Virtual meetings help minimize travel expenses and virtual offices can eliminate the need for physical space. While we certainly don't want to eliminate in-person contact altogether, save it for the instances when it's most beneficial.
- Manage your time and your employees' time. Remember, wasted time equals wasted dollars. (Refer to Chapter 9, Operations, for more insight to time management.)
- Go paperless. The cost of paper, ink, mailing supplies, and postage may seem minimal at times, but it can add up to a large business expense. Using a digital invoice and bill payment system and filing all important paperwork on your computer can help you reduce some of the most common recurring business costs.
- Save on marketing with customer referrals and word of mouth (see Chapter 6, Branding).
- Consider running your business from home:
  - Rather than waiting to raise cash to rent office space that will later be used as the business premises, it is advisable to run your business from your home or reach out to a friend or anyone who has a free room and use it to run your business.
  - If you absolutely must rent a space, make the most of it: sublease unused space to another business or individual.

- **Cut operating costs.** Operating costs are directly linked to the manufacture of your product or the delivery of your service. This includes the cost of material the product is made from as well as any tools or equipment used to manufacture it.
  - Try selling leftover materials like cardboard, paper, and metal or consider ways to use your waste to create another product.

  - Track and measure the operational efficiency of your business (see Chapter 9, Operations).
  - Don't invest in new equipment; consider buying used equipment or leasing it.
- **Check your business insurance rates.** Compare providers for the most competitive rate, then ask your current insurance provider to match that rate.
- **Negotiate everything.** Whether it's suppliers, consultants, or credit card companies, put your negotiation hat on (see Chapter 11, Legal and Regulatory). Share your budget constraints and negotiate products, services, and payment schedules to meet your budget. Ask for discounts or preferential payment terms, and politely argue for what you need.

DISCUSSION GUIDE

- Have you listed all your expected monthly expenses?
- What will each item cost?
- What are your total estimated expenses for your startup budget?
- How much have you allotted for variable expenses and an emergency fund?
- Do you have the funding to cover startup costs or will you need to borrow money or look for investors?
- Review your budget each week and compare your estimated to actual expenses; are you staying within your budget?
- Are there any expenses that you could trim, postpone, or eliminate?

Financial Projections

While your budget provides an estimate of your business expenses, three other statements reflect the health of your business: cash flow statement, profit and loss statement, and an assets and liabilities statement.

As we've said from the beginning, you need to track your business' money, both the incoming funds from sales and the outgoing expenses. These statements will help you estimate and track how much money you'll spend to make your products or services, how much you'll spend to run your business, and how much revenue you'll make from sales in order to determine how much money you will have leftover as profit.

Cash Flow Statement

The cash flow statement takes your budget a step further and provides a month-by-month snapshot of how your business is actually doing by putting your projected income and expenses on the same page. Positive cash flow indicates that your income is greater than your expenses and your business is making money—typically the end-goal for a startup.

Negative cash flow means that you're spending more than you make in a given period. It might indicate that the costs to make your products or services are too high or that you're spending too much to run your business. A cash flow statement can be backwards looking or forwards looking. If you project forward your cash flow to estimate your expected net profit or how much money you will actually make in the future, this is known as a cash flow projection. You'll need this if you want to fundraise for your business.

When you first complete the cash flow template, you may have some real numbers for some of your expenses and any pre-sales you've made. As you go forward month to month, update the cash flow statement to reflect your true expenses and income so that your predictions are valid. You'll track the following five areas on your cash flow statement:

- **Revenue** tracks how much money you made or expect to make by selling a specific number of products or services each month.

For example, if you sell 100 shirts in January for $20 each, your revenue is $2000.

- **Cost of goods sold** tracks how much it costs to make (or acquire if you're a reseller), the products you sell in a given time period. COGS comprises only material and labor. For example, COGS for a clothing manufacturer include the fabric, thread, buttons, and the labor to cut and sew the clothes. COGS does not include the cost of shipping the clothes to a store or customer. For example, if each shirt costs you $5 to make and you've made 100 shirts, your total COGS is $500—if you sell all 100 shirts within the year. Look closely at the name of this line item: cost of goods *sold*. If you sell only 80 of the 100 shirts in 2024, your COGS is $400 and you carry over an inventory of 20 shirts into the next year; the $100 of making those shirts is part of the 2025 COGS. For 2025, you would calculate the leftover 2024 inventory and any new shirts you manufacture and sell. For example, if you have 20 shirts and make another 100 and then sell 105, your COGS is $525 (105 shirts multiplied by the $5 cost to make them). The inventory and cost of the remaining 15 shirts would be carried over to the 2026 cash flow statement.
- **Overhead costs** tracks the cost it takes to keep your business running, like office supplies, space rent, equipment rentals, fees to apply for a business permit, etc. For example if office supplies cost you $200 per month and your website's monthly fee is $25, your overhead costs are $225.
- **Gross profit** is calculated by subtracting your COGS from revenue. For example, if your Revenue is $2000 and your COGS is $500, then your Gross Profit is $1500.
- **Net Profit** can be calculated by subtracting Overhead from Gross Profit. This is your real profit as it reflects your revenue, minus all the costs of doing business. In this example, if your Gross Profit is $1500 and your overhead is $225, your net profit is $1225.

Skysthelimit.org provides a cash flow template you can use to create your own snapshot of your business. Below you can see the line items that you would project for each month of the year (although we've included only two months).

Cash Flow Statement

See below for notes on how to do a financial cash flow projection. These are just estimates; you can't know for sure, so do your best and be realistic.	**January**	**February**
Revenue		
Revenue can be calculated by multiplying how many products or services you sell by the price you sell each product or service. For example, if you sell 100 shirts in one month for $20 each, your revenue is $2000.		
What is the BEST case scenario for Revenue?	$2,000	
What is the REALISTIC case scenario for Revenue?	$1,500	
What is the WORST case scenario for Revenue?	$1,000	
Cost of Good Sold		
Cost of goods sold (COGS) can be calculated by multiplying how much it costs to make each good or service by how many of those goods or services you've had to make. For example, if each shirt costs you $5 to make and you've made 100 shirts, your COGS is $500.		
What is the BEST case scenario for COGS?	$500	
What is the REALISTIC case scenario for COGS?	$500	
What is the WORST case scenario for COGS?	$500	

Gross Profit	January	February
Gross profit is calculated by subtracting your COGS from Revenue. For example, if your Revenue is $2000 and your COGS is $500, then your Gross Profit is $1500.		
What is the BEST case scenario for Gross Profit?	$1,500	
What is the REALISTIC case scenario for Gross Profit?	$1,000	
What is the WORST case scenario for Gross Profit?	$500	
Overhead Costs		
Overhead refers to costs not associated with making or selling goods or services. It's costs associated with advertising, rent, phone bills, etc. For example, if all of your bills not related to producing your shirts add up to $500, then that is your overhead cost.		
What is the BEST case scenario for Overhead?	$500	
What is the REALISTIC case scenario for Overhead?	$500	
What is the WORST case scenario for Overhead?	$500	
Net Profit		
Net Profit can be calculated by subtracting Overhead from Gross Profit. This is your "real" profit as it is how much you're making in revenue, minus how much it costs you to run your business. In this example, your real profit is your Gross Profit subtracted by your Overhead, which equals $1000.		
What is the BEST case scenario for Net Profit?	$1,000	
What is the REALISTIC case scenario for Net Profit?	$500	
What is the WORST case scenario for Net Profit?	$0	

Once you have an idea of how much it costs to make your products (or services) and an estimate of what your overhead costs will be, you can use a cash flow statement to adjust how much you need to sell in order to make your desired profit.

Profit and Loss Statement

When you have actual numbers, you can create a quarterly or yearly profit and loss statement, often referred to as a P&L. Investors and loan officers will ask to see your P&L if you request funding. While your cash flow statements can be used to make predictions about the future of your business, a P&L reflects the financial situation of your business during a specific time period.

The P&L reports the same information as the cash flow statement: Revenue, COGS, Gross Profit, Overhead Costs, and Net Profit but while the cash flow statement is a projection or prediction, the P&L represents the actual situation for a given period of time.

Statement of Assets and Liabilities

This statement is also referred to as a balance sheet. It simply lists all your business assets, such as equipment you own, product inventory, cash on hand, prepaid insurance, and outstanding invoices (money that's due to come in) with the value of each to attain a sum total of assets. The other side of the balance sheet lists liabilities, any outstanding expenses, loans, unpaid taxes, and wages.

Ideally, your assets total more than your liabilities, but when you have just started your business, often liabilities are greater than assets. The important thing is that you have strong, consistent cash flow and a plan to invert the balance over the long term.

DISCUSSION GUIDE

- Have you completed your cash flow projections for the next 12 months?
- Does your projected income cover your projected expenses?
- How much revenue do you need to not incur a loss?
- Do you see any places where you could reduce your spending, for example, renegotiating with other vendors?
- How much do you need to sell to make your desired profit?
- Are there any places where you could increase your sales?
- At the end of your first three months of business, create a P&L and then again at six months; have you seen growth or any other trends in income and expenses that have made you rethink your business?
- What assets and liabilities does your business have? If your liabilities are greater than your assets, how can you reduce your liability?

As you track your expenses and income, you need to also think about your taxes. In the next chapter, we present the legalities and regulations—including taxes—you need to consider as you launch and grow your business.

CHECKLIST

- ✓ Open a business bank account.
- ✓ Choose an income and expenses management tool, i.e., Excel, GoogleSheets, QuickBooks.
- ✓ Choose an invoice service.
- ✓ Create an invoice template.
- ✓ Automate invoicing and receipt generation as much as possible.
- ✓ Create a startup budget with estimated costs for each item.
- ✓ Create a cash flow statement that shows estimated expenses and predicted revenue.
- ✓ Create a profit and loss statement.
- ✓ Create a statement of assets and liabilities.
- ✓ Meet with a mentor or advisor to review your financials.

CHAPTER 11

Legal and Regulatory

> **When Should You Read This Chapter?**
> If you begin your business as a side hustle, as many entrepreneurs do, you probably won't think about structuring your business since you'll probably be working alone. If you decide to partner with someone or have a high risk business, read through the legal structure section. Regardless of your legal structure, at the start of your entrepreneurial journey, skim through the sections on taxes and licenses to be sure you have filed the proper paperwork. Then as you develop products or frameworks for your services, revisit the section on intellectual property. When you begin working with other people or vendors, the contracts section can help you negotiate wisely.

It would be nice to live in a world where everyone got along, we could all do what we want, no one sued anyone else, and we didn't have to pay taxes. But that's not the world we live in. In this chapter we present the concepts and terms you need to know to make sure your business is on the right side of the law and following the regulations dictated by your nation, state, or industry.

First we review the types of business entities and legal structures, then we talk about the permits and licenses you may need to open and run your business. We discuss the basics of insurance coverage to reduce potential exposure to risk. We dip into the idea of intellectual property, what it means, and what you can legally own. In closing we talk about negotiations and contracts. While much of this information will be more relevant to the United States legal system, there are some similarities with other western legal systems. Generally speaking, there are four levels of government that you'll want to pay attention to: national, state, county, and city. Many licensing and entity laws are specific to one or more of these levels of government. Generally, the bigger your company gets, the more legal risk you will have, though in certain highly regulated industries, you may have considerable legal risk from day one (e.g., pharmaceuticals, lending, etc).

The Legal Trap

It can feel intimidating and overwhelming to understand every law before starting your business. You can spend incredible amounts of money on legal advice, insurance, patents, etc., and it can bury your business before you even have a chance to get started. Understanding and balancing risk is a key part of the entrepreneurial journey. We estimate that 99 percent of entrepreneurs start their businesses without understanding every law that will affect their business. Indeed, many lawyers who make a profession out of studying business law do not understand every law that can affect any business. Our legal and tax codes in the United States could take a lifetime to read, let alone fully understand. There are some lines you should not cross, and you need to know what those are—but often these lines are pretty common sense. For example, a food business that poisons its customers, or a barber shop that seriously injures a customer, or an entrepreneur who commits fraud—all of these people are going to get into trouble no matter what. Generally, entrepreneurs try to understand just enough to stay out of trouble, and as their business grows and is exposed to more legal risk, they invest more in legal, insurance, compliance, and regulatory matters.

Disclaimer: Legal information is not legal advice. This educational material provides general information related to the law designed to help users safely cope with their own legal needs. This book does not provide legal advice and the authors are not lawyers. Although we go to great lengths to make sure our information is useful, we recommend you consult a lawyer if you want legal advice, or do your own research. You may explore Skysthelimit.org's community to find a volunteer legal expert who may be willing to provide pro-bono (free) support.

Legal Structure

Part of being in business is deciding on the form of business entity to establish. The business entity determines the rules you operate under, the tax return form you have to file, the amount of paperwork your business is required to do, the personal liability you face, and your ability to raise money—and take tax-deductible donations if you're going the nonprofit route.

There are two decisions to make regarding your business entity. The first is related to profit and the sociality of your business. You can choose one of the following:

- **For-profit organization:** This traditional business has the primary goal of making a profit.
- **Nonprofit organization:** The primary goal of a nonprofit is to fulfill a social, religious, or educational mission.

"Social enterprise" is a common business description you may have heard of. However, it is not a formal type of business in the United States (yet), they are either for-profit or nonprofit entities in the eyes of the law. This type of business combines the goals of fulfilling a social mission and making a profit.

Nonprofits typically form nonprofit corporations or associations in the state you're in, and later, many pursue a designation as a 501(c)(3) with the IRS. If you decide you are a for-profit organization, you'll have to choose from one of several types of legal entities or structures. Check your federal, state, and local legal and tax requirements for your preferred business entity before making it official. Consulting with a business lawyer and an accountant or taking advantage of the Small Business

Administration's services is often worth the time and cost when making these decisions, especially if you have a partner or co-founder.

We've provided an overview of business types below and the advantages and disadvantages of each. As a starting point, consider and compare three factors when deciding which entity type is your best choice: legal protection, tax treatment, and paperwork requirements from the government.

Sole Proprietorship

A sole proprietorship happens automatically when an individual starts conducting business. The government assumes you are a sole proprietorship until you tell them otherwise. You are the only business owner, and all debts of the business are your debts. There are no formal requirements to form or conduct business, the owner has unlimited liability, but taxes are paid by the individual. Typically, sole proprietors will use insurance to reduce their risk. If you work alone, you will likely be a sole proprietorship, but if you have a lot of potential risk or your business generates a lot of income, you might consider registering as an LLC or corporation. In fact, most entrepreneurs start off as a sole proprietorship.

Advantages

- You own it all.
- You have total control.
- You get all the profits.
- It is easy to form.
- It is easy to dissolve.
- Simple tax situation.
- No taxes on the business separately.
- You may deduct business expenses on your personal gross income.

Disadvantages

- You are personally responsible for all losses and debt.
- It is difficult to get financing.
- It is difficult to sell because the business is not separate from the individual.
- Few tax advantages.
- Dependent on the health and motivation of the owner.
- All business profit is taxed as personal income, even if you do not take the money out for personal use.
- You must pay additional self-employment taxes for Social Security Benefits.

Business Partnership (Co-Founders)

A partnership is a relationship existing between two or more persons who join to carry on a trade or business. Each person contributes money, property, labor or skill, and expects to share in the profits and losses of the business. Often the entity type for this route is a limited liability partnership, or LLP. You will conduct business under a Partnership Agreement. Two common types are general partnership and limited partnership.

- **General partnership:** A form of business in which two or more co-owners engage in business for profit. Usually the partners own the business assets together and are personally liable for business debts. Taxes are paid by individual partners.
- **Limited partnership:** A form of partnership similar to a general partnership, except that in addition to one or more general partners, there are one or more limited partners. These partners are only liable for the business' debts according to their registered investment, and they have no management authority. The limited partners, in other words, have some protection of personal liability.

Advantages

- Division of responsibility; you share liability with others.
- Some tax advantages.
- You have access to more resources, skills, energy, and financial assets.

Disadvantages

- Set-up usually requires a detailed partner agreement.
- You have less control.
- Making decisions is a more complicated process.
- Partners can incur liabilities because of something another partner does. They may not even know it is happening.

Limited Liability Company (LLC)

An LLC is a hybrid entity, bringing together some of the best features of partnerships and corporations. An LLC is a business structure that provides limited liability for the owners or members. This is a popular structure because it means the owners of the company are not personally liable for their company's debts or liabilities—in most cases, but not all. The LLC is a business structure that follows state statute. This means, each state may have different regulations, so you should check the .gov for your state if you are interested in starting a Limited Liability Company. LLCs were created to provide business owners with liability protection limited to the LLC's assets. Earnings and losses are included on the owners' personal tax returns and an annual fee must be paid. LLCs have no limitation on the number of shareholders and any member or owner of the LLC is allowed a full participatory role in business operations.

Advantages

- You don't need to have a lot of financial backing to begin.
- Structure can be used by individuals, partnerships or corporations.
- Owners not personally liable for debt or losses.

Disadvantages

- If you are not the sole owner of the LLC, you have less control and authority is divided.
- Decision making is more complicated.
- Set-up usually requires a detailed agreement regarding membership and participation.
- There are annual fees in many states to maintain your LLC, whether the company is earning or not. In states like California, this can cost you over $800 per year.

Corporation

A corporation is a business entity or type of business structure that provides its owners and shareholders with certain rights, privileges, and protections. The corporation may be set up as a for-profit business, a nonprofit organization, or a social enterprise.

The corporate structure is more complicated and more expensive than most other business structures, but it offers certain benefits that can make it worth the time and money to set up.

Advantages

- It's a separate legal entity from the owner(s).
- Profits are taxed separately from the owners' personal income.
- It's not dependent on the well-being of the owner(s).
- Owners are not personally liable for debt or losses.
- It may be easier to get financing.
- It may be easier to establish employee benefits, like retirement plans.

Disadvantages

- It's expensive to set up; includes fees to government agencies and probably legal fees.

- Salary and dividends are both taxed.
- There are annual fees in many states to maintain your corporation, whether the company is earning or not.
- It's complex to set up: owned by stockholders and highly regulated by IRS and state Tax Boards.
- Must register with the state.
- You have less control.
- It's complex to operate and requires more paperwork.
- Decision-making is complicated and less flexible.

Choosing the right type of entity for your business will impact everything from day-to-day operations, to taxes, to how much of your personal assets are at risk, to the ease with which you can get a small business loan or raise money from investors. And if someone sues your business, your business entity structure—along with your insurance—determines your risk exposure. You should choose a business structure that gives you the right balance of legal protections and benefits.

You'll need to choose a business structure before you register your business with the state. Most businesses will also need to get a tax ID number, or EID, and file for the appropriate licenses and permits. The next sections cover these topics.

DISCUSSION GUIDE

- Will your business be for-profit, nonprofit, or a social enterprise?
- Will you be working alone or starting your business with one or more other people?
- What are the advantages and disadvantages specific to your business related to each type of legal structure?
- What kind of company are you?

Federal and State Tax ID

You will want to avoid getting in trouble with the IRS, and generally one of the best ways to do this is to pay your taxes. Registering with the government and getting the proper identification is necessary to do basic things like reporting your taxes, or selling past a certain dollar amount each year, or getting a license. You will need an Employer Identification Number (EIN) if you answer "Yes" to any of the following questions.

- Do you have employees?
- Do you operate your business as a corporation or a partnership?
- Do you file any of these tax returns: Employment, Excise, or Alcohol, Tobacco and Firearms?
- Do you withhold taxes on income, other than wages, paid to a non-resident alien?
- Do you want to apply for loans or grants?

Generally, businesses need an EIN or a Federal Tax Identification Number; both are used to identify a business entity. This number appears on your tax forms and W2 forms. You will need it for almost everything—opening a business bank account, filing taxes, paying employees, being a legitimate corporation or partnership, applying for business licenses and permits, etc. It's free to apply for an EIN online and you can get your EIN immediately. You will just need your name, social security number, address, and your fictitious or Doing Business As (DBA) name.

Getting a state tax ID is a similar, simple process as getting a federal tax ID, but guidelines vary by state.

Most states, 43 in fact, require businesses to pay additional state taxes. Only seven states have no income tax: Wyoming, Washington, Texas, South Dakota, Nevada, Florida, and Alaska. Tennessee and New Hampshire have income tax only on business dividends and business interest payments. Your state income tax will also vary by the type of business structures. In addition to income tax, your state tax ID also impacts business insurance for you as a business owner and for your employees.

Licenses, Permits, and Qualifications

While relatively few industries are regulated by the federal government, almost all types of businesses require permits or licenses issued by the state. Business licenses are simply an approval from your city, state, and/or country that lets you operate a business. Some of these permits and licenses are for tax purposes, while others aim to protect the safety and health of customers and the general public. Some are optional and some are required. Potential licenses a business may need include: health and safety regulation, food hygiene and safety, online and distance selling, etc.

Below, we put together the basic steps you'll need to take to get a business license.

1. Visit your state's website to find out which permits and licenses you need. Usually you can download the application form from the site. You may also need to check the city and/or county for permits and licenses.
2. Complete an application, online, in person or through the mail. This will vary depending on your business location. Typically, you will be asked
    - Business name and ownership information
    - Business address
    - Square footage of the business location (if applicable)
    - Detailed description of all business activities conducted on, and off, the business location
    - Identification from all of applicants/owners, such as a valid driver's license, state ID card, or other government-issued photo ID
    - Your Department of Revenue Number (if applicable)
    - Employer Identification Number (EIN) (if applicable)
    - Some business license applications require a fingerprint-based criminal history investigation. There are usually fees associated.

  - Names of every owner or any person with a 25 percent or more interest in the business
  - Names of every on-site manager
  - A separate license is required for each separate business location (if applicable)
3. Pay the filing fee. Each city has its own requirements regarding the filing fee that goes with your business license or permit.
4. After you apply, a zoning review may be conducted to determine if your business activity is permitted in the zoning designation of your business location. You can use the online interactive zoning map to check any business location's zoning designation ahead of time.
5. Depending upon the license type, an inspection may be required by one or more city departments prior to license or permit issuance.

For more information on federal requirements for licenses and permits, visit the Small Business Administration (www.sba.gov).

Most licenses and permits also cost a small fee (typically ranging from $50 to $400) to apply and to get, and they expire at some point, so know those costs when minding your budget and finances. Approval for applications can take anywhere from a couple days to multiple weeks. You may even be required to display them at your place of business or make them available on your website. Some common business licenses include:

- **Fictitious Name or Doing Business As (DBA) licenses:** This is required (in most states) when you decide to use a business name that differs from your legal name. Typically they are used by sole proprietors and unincorporated partnerships. For example, if Joe Smith wants to conduct business as Smith's Shoe Repair, they would file a DBA with the business name. Likewise, an LLC or corporation may want a business name that differs from their corporate name for brand differentiation. The DBA doesn't offer any legal protection (like an LLC would) but does allow businesses to open bank accounts under the DBA name. When choosing a DBA, search through the Secretary of State's office to make sure no one else is using your chosen business name. Steps also vary from state to state and filing may occur at the state, county, or city level.

- **Business licenses:** These are issued by the local and state government for all businesses and require two separate licenses. If you're working in multiple states, be sure to know federal rules as well as the rules for each state you operate in.
- **Federal licenses:** These are specific to some categories of businesses that need permission from the federal government. Most small businesses don't fall into these categories, but double check by searching your industry and the keywords "federal business licenses."
- **Industry specific licenses:** These are required for health or professional services, like for restaurants to serve food and for lawyers to give legal advice.
- **Sales tax license:** This is applied on top of goods (and sometimes services depending on the state and type of service) that are sold. You will likely have to attain a sales tax license unless your state does not have sales tax. If you sell and ship your products to states other than where you reside, you may have to pay sales tax to the state where your customer lives. Many e-commerce services calculate the sales tax automatically for you, depending on where your customer is. The variables are many, so do your research (or consult with a tax expert) for both your state and industry to determine the licenses you need and the taxes you have to pay.
- **Seller's permit:** This allows you to buy wholesale goods from a manufacturer without paying sales tax. Buyers pay the sales tax when they buy the goods that you are reselling. If you make three or more sales in a 12-month period, you may be required to hold a

seller's permit. For both wholesale and retail business, this is your permission to do business in the state.

- **Home occupation permits:** These are required for businesses that are run out of a personal home. If your neighborhood is not zoned for home businesses, you might have to file for an exception.
- **Zoning permit:** This sets guidelines on what businesses can operate in a certain areas. Residential zones, commercial zones, industrial zones, etc. all have different rules.
- **Fire inspection permits:** These are usually granted from your local fire department and give you permission to have, store, use or handle materials and to do activities that may be potentially dangerous.
- **Public safety permits:** These are usually granted by the police department and they can include parking permits, food serving permits for food trucks and restaurants, or even to provide electric scooters. If your business or company provides services that might affect your customers' health, like with food and drink or with physical activities, then you may need public safety permits from your city and state.
- **Building inspections and permits:** These are usually granted by the city government for making any changes to a building and to assess if your workplace is up-to-code.

Most small businesses need a combination of licenses and permits from both federal and state agencies and some require permits from local governments as well. Learn more about the requirements, fees, and application process through the Small Business Administration and your local municipality. It is important to note that laws change over time in the United States and in other countries, so check government websites for the latest information if you are concerned.

DISCUSSION GUIDE

- Which licenses and permits do you need to run your business?
- What is your deadline to complete the applications?
- Are you required to display any of the licenses and permits?
- What are the costs for each license and permit? Have you added those to your startup budget and cash flow statements?
- Do you need any specific qualifications? If you do not already hold this, how and when will you obtain this? Is there any cost associated with this?
- Also, have you filed a Fictitious Business Name Statement or acquired a federal Employer Identification Number?

Insurance

Generally speaking, insurance is often one of the better forms of protection for a small business, in our experience. Protecting your business and yourself as an entrepreneur from risk can take several forms, and, much like risk, protection comes in many forms. You can get insurance for your equipment and working space in the case of a fire or natural disaster, for your personal liability in case of injury or slander. If a risk of loss exists for your business, you can very likely purchase insurance that will cover your financial loss if that risk becomes reality. It is important to make sure you are not over- or under-insured, you'll likely want to adjust your insurance levels as you grow and as new risks emerge for you and your company.

Business insurance coverage protects businesses from losses due to events that may occur during the normal course of business. When exploring the type of insurance you should get, consider the risks you're facing: Are you trying to ward off accidents, natural disasters, lawsuits, or all of the above? Shop around because different insurance companies offer different coverage types and prices. The same goes for insurance agents who receive commissions from insurance companies, so shop around for licensed agents as well. Your needs will change and evolve over time, but start with the basics when trying to find the right insurance for your business. We've put together a brief description of the different types of insurance you want to consider.

- **General liability insurance:** This applies to any business and insures against financial loss resulting from injury, property damage, medical expenses, libel, slander, lawsuits, and settlements.
- **Product liability insurance:** This insures against financial loss resulting from a defective product that causes injury. If you manufacture, sell, or distribute a physical product, you'll want this insurance.
- **Home-based business insurance:** This offers additional insurance on top of homeowner's insurance to cover some business equipment and liability for third-party injuries. Businesses that are run out of the owner's personal homes should check this out.
- **Professional liability insurance:** This applies to businesses that provide services to customers and insures against financial loss resulting from professional malpractice, errors, and negligence.
- **Commercial property insurance:** This insures against lost or damaged property resulting from disasters like fire, floods, looting, and vandalism. Businesses with a lot of equipment, real estate, or physical assets should have this insurance.
- **Business owner's policy:** This type of policy offers a comprehensive combination of common business insurance options. This policy benefits most small business owners, but especially home-based business owners.
- **Cyber insurance:** This insures against data breaches from hackers and other related nefarious actors largely on the internet. This is mostly applicable for tech companies or companies with sensitive data.

You should also consider having a release of liability form or waiver, that is an agreement between you and the signer that the signer will not sue for any specific reasons listed on the form. This is especially important if you have customers engaging in risky activities where they might get hurt.

DISCUSSION GUIDE

- What kinds of accidents, natural disasters, or lawsuits could damage your business?
- Which types of insurance would be most useful to your business?
- Have you insured yourself and your company, and if so, is your insurance at the right level? If not, how are you protecting yourself and company?
- Do your customers risk injury or loss when they work with you? Would you sleep better at night if you had customers sign a liability waiver?

Intellectual Property

When you have an idea and turn that idea into a new, previously non-existent product or develop a framework for a service, you have intellectual property. Intellectual property is any product of the human intellect that the law protects from unauthorized use by others. The ownership of intellectual property inherently creates a limited monopoly in the protected property. Intellectual property (IP) traditionally comprises four categories: copyright, trademark, patent, and trade secrets.

The IP Trap

You can spend a lot of money on these IP protections; the key is to know when the right time is to make these investments. If you pay for a patent too soon, you may be wasting money. Too late, and you may have someone copy your idea. And even if you have a patent, you will still likely need to take the person who copies your idea to court, which can cost a lot of money even if you win.

The risk of someone stealing trade secrets may seem far-fetched for a new entrepreneur, but if you've come up with the solution all the big players want, that risk grows and filing the forms to protect your intellectual property may be wise—when the time is right. You may want to protect yourself in the event that somebody copies or uses your logo, designs, writing, etc. without your knowledge or passing it off as their own work. You can file for a trademark or patent for your own intellectual property like a logo or secret recipes, so that people cannot use your trade secrets without your permission. That said, the process can be long, complex, and costly. Consider the benefits of copyrights, trademarks, and patents as outlined below and then decide whether or not you want to invest the time and money in the process. For more information, read all about copyrights, patents, trademarks and more through the US Patent and Trademark Office (www.uspto.gov).

Copyright

Copyright is a form of protection for original works such as books, music, paintings, movies, photographs, recipes, and certain other intellectual works, both published and unpublished. Copyright protects you from others reproducing, distributing, displaying, or making money from your original work without your permission.

You must register if you plan to bring someone to court for infringement. Copyrights are exclusively regulated by federal law and must be registered with the US Copyright Office to be enforceable. A work must meet certain minimum requirements to qualify for copyright protection.

The length of protection also varies depending on when the work was created or first published. Generally, a copyright protects your work for your lifetime plus 70 years.

Indicate your copyright by putting the copyright mark ("©") on original and reproduced pieces. The process for registering a copyright is:

- **Online:** Applications take about four months to get processed by the US Copyright Office for a $35 fee.
- **Mail in:** Applications take about seven months to get processed. Download the form from the internet or pick up a copy at your Small Business Administration office and mail it in with the $65 fee.

For more detailed information, consult the website of the US Patent and Trademark Office (PTO).

Trademark

A trademark is a word, name, symbol, or design, or any combination thereof, used to identify and distinguish the products of one manufacturer or seller from others. A service mark is the same as a trademark except that it identifies and distinguishes the source of a service rather than a product. The terms "trademark" and "mark" are commonly used to refer to both trademarks and service marks. For example, the Nike Swoosh logo is a trademark of Nike. In this way, other brands can't just use the Nike Swoosh on their shoes or apparel and pass it off as a Nike product without express permission from Nike. If a company is caught using this trademark without permission, Nike can sue if necessary. Other common trademarks are logos and slogans. You should search for existing trademarks to double check your idea is not already taken.

The PTO is responsible for issuing and monitoring federally registered patents and trademarks. In the United States, you are not required to register your marks to obtain protectable rights. You can establish "common law" rights in a mark based solely on use of the mark in commerce, without a registration. For local protection, use the trademark symbol (™) on printed and digital materials, i.e., placed after your logo, word or phrase. Use the register symbol (®) to provide nationwide protection.

Registering your marks gives you additional rights beyond common law. These include the right to:

- Sue in court
- Let others know you own the mark
- List your mark in the USPTO's database
- Register with US Customs and Border Protection to prevent importation of infringing foreign goods
- Use the federal registration symbol ®
- Obtain US registration as a basis to get recognized/registered in foreign countries

When you begin developing a logo or slogan that you want to use and eventually trademark, first search the USPTO database to make sure no one else is using the same trademark. Then, two basic requirements must be met for a mark to be eligible for trademark protection: it must be distinctive and it must be in use in commerce—yes, as odd as that is, you must be using the image or words you want to trademark when you apply for a registered trademark. Because of the searches involved, you may want to hire a trademark attorney to manage the process. If you decide to do it yourself, you can apply.

- **Online:** Applications take about three months for review and approval. The non-refundable fee ranges from $225 to $400.
- **Mail in:** Mail or hand deliver a paper application to the USPTO. You can call the USPTO's automated telephone line at (800) 786-9199 to obtain a printed form.

Patents

New devices, methods, or processes can be protected by a patent. A patent gives the owner the right to be the exclusive maker and seller of the invention covered by the patent, meaning that the patent owner has control over who can use the invention for a limited length of time. This period is usually 20 years for utility and plant patents, and 14 years for design patents—both are effective from the filing date. US patent grants are effective only within the United States, US territories, and US possessions.

There are three types of patents: utility, design, and plant. Consult the USPTO fee schedule online to learn about associated fees.

- **Utility patents** apply to a process or machine. Most patent applications are for a utility patent. A utility patent protects any new and useful process, machine, article of manufacture (items that can be made), composition of matter (mixtures of ingredients or new chemical compounds), or any new, useful improvements to an existing invention. They cost around $1,500-$15,000 and unlike other patent types, utility patents have maintenance fees.
- **Design patents** apply to original graphical representations. They cost around $1,500-$3,000. A design patent gives you legal claim to your original design, the ability to use and sell it, and the right to profit from the unique look of an object. Design patents only protect the look of an object. They aren't the same as utility patents, which cover how objects work and how they're used. A design has to meet some basic requirements to qualify for a patent:
    - It doesn't affect the function of an object.
    - It is integral to an object and can't be removed.
- **Plant patents** apply to newly invented strains of asexually reproduced plants. To be patentable, the plant must have been asexually propagated. These are plants that reproduce by means other than from seeds, such as by the rooting of cuttings using layering, budding, grafting, or inarching. They cost around $1,500-$10,000.

Applying for a patent requires extensive research and documentation, not to mention fees. We suggest doing some preliminary research to make sure your idea is original and then engage a patent attorney to manage the process. If your invention is worth patenting, it's worth the expense of a legal professional. Following are the high-level steps to apply for a patent.

1. Keep a written record of your invention.
2. Make sure your idea is original and that it is not already patented; research is key!
3. Determine which application to file.
    - **Provisional Patent Application (PPA):** Allows you to claim "patent pending" status for the invention and involves only a small fraction of the work and cost of a regular patent application. Include a description of the invention that details how to make and use it, and an informal drawing. You must file an RPA within a year of filing the PPA.
    - **Regular Patent Application (RPA):** The key elements of a patent application are specification, claims, abstract, and drawings.
4. Submit your application to the US Patent and Trademark Office.
    - Online applications require payment of four types of fees: application, examination, patent search, and issuing. Allow three months for the application review.
    - Mail or hand deliver a paper application to the USPTO. You can call the USPTO's automated telephone line at (800) 786-9199 to obtain a printed form.

Before getting started, make sure you have the budget to pay for the fees associated with patents, which can be pretty hefty. Make sure you have an actual working model or a design on paper of your useful invention and consider hiring a patent attorney or patent agent, which the USPTO strongly recommends.

DISCUSSION GUIDE

- What intellectual property have you developed?
- Do you have an original product or process?
- Do you have any material that would benefit from a copyright? If so, will you register for copyright?
- Is your logo or slogan at risk of being reproduced? Have you registered for a trademark or service mark?
- Have you invented a process, product, or plant that could be patentable? What steps have you taken toward getting a patent?

Contracts

Few entrepreneurs start a business without signing any contracts. If you have mobile phone service, an internet host, or Netflix, you have to click the Accept button at the end of their Terms and Conditions when you sign up for the service. Chances are you didn't read those contracts, (who does?) but you'll want to pay more attention when you begin to contract with clients, vendors, landlords, contractors, or employees.

First and foremost remember this:

Everything is negotiable.

Negotiating

When you begin discussing a contract with someone, your options are wide open. A friend once said, "It costs nothing to ask." Negotiating is all about asking for something in return for something else—give and take. The goal of any negotiation is a win-win outcome—that is, an agreement that leaves both parties feeling like winners. A good negotiation relies on trust, and if either party feels like they've made a compromise, the risk of resentment or future disputes is high. Whole books have been written about the art of negotiation; we'll give you a few tips for successful negotiating and then walk through the standard parts of a contract.

When negotiating, first figure out what matters to the seller. For example, if the seller wants you to pay full price and won't budge, can you negotiate for an interest-free payment plan or a longer warranty? If you can't come to an agreement, you may have to contract with someone else for the same thing.

To that end, when negotiating with a manufacturer, vendor, or service provider—anyone who is giving you something you're paying for—get multiple bids. Look for sellers who are new to the industry as they may be more willing to offer great service at a lower price to get started in the business, but keep in mind that there is some risk involved because they have less experience or volume. Consider high-end or high-volume sellers who may provide more security and options; a vendor with high-volume may be able to offer a greater discount whereas a high-end seller may charge more but offer better quality. And, inquire with a seller who lands somewhere in the middle, someone who has more experience and stability than the newbie, but perhaps less volume than the high-end/high-volume seller. Think about your needs, the price you can pay, and the level of service and stability you require.

Thirdly, protect yourself. Until the contract is signed, you aren't under any obligation to the seller. Ask all the questions you have of the seller, seek full clarity about the product or service they offer and the costs involved. If the negotiation is for a large sum (relative to your capacity), negotiate for a payment plan wherein you make payments as milestones are reached. Likewise, if you're working with a new company that doesn't have an established track record, make your payments in stages to reduce your risk. If a company goes bankrupt, you are generally better off forgetting about it and moving on, there's not much you can do.

For full assurance, you may want to ask a contract attorney to review the terms to make sure you are getting a fair deal and are protected if a dispute arises. Contracts aren't always worth the paper they are printed on, meaning if there are loopholes or circumstances left undefined in your contract, you will be defenseless in legal dispute. What's more, if you have to enforce a contract in a legal proceeding, you have both already lost—you're both losing precious time and usually money if you need to go to court. The contract should define how each party will behave and hold the parties to that behavior. In business legal disputes, the lawyers are usually the only ones winning.

Elements of a Contract

In simplest terms, contracts define how two parties will interact to reach a common outcome. For example, Seller provides fabric to Buyer for an established price; the Buyer needs fabric to make their product, in exchange the seller needs money to stay in business. Most contracts include specific information and then some contracts have other information specific to the type of contract, parties, or the object/service being contracted. The basic parts of a contract include:

- **Definition:** Who is involved?
  - Who are the two (or more) people or entities entering and signing the contract?
  - What are they contracting for?
- **Duration:** When will the contract begin and when will it end?
- **Cost:** What is the total cost of the product or service?
- **Payment terms:** How and when will the buyer pay the seller? Will there be multiple staged payments? A deposit at the beginning of the work and the rest upon delivery? Will payments be made in cash, through bank transfer, or some other payment system? Are any discounts applied for prepayment?
- **Penalties:** What happens if either party doesn't honor the terms of the contract? If a dispute arises, under the laws of which state or country will it be mediated or settled? Will a discount apply if the seller is late with delivery?

- **Signatures:** All parties sign the contract and note the current date. Many contracts are signed electronically via online services like Docusign or Digisigner and most offer a free version for a limited number of contracts each month. Use your local search engine or AI assistant to find the service that best meets your needs.

Typically, the seller, manufacturer, or employer creates the contract. If you are the buyer, you will receive a contract from the other party, which you should review closely—or have your attorney review—before signing. When you are the seller or employer, you'll create the contract. Listed here are some common business contracts and what that contract really means.

- **Independent contractor agreements:** A written contract showing that you have hired a company or a person to perform a specific service for a specific length of time.
- **Rental leases:** A written contract between you and a property owner showing an agreement to rent, maintain, and insure their property for a specific length of time at a specific monthly price.
- **Equipment leases:** A written contract between you and an equipment owner showing an agreement to rent, maintain, and insure their equipment for a specific length of time at a specific monthly price.
- **Purchase and sales agreements:** A written contract between you and a seller to purchase equipment or their business at a specific price and by a certain date.
- **Credit agreements:** A written contract between you and a customer showing an agreement to provide him or her with products or services before being paid for them. The agreement states how and when the customer will pay for the products and services.

Starting with a template makes the contract-writing process easier. Search for "contract templates for small business" or for your industry and the type of contract you need. There may be a fee associated with downloading the template, but there are also many free versions, often written by lawyers. You may need to look at several different samples to find one that most closely matches your needs. You then fill in the blanks on the template to reflect the details of your negotiation.

You may use the same type of contract multiple times. For example, if you are a life coach, your clients sign a contract with you that defines the outcome, the number of sessions and costs, and terms. The client name and number of sessions might change but the rest of the contract will always be the same. Create templates for the contracts you'll use frequently, so when you need to create a new contract with a client or contractor, you're not starting from scratch.

DISCUSSION GUIDE

- Who might you need to negotiate with in the next three months?
- What outcome is most important to the other party?
- What outcome is most important to you?
- What are your strengths in the negotiation?
- What are your weaknesses?
- Who might you contract with in your business? Clients? Vendors? Contractors? Others?
- What types of contracts do you need? Create templates for the main three contracts you'll use.
- Can you use an online template to get started?
- Do you need to have an attorney review your contracts? If so, who will you ask?
- Which online signature services have you researched? Which one did you choose?

One of the primary contracts you'll write as your business grows are those with partners, contractors, and employees. You'll learn about building a solid team in the next chapter.

CHECKLIST

- ✓ Decide on whether you want to be a sole proprietorship or some other business structure, weighing the pros and cons.
- ✓ Check on the licenses (from the city or state or federal government) and permits you need for your business.
- ✓ File for a business license and a Doing Business As (DBA) or fictitious name if your state requires this.
- ✓ Request an Employer Identification number (EID) from the IRS.
- ✓ Explore getting insurance for your business.
- ✓ Explore whether or not you need to create liability release forms for customers or partners.
- ✓ Consider whether or not you want to invest the time and money in trademarks and copyrighting.
- ✓ Remember, when you sell your service to people, it is usually a good idea to have a contract.
- ✓ Create contract templates for the types of contracts you use most.

CHAPTER 12

Building a Team

> **When Should You Read This Chapter?**
> Come to this chapter when you've reached the point of needing help. This may be at the very beginning where you find you need a partner or it could be several years into your business when you've left your day job, and you want to expand your business—or focus on the parts you love to do—and need assistance to meet those goals.

As the business grows, most entrepreneurs find themselves wishing there were more hours in the day or that they had a clone. Or, they find themselves turning customers away and saying no to projects they'd like to do but don't have the bandwidth to support. In these situations entrepreneurs begin to think about getting help, whether that means hiring an employee, bringing on a contractor, or looking for volunteers.

In this chapter, we talk about deciding when it's time to get help, finding the right person, and hiring (and firing). We also offer some tips for being an effective leader and creating a strong and positive culture that keeps your team motivated and performing.

Do You Need Help?

Many entrepreneurs resist getting help because they believe they can't afford to hire someone or that no one can do the job as well as they can. These beliefs may be true at some time in the course of your entrepreneurial journey but we all have blind spots. At the very early stages of your business, unless you have substantial funding, you probably can't afford to hire someone.

As your business grows, however, and the number of tasks you have to do grows, hiring someone can actually help you make money. If you think about the value of your time, you quickly see that it makes sense to pay someone to do repetitive tasks like data entry so you have more time to make sales calls. Likewise, contracting a social media expert for 10 hours a month may grow your audience far more than you're able to do in the same 10 hours, leaving you time to concentrate on product development or take on more clients for your service. It's essential you lean into your talents, and invest in areas where someone can do a better job than you.

How do you know if you're ready to add an extra set of hands to your team? If you answer yes to any of the following, it's time to consider getting help:

- Do you feel like you're always behind in your tasks?
- Do you wish you spent less time on repetitive tasks and had more time to strategize?
- Are there tasks that you simply HATE doing?
- Do you have an upcoming life situation or contributing factor that will reduce the time you can spend on your business? For example, if you and your partner run the business together and one of you is going to work less to spend more time with your children.
- Do you lack knowledge or skills that would enable your business to grow?

You also need to look at the state of your business and answer the following questions:

- Is there enough money to bring on and pay for the new employee(s)?

- Is there enough work for new employee(s) to do full-time, or can this be a contractor, an intern or part-term position? You can, and should, try before you buy (with new hires).

If all of the above are yes, don't hesitate! A one person show can only last for so long, and the more you can focus on what you truly enjoy in your business, the less likely you are to get burned out.

As you begin hiring people, think about your own zone of genius—those things you do best—and begin to specialize. Entrepreneurs acknowledge the skills the business will require but that they don't currently have. By identifying these skill gaps early, they can make a plan for how to fill those roles in your company. They can fill those needs by either developing those skills, taking on a partner, hiring someone who possesses those skills, or contracting that work out. It's an old adage, but you are the sum of the five people closest to you; improvement to your life or business environment happens when you surround yourself with people who are better than you.

What Will They Do?

Before you start the process of hiring an employee or contractor, figure out the kind of support you need. Think about the tasks and responsibilities you'd like the person to take on now and in the future—people often like to know there's potential for growth when they take on a new position. Companies hire employees or contractors to fill two kinds of gaps: capacity and capability.

- **Capacity:**
  - Make a list of the most important tasks you need help with. Is it someone to help with sales, social media marketing, or bread baking?
  - Make a list of things that you simply don't want to do. Are there certain things that you dread doing? Accounting, Sales, Customer Support?

- **Capability:** Make a list of things that you don't have the experience to do or simply don't know how to do. Do you lack experience running marketing and sales campaigns or designing your website?

With your lists in hand, group the tasks to be completed by skill set. If you find that you need people with distinct skill sets, (for example, a baker and a social media manager) think about which tasks either have priority or will free up more time for you and hire for that position first. For many entrepreneurs, a part-time virtual assistant (VA) is the first hire they make. An experienced VA can see ways they can help that an entrepreneur might not have identified. And, you'd be surprised how much you can accomplish when you get back as little as two hours of your time a week—it's like having an extra day each month.

As with any business decision, you have to determine how much it will cost you. The salary (for an employee) or contract rate (for a contractor) depends on the kind of work they will be responsible for, the role's seniority, your location, and your budget. When you make the decision to hire an employee or contractor, it is crucial that you can afford to pay them without going bankrupt!

Once you've done this legwork, you're ready to think about whether you want to hire an employee or a contractor and then write a much more detailed job description to begin the search for candidates.

The Hiring-Too-Soon Trap

Getting help can seem like the solution to all your business problems—and lack of sleep—but hiring new employees will have hidden costs you should be thinking about. You will need to spend time researching, writing job descriptions, and interviewing each job candidate, which means you'll lose valuable time you can be investing in your business. New teammates take a while to get to fully operational, but you'll have to pay them their full salary while they get the hang of things.

We're all for getting help, but if the problem you want to solve is short-term, a contractor may be a better solution rather than a full- or part-time employee.

What Kind of Help Do You Need?

When you are in the early stages of your entrepreneurial journey, spend some time imagining your future company: What type of company do you see in six months? One year? Five years? Are you still working alone or do other people work with you? If there are other people, how many are they and what do they do? Even before you reach the point of overwhelm and exhaustion, you can sketch out the future of your company with projections for sales, revenue, and growth. Make a list or chart of the roles you see and outline the skills and tasks the people in those roles will have.

Hiring is a major risk for a company and generally where you spend the most money. It is hard to get right, but you must. When you're faced with needing to bring someone into your business, you want to think about why you want someone now and what tasks or responsibilities you want that person to take on. (The playbooks discussed in Chapter 9, Operations, can be a great resource for identifying specific tasks that need to be done.) The answers to those questions can help you decide whether you want a business partner, a contractor, or an employee. Hiring is part science, part timing, part luck, and a lot of responsibility to help your colleague achieve their potential once you bring them on board. You will not always be successful. We've hired thousands of people; sometimes it just doesn't work out, even if you've been careful. We'll go into more detail below.

Partner or Co-founder

When you first start talking about your idea, you may have friends or colleagues who express interest in creating a business with you. There are situations where this makes perfect sense and entrepreneurial history is filled with co-founding teams like Jobs and Wozniak, Hewlett and

Packard, Ben and Jerry. Co-founders should have complementary skills; if you're good at product development, working with a co-founder who excels at sales can be ideal.

Having a co-founder means you have someone to share the risk and rewards, the decisions and the consequences. Like a marriage, it can be great and/or it can be tough. Choose your co-founder with caution. In many ways, getting a divorce from your co-founder may be harder than from a spouse. This relationship needs to be ride or die, and a total commitment. It won't be easy, but it's very important you cover the hard questions between roles and responsibilities early.

Even if you started your business as a solopreneur, you may decide that more than a contractor or employee, you need a partner who can be equally invested in the development and outcome of your business. Much like hiring someone, you'll want to develop a description of the skills and responsibilities you want in a business partner and consider how you can entice this person financially, perhaps with equity in the business and an equal share of the profits. If you're bringing more to the table, you should earn more of the upside. It's key to negotiate partnership economics very early on.

Contractors

You may have heard of the gig economy—maybe you're part of it. The gig economy runs on people who offer services to companies or entrepreneurs and instead of having a full-time job, they go from gig to gig. The contractor trades the stability of a traditional job for flexibility in the hours they work, the way they do their tasks, and the rates they can charge.

For an entrepreneur, hiring a contractor can be a great solution. Contractors have experience, skills, and knowledge to do a task without much direction. In general, you cannot tell a contractor when or how to do the job. You agree to a deliverable or outcome and a due date.

Employees

Although employees can help an entrepreneur increase both their time and their earnings, employees can also be the biggest cost center of a business. When you hire an employee, the costs involved in the employee's salary include contributions toward social security and healthcare, vacation time, and personal days—meaning there will be days when you pay your employee but they aren't working, so you may have the added cost of paying someone to cover for them. During the initial working days, referred to as onboarding, you'll spend your time (or another employee's time) training the new employee. Although you hire people who have the skills you need, they don't know how you run your business; they won't be at their capacity on the first day, but instead will have a learning curve. Some statistics state that it takes up to a year (!) before an employee's contribution to a company reaches 100 percent of their potential—all the more reason to do your best to hire the right people and create a situation where they want to stay for a long time.

The best advice we can give for employees is to hire slow, fire fast, which means taking the time to write an accurate job description, be demanding in your recruiting and interviewing, and hire only when you're fully convinced you've found the right person. If that person doesn't work out, don't hesitate to let them go quickly. Most companies today require a 30 to 90 day trial period so if things don't work out, the employee and employer will part ways without dire consequences.

Alternative Help

Many entrepreneurs, especially in the bootstrapping stages, get creative about where and how to find help. Building a strong and varied network is critical to finding help outside of contractors or employees. As Mister Rogers advised children who are lost or alone: look for the helpers. Tell people about the type of help you need; you'd be surprised where that help may come from.

Mentors sit at the top of our list of alternative help. While a mentor probably won't roll up their sleeves to do the actual work with you, their experience, guidance, and advice offer priceless insights to help you make decisions, reduce risk, and increase efficiencies in your business. When you have an established relationship with a mentor, you may also be able to tap into their network for partners, contractors, employees, or investors.

Another place to look for help is from volunteers. Look to your group of friends or followers, college campuses, alumni organizations, or relevant industry groups or trade associations to find volunteers to help you. Many people have the time and experience they want to share while others have the time and willingness to learn new skills. Hala Taha, founder of YAP Media, had a crew of 20 volunteers when she first started her podcast. As her business grew, she hired many of those volunteers.

If you have specific skills or a framework you can teach, taking on an apprentice or intern often creates a win-win situation. Many entrepreneurs pay a small stipend to apprentices or interns. Training an apprentice or intern gives you the chance not only to teach someone your specific way of doing something, but also an opportunity to test that person as a potential future employee. In exchange they should gain skills and experience, so make sure you're willing to invest in them.

Don't forget about your entrepreneurial peers. Many entrepreneurs are in the same situation: lots of ideas and desire for growth but a lack of skills or time to bring them to life. Swapping skills or services generates goodwill and a supportive relationship with entrepreneurial peers. These swaps may happen remotely or locally, depending on the skill or service you both bring to the table. You can meet people in groups online, through associations related to your trade or field, or in local organizations.

DISCUSSION GUIDE

- What is your future vision for your company, i.e., are you working with other people and if so, how many and what do they do?
- What do you need to accomplish right now that you aren't able to do without help?
- How did you become aware of this need?
- What gaps do you have in capacity? In capability?
- How does the role fit into the current team structure?
- Do you need an employee or a contractor?
- Is there an alternative type of helper you could recruit, i.e., volunteer or intern?
- What is the priority of this role?

Job Description

A job description is a useful, plain-language tool that explains the tasks, duties, function, and responsibilities of a position. It details who performs a specific type of work, how that work is to be completed, and the frequency and the purpose of the work as it relates to the business. It also lists the training, education, and experience required to do the work and includes a description of the essential functions to be performed. Job descriptions also detail salary ranges and any benefits that are offered to employees in the position. In many cases a job description also outlines how the position fits into a larger organization as a whole.

Look at the list you made of the tasks you'd like someone to do and the skills they need to do the job. Then, revisit your core values, which inform the job description. The employee-employer relationship stands on shared values; when a potential candidate reads your job description, they should also get a sense of the values your business stands for. In today's employment market, a candidate interviews the company as much as the company interviews the candidate and both sides want their values to be aligned. Your values and principles drive the culture of your company and although you seek diversity among your employees in terms of skills and background, you want alignment with values.

An effective job description—one that helps you find the right person—details the role, the responsibilities, and the expectations (RREs) and includes the following:

- Description of your company or organization
- The role title
- Responsibilities or duties of the role
- Expectations or outcomes of each responsibility
- Required qualifications ranging from education, experience, skills, etc.
- Preferred qualifications that would set apart stronger candidates
- Location information or expectations
- Optional: Salary, this can be discussed during the candidate interview

Remember, you can sketch out job descriptions before you begin looking for people as part of your business planning and projections. When you are ready to hire, the job description helps you find qualified candidates and guides the interview process. Keep in mind that the job description details the ideal, and you may not find a candidate who meets all your requirements. Before you begin interviewing, think about the qualifications that are an absolute must—the must-haves—and those that would be good but could be learned or would be a bonus—the nice-to-haves. As you write your job description, we suggest looking at job postings for similar jobs to see if other companies are using the same titles or offering similar salaries. Candidates will be applying for more than one job so you want to identify your competition and adjust accordingly.

The Job Description Trap

When a candidate reads a job description, they run through a mental checklist to determine if the job looks interesting, if the company seems like a good fit, and if they meet the qualifications of the position. A clear and precise job description helps candidates self-identify, ideally screening out unqualified candidates, which saves you the time of reviewing applications or interviewing people who aren't fit for the job. While many companies don't post salary ranges, we think it's better to be up front about your budget and what you're willing to pay. This way you're not wasting time negotiating late into the process and you screen out candidates who are playing multiple offers off different companies to get the best outcome they can.

A job description serves many purposes beyond recruiting candidates for the job. As your company grows, job descriptions provide a guideline for evaluating employees, making salary comparisons, and strategizing for organizational growth.

DISCUSSION GUIDE

- What are the essential duties and responsibilities?
- What are the key projects this role would contribute to in their first 30, 60, 90 days?
- What are the "must have" qualifications?
- What are the "nice to have" qualifications?
- In what areas of knowledge or skills are you willing to take risks or make trade-offs?
- What could growth look like in this role?
- Who would be a good person to model the ideal candidate after?
- What titles in the marketplace have similar requirements and responsibilities?

Recruiting

Chances are, you are running a small business and company with lots of potential, but not a lot of revenue yet. So how do you attract and recruit the best team without the fancy perks and amenities offered by bigger companies. The answer is looking at you in the mirror—it's you! There are lots of people who would rather work for a leader and business they admire than to work for an average company with free beer on tap. You're looking for people who want to help the company grow and to grow with it, not for people who want free perks. There are several components that help immensely when it comes to recruiting top talent:

- **Good attracts good:** Good talent naturally attracts other great talent. You and your founding team are the forces that will cultivate and shape your culture.
- **Challenges and ownership:** Offering qualified candidates the chance to solve hard problems and growth opportunities draws in some of the brightest candidates who want startup experience. A lot of people don't just want to work somewhere, they want to feel like they can claim or own some part of its success.
- **Flexibility:** Taking risks can have big rewards. It may pay off to adopt innovative hiring models like remote work or flexible working hours as long as you are confident this will not affect the employee's productivity and work results.
- **Pay and benefits:** Make sure you offer a reasonable salary for your location. Define a minimum and maximum salary to create room for negotiation.
- **Revisit your values:** Communicate your brand and purpose to attract candidates who are better matches and are more engaged; engaged employees are much less likely to leave over time.

The act of recruiting people is a major commitment of time and money. It costs money to use recruiting sites or recruiters and to find, interview, train, and manage additional team members. Check out some common ways you can go about spreading the word to qualified candidates.

Use your network to recruit first. Let your mentors, peers, even friendly competitors know you're hiring. Then begin to spread the word through various channels:

- **Your website:** This is where your customers and fans may first find you and your story, so you can easily make a page for job postings.
- **Social media platforms:** Platforms like Facebook or X (Twitter) are where your followers can see and apply to a position or to spread the word to their network.
- **Professional job sites:** Consider LinkedIn, Handshake, or Monster for companies and Idealist for non-profit or social good organizations.
- **At events:** Having a booth at college job fairs, conferences for your trade or industry, roadshows, etc. are good ways to meet lots of qualified people who are already interested in your type of business or organization.

We recommend setting a close date for applications so you can review the candidates and begin to set up interviews with those who meet the minimum requirements.

DISCUSSION GUIDE

- Are there partners or other connections who can make referrals?
- Which job boards will you post to?
- What professional organizations can you post to or tap into for referrals?
- Which organizations or companies have similar talent?
- Are there any specific people you know through your network that you believe would be a good candidate for the role? Have you reached out to them directly to set up a time to talk?

Interviewing

Most first-time entrepreneurs or small businesses do not have a solid, easily-repeatable process for interviewing candidates. Fortunately, we can help you establish one! A defined process for interviewing candidates will help you identify the best candidate quickly. And in addition to having a robust method of screening, interviewing, and reviewing the best candidate for the role, you will need to keep track of certain legal information for tax and recordkeeping purposes.

The Interview Process

As the applications start to come in, review all the resumes you get from all the portals where you have posted your listings. Because of time restraints, you can't talk to everyone who sends in a resume, so use the portal's AI features to set parameters the candidates must have like minimum years of work experience or must-have skills. Candidates who don't meet those requirements will be declined and their resume won't cross your desk. (This is why you sometimes never get the minimum acknowledgement from a company when you apply for a job.) Consider blind recruitment—hiding applicants' names, education and even years of experience—to overcome unconscious bias and promote greater workplace diversity.

When you have a handful of candidates, you can begin to have preliminary conversations with those candidates. We've outlined the stages here, followed by our suggested interviewing method, and key points to remember when you present your chosen candidate with an offer.

- **First screening:** At this stage, you will be calling some qualified candidates that pass your hard cutoffs. This is usually a quick call over the phone where you can describe the role and your company and ask the candidate to walk through their resume. A good candidate can explain their resume quickly without hesitation. Ask for their interest in the role and company, then proceed to next steps if they are interested and seem like a good fit. Remember to screen for a values match at each stage.

- **Technical screen:** This step is optional, but if technical skills are critical to the role, you may ask candidates to take a test. If the test is substantial, you could consider paying the applicants for their time. For example, publishing agencies often request candidates to take a writing or editing test. A common way to test coding skills is to ask for a Github portfolio or for previous work samples.
- **First round interview:** Candidates who pass the screening stages are called in for a longer, formal interview, usually in person or through a video call. Most companies do at least two formal interviews. Here you can drill into the candidate's resume and experience to make sure nothing is exaggerated.
- Look out for candidates who criticize past employers, and look favorably on candidates who ask a lot of questions and show that they've done research on the company.
- **Second (or final) round interview:** Only candidates who meet all of your minimum requirements will be called in for a second interview. While the goal of the first interview is to confirm a candidate's qualifications and experience, the second interview looks for company and culture fit.
- Give other members of your current team a chance to talk to these candidates to gauge if they are a good fit. You can have a third and final round of interviews to get opinions from as many people as possible.
- **Reference check:** When you choose the candidate you want to hire, ask for their references if they have not provided them already. Schedule brief calls with the references to double check the candidate's past experience. References can expose red flags but a candidate's responses in an interview tend to be a better indicator of their skills and fit. You may also want to run a background check if you have any suspicions about the candidate's background or need to run one for your insurance or because of your type of business.

(You must ask for the applicant's permission to do this.) For example, if you are hiring a teacher or aide for a nursery school, your state may require that you run a background check on all potential employees. Have one or two backup candidates in case you need to make a different choice.

- **Offer:** Present your offer to the candidate of your choice. If they accept, move forward with your confirmation and the next steps of hiring. If they decline, go back to the clients you identified as second and third choice.
- **Follow-up:** After your candidate has accepted your offer. Follow up with everyone who applied and interviewed to inform them you closed the role and to thank them for their time.

Interview Tactics and Questions

When developing interview questions, consider three rules of thumb: Ask only for information that will serve as a basis for the hiring decision, know how the information will be used to make the decision, and do not ask for information that will not or should not be used to make hiring decisions.

Write down your questions, and be sure to give yourself enough blank space to jot down notes. Doing this in advance and using the same set of questions for each candidate will make the interview process flow much more smoothly. We recommend that you use the job description as a roadmap for creating questions.

The best predictor of future behavior is past behavior in similar situations. Case studies are helpful to assess whether or not someone can do the job you need them to do. We recommend asking STAR questions: Situation, Task, Action, Result. You will be asking how they handled a specific situation when they encountered it in the past rather than asking hypothetical questions about how they would handle a situation if confronted with it in the future.

Ask the candidate about a situation or event that focuses on his or her past experiences, behaviors, knowledge, skills, and abilities. Present them with a specific type of task, ask about the action they took or contributed, and the result or outcome. For example, you can lead with questions like:

- Describe a situation in which you were able to use persuasion to successfully convince someone to see things your way.
- Describe a time when you were faced with a stressful situation that demonstrated your coping skills.
- Give me a specific example of a time when you used good judgment and logic in solving a problem.
- Give me an example of a time when you set a goal and you were able to achieve it.
- Tell me about a time when you had to use your presentation skills to influence someone's opinion.
- Give me a specific example of a time when you had to conform to a policy with which you did not agree.

This type of questioning reveals how an applicant thinks and reacts in a particular situation and can be very helpful to compare experience with scenarios which you have experienced in your business.

You're listening to their answers not only to learn about their capability but also to determine if their values align with yours. You can tell a lot about a person's values by how they describe a situation and their involvement in it. For example, if one of your values is teamwork, when you ask about a situation, you would look for a candidate who discusses how they worked with other people, who perhaps uses "we" instead of "I" when talking about solving a problem. If you have a clear understanding of your values, you can ask questions and interpret answers through the lens of those values.

You can also ask specific questions to determine culture alignment and fit. Company culture is explicitly defined in a company's mission statement, HR handbook (if you have one), and workplace policies—you want to hire candidates who exhibit the best fit within your organization's culture. Company culture develops organically, guided by the founder's values and reinforced by their behavior. For example, the way a company engages and supports employees; the style, level of formality, and transparency in communication; and the common attitudes and work habits among employees all contribute to the underlying culture of an organization. An employee who will fit into the existing culture will likely be more satisfied, exhibit superior job performance, be more engaged, and less likely to leave the company than someone who clashes with the culture. To interview for culture fit, ask questions like these:

- Describe the work environment or culture in which you are most productive and happy.
- What can your hobbies tell me that your resume can't?
- What are your three ideal job qualities?
- What are you passionate about?

Effective interviews expose potential red flags, reveal strengths, ensure that there is a fit with salary, compensation, and personality, and verify qualifications, skills, and abilities. They're an essential part of the hiring process.

The Just-Like-Me Hiring Trap

When hiring employees, you'll want to avoid the trap of hiring people who are just like you or "clones" so to say. A new employee is your opportunity to bring new ideas and direction to your organization. Don't eliminate the opportunity by picking only employees who will agree with your thinking or who could become your new best friend. Make sure they have the right skills and that their values match your company's values.

The Offer

The offer process should happen in two steps: an initial informal job offer and an official job offer. The first is typically a phone call and the latter is in written form.

The following framework outlines the elements of a strong, effective informal job offer to make candidates cancel their job search and begin the onboarding process with your organization.

1. **State your excitement.** Everyone likes to feel wanted, and your newest potential hire is no different. Let them know how excited you are to have them join the team.
2. **Remind them why they like your company.** Talk to them about how they'll fit in at your organization. What made you realize they'd be a good match for your culture?
3. **Show them the money.** Let them know the base salary you're prepared to offer, as well as any other major benefits.
4. **Be ready to negotiate.** Oftentimes, candidates may want to negotiate everything from start date, to salary, to vacation days and everything in between. Make sure you've thought through your needs and if you don't know, let them know you'll get back to them with an answer.
5. **Get a response.** Whether you're communicating via email or phone, it's completely appropriate to ask for the recipient's initial response. Be aware, however, that many people may want to see the official, formal offer before making a commitment. Make sure you let them know if they'll be receiving it through email, mail, or any other method you choose.

After the initial call, you'll want to send the candidate their official written offer letter through email or mail.

When the candidate accepts the written offer, the official hiring and onboarding process begins.

DISCUSSION GUIDE

- What interview questions will you ask to address a situation?
- What questions will you ask to learn about behavior?
- What questions will you ask to reveal outcomes?
- How will you know if a candidate aligns with your values?
- Have you defined the salary and benefits of the position you have open?
- Are you prepared to make a verbal offer followed by a written offer?

Hiring

When a candidate accepts your offer, your first step is to set up your records for the government. As an employer in the United States, you'll need to ask your employee to complete:

- Form I-9 confirms their eligibility to work in the US. You don't need to submit this form but keep it on file for three years after the hire date or for one year after the employee stops working for you.
- Form W-4 confirms the state and federal withholding taxes and needs to be filed once a year.
- Form W-2 must be submitted to the Social Security Administration along with the payroll taxes (FICA, the Federal Insurance Contributions Act) once a year to the state and federal government.

We recommend using electronic versions, or scanning any documents to make sure you have a secure copy.

Remember to update your business insurance coverage to cover new employees with workers' compensation, disability insurance, and unemployment insurance. Requirements for employers vary from state to state so make sure you read up on what you need to do to be compliant.

Onboarding

Onboarding is the period of time from when a person accepts the offer through when they're able to do their job fully and independently. The length of time depends on the complexity of the role, the employee's experience, and the preparedness of the employer—that's you!

The first few weeks are some of the most crucial because you're setting expectations and building their personal investment in your business or organization. Start with a simple overview of your business, share your mission, vision, expectations, and a training plan. If you've created playbooks, share them with the new employee; they reinforce your way of doing things and give the employee a sense of independence and learned competencies because they don't have to ask you how to do something at every turn.

Consider having a 30, 60, and 90 day plan with clear goals for them to achieve to evaluate their success in meeting expectations. Make sure you ask them how they're doing regularly so they feel supported as they acclimate to a new job.

First impressions matter, so think of onboarding as a part of your business's brand development by being as thoughtful about the employee experience as you are about the customer experience. Your efforts will pay off with higher employee engagement and retention, and your business will quickly benefit from employees that are giving their all each day.

When your employees are excited about their job and the company they work for, they share their enthusiasm with people they know and become part of your marketing efforts. Customers like to support companies that treat their employees well.

Firing

As we mentioned before: hire slow, fire fast. Some hires just don't work out and the best solution may be to cut your losses and let the person go. Don't let deadweight sit around. A bad apple spoils all the other apples and a poor performer demoralizes the other contributing employees.

These conversations challenge many entrepreneurs; no one wants to tell someone else they're not doing a good job or that they're fired. This may be the toughest part of the job for many founders. Consider writing a script for a firing conversation. Be clear about the reason you are firing the individual, and make sure this is a legal reason. Many times, an entrepreneur won't be able to afford the role any longer, so the reason for firing would be "eliminating the role" at the company. Be direct and keep it short but maintain the dignity of the person. You can refer back to the original job description and the offer letter to compare the agreed upon expectations for the job and the actual performance of the employee.

Frequent communication with employees keeps you informed about their challenges so as soon as problems arise, you can determine if the employee needs more support from you and whether they can come back from their poor performance. Consider creating a Performance Improvement Plan (PIP) together and set deadlines. If their performance improves by the established date, they keep their job, otherwise it's time to part ways.

If it comes to that, consider consulting with an employment attorney or human resources specialist to make sure you follow the laws of your state.

DISCUSSION GUIDE

- What federal and state forms do you need to complete and file when you hire a new employee?
- How will you help your new employee learn about your company culture?
- Who will manage the employee onboarding?
- How long will the trial period of your new employee be?
- How will you determine if your employee is doing their job or not?

Building and Maintaining a Healthy Team Culture

As people join you in your entrepreneurial efforts, whether as partners, contractors, or employees, you want them to embrace and mirror your values in the work they do. You share your vision and mission in words, but set the tone of your values and culture with your actions. We've worked from the beginning to create an atmosphere of learning and diversity at Skysthelimit.org, and here we share some ideas about how entrepreneurs who become leaders and managers can do the same.

Leadership vs. Management

Early stage businesses are fragile and rely on you as the founder to do a LOT. In the beginning you will both lead and manage your employees. As your company grows, your role shifts more toward leadership and away from management. Leaders drive the culture of the company by developing and communicating the vision and mission. They decide on the company goals as well as the strategies to reach them and the measurements to determine the team's success. Leaders make sure that your company has the right employees in the right roles, especially your management team, who can execute on your vision.

Managers take action to fulfill the strategy and meet the company goals. They also oversee others and delegate the tactics and tasks that apply to the strategies. Managers have the responsibility for holding team members accountable, increasing their performance, and providing candid but constructive feedback. They work with employees on their professional development through mentoring and training.

In terms of strategic delegation it's helpful to follow Maxwell's 10-80-10 Principle, which suggests devoting your energy to the crucial first 10 percent of a process, allow your team to handle the middle 80 percent, then return to tackle the vital last 10 percent with them.

Power Skills

Both leaders and managers need to develop their soft skills—or as we prefer to call them, power skills. Soft skills comprise the capacity for interpersonal relationships, problem-solving, collaboration, communication, and decision making. The hard skills counterpart points to the technical or job-specific expertise required to perform a specific role. In business today, where AI can do many of the technical tasks, the power skills need a human touch, making them often more important to the success of a business.

Following are power skills you should have—or strive to develop—that are important to running a business:

- **Communication:** Clear and effective oral, written, and visual communication skills—and active listening—will help you sell your product, pitch your business, and recruit and lead a team.
- **Courtesy:** Meeting people with respect and gratitude will make them more likely to buy from you, invest in you, and want to work with you.
- **Adaptability:** The ability to embrace change and stay open to new things or new ways of doing things impact the capability of your business to overcome obstacles.
- **Positive attitude:** Displaying enthusiasm, encouragement, and confidence in your business will help others believe in you. Adopt a growth mindset toward your tasks.
- **Responsibility:** Business leaders who are accountable, reliable, and respond to challenges with resourcefulness and a desire to get the job done will find more success in the long run than those who look for excuses or scapegoats.
- **Teamwork:** Even if you are a "solopreneur," the ability to work well with others is essential. At some point you'll need to work with a mentor, a vendor, or a client to get something done, so if it doesn't come naturally, learn to be supportive, helpful, and collaborative by practicing collaborating with others.

- **Consistency:** As you start to build your business, think about how your values and voice are represented in your business and your actions.

Employee Morale

Good employee morale translates into a positive company culture. Create the conditions that enable the team to perform their best work. You may have heard or read about the Love Languages developed by Gary Chapman. The idea is that every person has a specific way they like to be recognized or rewarded. With an employee, seek to understand if they feel validated through public recognition, by receiving a gift or bonus, or when asked to take on more responsibility.

DISCUSSION GUIDE

- Do you spend more time leading or managing? Does the ratio between the two responsibilities feel right for this stage of your business?
- What are your plans to shift more of your time and effort toward leading?
- Who will you delegate the management responsibilities to as your company grows?
- Which power skills do you feel strong in?
- Which power skills do you need to develop?
- How will you develop and strengthen them?
- What incentives will you use to recognize and reward your employees?

Next up is the chapter you've been waiting for, Funding and Finance. If you've reached the point of hiring contractors and employees, chances are your business is on solid ground and you're in a position to seek funding to expand. We present funding options and how to write a business plan in the next chapter.

CHECKLIST

- ✓ Make a plan to decide when you might bring on help.
- ✓ Write job descriptions for the different roles you see in your company.
- ✓ Distribute the job description to your network and job boards.
- ✓ Make a list of potential interview questions.
- ✓ Draft an offer letter.
- ✓ Determine which state and federal tax forms you need to file.
- ✓ Make an onboarding plan.
- ✓ Plan your transition to leader.

CHAPTER 13

Funding and Finance

When Should You Read This Chapter?
Here it is: the chapter you've been waiting for! After you've defined your idea and your customer and thought about your budget, you're ready to pursue funding to cover startup or expansion expenses that you can't pay for on your own. This chapter includes guidelines for creating a business plan and pitch deck, which includes information from the exercises and processes you've done in all the previous chapters in the book.

If you're like most entrepreneurs, the thought that follows your brilliant business idea is *I need investors; how do I get funding?* Before anyone will invest in your idea—which is what any funder does—you have to have gone through the thought processes described in the first 12 chapters of this book. When you ask for money, whether it's a loan, an investment, or a presale, you're asking the other person to believe in your idea and your ability to make it a viable business, and you need to prove that viability to them.

The reality of getting funding for your small business is that you often need to have already built a profitable business before you can attract investment—what's more convincing than already demonstrating success? We have seen way too many earliest-stage entrepreneurs spend far too much time looking for investment instead of working on making their products or services more valuable and finding paying customers. That's why this chapter is at the end.

In this chapter, we introduce the different types of funding to consider seeking. We then walk you through creating the long pitch we mentioned in Chapter 6, Branding. This document helps a loan officer or investor get the information they need to make a decision about funding your business.

Funding Options

As we discussed in the opening chapter, entrepreneurs usually fund their business initially through personal savings, partnerships, and pre-sales. As the business grows, investors and creditors become realistic fundraising options. Going as far as you can on your own is beneficial because you retain control, and you're responsible only to yourself. As soon as you have someone else's money, that whole dynamic changes. However, having other people's money can reduce your personal risk. Understanding the types of funding available helps you decide which to pursue at different stages of your entrepreneurial journey. Funding falls into three main categories: traditional, loans, and investors.

Traditional: Personal Savings, Credit, Partnerships, Pre-sales, and Donations

There are several different ways an entrepreneur accesses funding at the beginning of their journey. Many of them pay for startup expenses with their personal savings or credit, i.e., maxing out their credit cards. This is risky business and we advise that you don't spend money you can't afford to lose. A more prudent approach might be a partnership, which allows you to share the risk and responsibility of your venture. The most favorable funding comes from pre-sales of your product or service that help you get off the ground without ever having to take money from a third party. Lastly, donations come from individuals and organizations that support entrepreneurs financially without asking that the money be repaid.

Pre-sales and Crowdfunding

This may be one of the best ways, in our opinion, of getting funding for your new business. Pre-sales take more work up front and you have to make or do something people *really* want, but it reduces your risk of creating a product or service that no one wants—and you can get paid up-front so you get the money you need.

A presale or pre-order is a targeted sale before your product or service actually goes live. You sell the idea to a small group of customers before you've created it. It is a great way for businesses to spark interest about new products, plan for inventory management, and raise money for production. Think about potential customers; imagine how much less risky your business would be if you got a commitment from a customer to buy your product or service *before* you risk a ton of money and time building the whole thing! Access to capital is really limited. It can be easier to pre-sell your product or service rather than raising money.

You can pre-sell by generating a simple website with images and descriptions of your product or service, and shop this website around to a list of potential customers. If you don't have a list, your marketing efforts should focus on gathering customer leads and gaining publicity for your product/service. Refer to Chapter 5, Marketing and Sales, for more information about creating a product/service launch campaign.

Crowdfunding sites like Indiegogo or Kickstarter offer the opportunity to pre-sell to strangers. Entrepreneurs create crowdfunding campaigns that demonstrate the product idea and then customers can pre-order, typically at various prices. For example, pre-sales packages may range from a very high price that includes an invitation to the product launch party, to a multi-item purchase that includes a free T-shirt, to a single item at a discounted early bird price. Typically, the product will be manufactured if enough pre-sales occur. If they do not, the customers receive a refund and the product is canceled. Crowdfunding has become quite competitive and the most successful campaigns include product videos and a robust marketing campaign to drive traffic to the site.

In addition to your customer interviews (see Chapter 3, Customer Development), pre-sales reduce the possibility of failure because they allow you to collect feedback to change and improve your product/service. You also learn how much demand exists for your product/service and the price your customers are willing to pay. This is the kind of work you would need to do anyways in the earliest stages of starting a business, why not do it before you risk a lot of your money?

Personal Savings

If you have personal savings you can tap into, it offers the easiest and most cost-effective way to provide your own financing for a new business. Self-financing your business gives you full control and ownership of the business, which in turn means that you will receive 100 percent of future profits. You will know exactly how much money is available to run your business, and you will not have to spend time trying to secure other forms of funding from investors or banks. If you fund a business yourself, you will be forced to live within your means, only investing in business equipment and marketing when you need to. This can help you to prioritize your business expenditures and avoid excessive spending. On the other hand, it can put a strain on your family, and if your business were to fail, you could lose your home and other personal possessions. At the very beginning of this book, we discussed the concept of "affordable loss"—as an entrepreneur, you need to balance the risks and generally should not invest more time and money than you can afford to lose. This is a highly personal calculation that only you can do, and it changes over time as your circumstances change.

Partnership Funding

A partnership is a business owned by two or more individuals (as explained in Chapter 11, Legal and Regulatory). Before creating an official partnership, talk about expectations: Who will be contributing financially? How much capital will be expected from each partner? When does that investment have to be made? How much time will each party contribute to the business? Keep in mind that while the specifics of who will contribute what financially are important to your partnership agreement, financial resources alone are not a worthwhile reason to bring in a small business partner (see the False Partner Trap below).

All partners share in the profits, managerial responsibilities, and liability for debts equally. Your partner will help with the financial burden, decision-making, workload to develop the business, likewise, a partnership adds another opinion and say to decisions made for the business, so you will no longer have full control and authority. One of the most important things you can do in a partnership is to be crystal clear about who is doing what—write it down!

The False Partner Trap

Keep in mind that if your partner only brings financial capital to the table, then they are not a business partner—they're an investor. Make sure you understand the difference, and structure your business relationship accordingly.

Donations

Donations are free contributions and they can come as monetary donations, volunteer time, or anything else that might be helpful to your business. This can be a very difficult path for businesses, even nonprofits. Sometimes, you can spend more time chasing donations and get less money than if you worked a minimum wage job.

A local church or business may be willing to donate the use of a building for your first year of business. A local charity might be willing to offer manual labor necessary for your opening. Or a local school might be willing to help organize a coupon drive to generate advance sales before opening day.

Speak with other local businesses, local churches, charities and nonprofits about grants and contributions. If your business will provide a valuable service to the community, you will likely find that many in the community will be willing to support your effort.

Regardless of what you're asking for, asking for donations can be an intimidating prospect. Identify individuals and organizations that align with your values. Think about what you can offer in return. Depending on your existing relationship with the donor, how much they donate, and your available resources, this could take the form of including their logo and name on banners or publicity with a "sponsored by..." line, references on your website, social media, or newsletter, and tax benefits. Tailor your approach to the person or business you're asking, craft a formal letter, and meet with them in person to discuss your project and the reasons they should donate. Follow up in a couple weeks if they haven't communicated their decision. Whether they make a donation or not, express your appreciation for their consideration.

DISCUSSION GUIDE

- How much money do you need to start or grow your business? (Refer to Chapter 10, Accounting and Bookkeeping)
- Do you have enough personal funds to start or grow your business?
- Do you need funding to start or grow your business?
- What kind of traditional funding can you tap into?
- Have you made any pre-sales to fund your business?
- Which customers might you approach for pre-sales?
- Have you considered crowdfunding as a possible solution?
- Would a partner be a good idea to share the costs and workload of your business?
- Are there any individuals or organizations that might offer financial or in-kind donations?
- What benefit can you offer potential donors?

Loans: Personal Loans, Crowdlending, and Bank Lending

Loans are money you borrow from someone else in the form of personal loans from people you know, crowdlending from strangers via online platforms that match people who are willing to lend money with people who need it (i.e., www.kiva.org), and loans from lenders such as banks or financial institutions. These forms of funding rely on three major concepts: risk assessment, leverage, and your ability to pay off a debt.

Loans come in many forms; we've listed some of the most common here:

- **Small Business Administration loan:** The SBA works with lenders to provide loans to small businesses. The agency doesn't lend money directly to small business owners. Instead, it sets guidelines for loans made by its partnering lenders, community development organizations, and micro-lending institutions. The SBA reduces risk for lenders and makes it easier for them to pre-qualify borrowers. That makes it easier for small businesses to get loans—however, many entrepreneurs don't qualify for these loans until they've purchased a building or have a great deal of established revenue. Pursuing SBA loans with a bank can make sense for certain types of businesses, but they can be a waste of time for many entrepreneurs.
- **Business term loan:** With a traditional-term business loan, you are lent a lump sum amount upfront, which you pay back (along with interest) over a set period of time.
- **Business line of credit:** With a business line of credit, you can borrow up to a maximum credit limit and only pay interest on the amount of capital that you borrow from your credit line.
- **Personal loan for business:** Personal loans can actually be helpful for newer businesses that don't have any financial history. You personally guarantee repayment for a personal loan, which means your personal assets are at risk if you can't repay the loan. On the

positive side, personal loans can have lower rates than business loans.

- **Invoice financing:** Invoice financing lets you sell invoices to a lender, who fronts you a portion of the invoice amount. The remaining percent (usually 20 percent) is held until the invoice is paid.
- **Startup business loan:** Startup loans offer newer businesses capital to grow. Business credit cards, lines of credit, and equipment loans are great startup loans if you have strong personal credit.
- **Equipment financing:** With equipment financing, the lender will front you cash to help purchase the equipment outright. You then pay back the total amount lent, plus fees, for a set period of time.
- **Short-term business loan:** With a short-term small business loan, you borrow a set amount of capital upfront, which you quickly pay back (along with fees) over a short period of time. This is sometimes known as a "swing loan" where you know you have money coming in in the future and the bank lends you money which you immediately repay when the payment comes in.
- **Merchant cash advance:** With merchant cash advances, a financing company fronts you a lump sum of capital, which you repay (plus their fee) with a set percentage of your daily credit card sales.

Regardless of the lender, the process to apply for a loan follows these steps:

1. How much do you need? Figure out exactly how much money you need and when you'll need it (refer to Chapter 10, Accounting and Bookkeeping).
2. Prepare and have a business plan (as detailed later in this chapter). This will help you demonstrate knowledge of your industry, be able to articulate the opportunity you're going after, and highlight

your competitive advantage. You should also have a firm grasp of what you plan to use the money for, and how this investment will impact your bottom line.

3. Check your credit. Your credit is an important indicator of your creditworthiness. Request a copy of your personal credit report and score. Contact the credit bureau to resolve any issues, and if your score is lower than 700, take steps to improve it before you approach lenders. The credit reporting agency can offer tips to do this.
4. Educate yourself and research whether you actually qualify for a loan. There are Five C's of Credit used by lenders industry-wide to determine the creditworthiness of potential borrowers.
   - Character: What is your reputation and track record for repaying debts?
   - Capacity: Do you have the financial ability to repay the loan?
   - Capital: How much "skin" in the game do you have? If this business fails, what do you lose?
   - Collateral: What assets can you pledge to support your loan?
   - Conditions: What are the important circumstances surrounding your business and the economy?
5. Ask about the terms. Here are some thing you should be asking:
   - Interest rate
   - Upfront fees, i.e., origination, application, and guarantee
   - Loan term
   - Full cost of the loan over its lifetime
   - Payment amount and frequency
   - Prepayment penalties
   - Check processing penalties

  - Broker fees (if using a broker)
  - Time to access the funds

6. Prepare your documents. These include:
   - Business bank statements
   - Financial statement or balance sheet (see Chapter 10, Accounting and Bookkeeping)
   - Profit and loss statements, also known as your income statement
   - Any business debt payment details
   - Your most recent personal tax return to verify your income
   - Your business tax returns from the last two fiscal years
7. Prepare your investor pitch (see the next section).
8. Apply and wait for a response.
9. Choose to accept or decline your loan.

With a small business loan, you maintain full control of your business and any potential profits. Small business loans will help you grow and expand your business without any hassle, so you have financial flexibility for your daily operations.

Small business loans are difficult to obtain as many lenders are leery of lending money to startup businesses and prefer to lend to established entities that are in a solid financial position. A lender may require that you put up some form of security to obtain the loan. If you do so and you default on the loan, you face the possibility of losing not only your business, but also your home, car or other property.

DISCUSSION GUIDE

- What kind of loan might you apply for?
- What is your credit rating? What steps can you take to improve it?
- Do you understand the terms of the loan?
- Have you prepared the various financial statements and tax returns that a lender will likely ask for?
- If your loan application is accepted:
- Can you repay this loan?
- Are you comfortable with the payment, whether it has daily, weekly, or monthly payments?
- Can you confidently say this is the lowest rate you will find?
- Do you know all potential fees associated with the loan?

]Investors: Friends and Family, Angels, Venture Capital, Accelerator

There is a lot of talk about investment in the entrepreneurship space, but the truth is investment can take many forms. Sometimes friends or family members will invest in your business with the expectation that you will repay them with interest when your business reaches a certain financial milestone. Like any investment, the risk is that your business will fail and they won't see any return on their investment.

In exchange for money from investors, you must give them a portion of ownership and control in your business. Angel investors are high-net-worth individuals who get an equity stake in return for their financing, while venture capitalists are firms or fund managers that take equity in your business in exchange for financing. Accelerators offer both funding and other types of support such as mentoring, workspace, or equipment in exchange for equity.

Finding an investor is a full-time job. It takes hours of work, many conversations, and skin thick enough to withstand a lot of nos. We want to keep it real: The percentage of minorities and women who procure investment funds is woefully low—although Skysthelimit.org is trying to change that by educating these entrepreneurs. That doesn't mean you shouldn't try, but that you will need to give your all to your efforts. Show investors you are going to make this business work whether they're on the train or not. Even better if you can make them feel that they might miss out on a great opportunity to be a part of an incredible story. You should try to invoke FOMO for every type of investor or lender.

Before you start looking for funding, complete your business plan and include a well thought-out and researched business timeline. This will help you more accurately estimate how much money you will need and when you will need it. Then, prepare your long pitch deck, which presents the pieces of your business plan to potential investors and demonstrates the validity and viability of your business. (Details in the next section.)

The Funding Trap

You think you need a ton of money to get started, but how can you work with what you have? Rather than spending too much time looking for funding, focus on building your business and getting sales.

DISCUSSION GUIDE

- Do you want to approach investors?
- What kind of investor will you approach: friends and family, crowdfunding, angels, or venture capitalists?
- How will you identify and find potential investors?

Business Plan and Pitch Deck

Whether you're applying for a loan, pitching to investors, or looking to sell your business, you need to create a business plan and pitch deck that showcases the current situation and future potential of your business. Both documents pull together information from all the previous chapters of the book and present a 360 degree vision of your business. Aside from sharing these documents with others, taking the time to create them forces you to review all the pieces of your business and can help you identify gaps or misalignments and find the clarity that helps you strategize and move forward with less stress and more ease. And it forces you to start thinking about the future, like how you will deal with your competitors after your business launches.

In Chapter 6, Branding, you developed your short pitch and we explained the top-level concept of the long pitch. Here we walk through it in more detail.

Your long pitch will be based on your business plan, so you should formulate the latter first. A business plan can be a one-page summary or a longer detailed document. The length depends on the audience for your plan. If you want to clarify and state your business purposes for potential employees or begin preliminary conversations with partners or investors, the one-page summary may be enough. If you're going to use the plan to search for potential bank loans or equity capital from a potential investor, then you'll want to write a detailed business plan.

Meanwhile, the long pitch is an abbreviated version of the business plan created as a series of slides; we suggest ten slides. When you share the long pitch, you are making a presentation and verbally share the details.

Below we take an in-depth look at both the business plan and pitch deck.

One-Page Business Plan

Writing a business plan will make you look closely at your idea and how you will turn it into a business. A business plan describes what you want to do with your business and how it will be done. By writing down how to bring your idea into reality you will have figured out answers to why, what, who, how, where, when, and how much for your startup. The one-page business plan answers the following questions about your customer and product/service; the work you did in the first three chapters will help you answer them. Remember, you want to demonstrate the value your product or service brings to your customer by solving their problem:

- Describe your business idea and why it's unique in a sentence or two.
- Define the customer you want to help.
- Describe the problem your potential customers have.
- Detail the way your business idea will help these customers by solving their problem.

Detailed Business Plan

The person reading your business plan will need a full description of what your product or service will be to get a better understanding for how to support you or even to decide whether or not to provide you with funding. We developed a nine section approach to give your audience all the details they need.

1. The Product or Service

What product or service do you provide that people need or want?

Describe your product or service and how it will be used. You can also identify cool and unique features and benefits, and discuss the needs or problems they address in the market. In this section, you can include a general description, including the business idea (new or existing) and objective. For example,

- **Business idea:** Sell T-shirts online (only) with unique logo designs on the pocket, 20 percent of profits will go to a Chilean orphanage.

- **Example business objective:** I want my clothing line to help people feel like they stand for something.

2. The Customer and the Market

Who is your customer? What is the current demand and growth potential for your target market?

Discuss the market you want to enter. This foundation will help you prove that a market exists for your product or service and narrow the range of potential customers to the ones who are willing and able to buy your product. Here, you will define your target market, provide evidence of demand, and research the potential for your target market to grow. For example,

- **Target market:** My products will be used by middle-class men and women in their twenties and thirties.
- **Demand:** Reports from "All Knowing Research" have proven a 20 percent growth in the t-shirt market for the next five years. Include an example that shows this.
- **Growth potential:** I can grow my clothing item selection to tanks or even create a new logo "series" to attract other customers.

3. The Competition and the Industry

Who are you up against? What is your strong competitive advantage and unique selling point for your business offering?

Discuss your approach to your market. This section recognizes that your efforts to reach your potential customers and make money will be limited by similar businesses. Here, you will describe your competitive advantage, unique selling point, competitors, and trends. To find out more information on your competitors and trends, you can easily run an online search on your product or service type, just make sure to use reports and articles from reputable sources. For example,

- **Competitive advantage:** I will provide high quality materials and shopping with a purpose.

- **Unique selling point:** 20 percent of our profits will serve to clothe children in a Chilean Orphanage. The T-shirts will be unisex and the cut style will be longer in the back than the front. The back part of the shirt will also have a center slit and the short sleeves will be folded.
- **Competitors:** Direct competitors include charitable clothing brands in store and online only retailers.
- **Trends:** Findings from Accenture's Global Consumer Pulse Survey revealed that at least 50 percent of consumers prefer to buy from brands that "support and act upon causes they have in common (e.g., social, charitable)."

4. Sales Channels and Marketing

How will you reach your customers? What platforms do you plan to use to execute your sales? What is your marketing budget?

Write a general description of your marketing strategy and sales channels for reaching your customers. A good marketing plan should have a defined budget and focus on your target segment. On the other hand, distribution decisions should concentrate on the methods and channels that will optimize your sales and profits. In the marketing strategy section, will define how you will attract new customers, the steps you have already taken, and your future budget. In the sales and distributions section, you will define your business reach, channels, and strategic partnerships. For example,

- **Attract new customers:** I will market my business on social media, specifically on Instagram.
- **Steps already taken:** I have created an Instagram business account.
- **Budget:** A quick online search revealed that typically, businesses spend between $200 to $350 per day, so I will start with $200 per month as a test and build from there.
- **Reach, Local:** I will sell T-shirts only in San Francisco.

- **Sales channels:** I will sell online only.
- **Partnerships:** Ideally, I would like to partner with a local San Francisco department store to carry my T-shirts.

5. Pricing Model

What do you charge and why? Which sales and pricing model do you use: single-time, recurring subscription, free and premium memberships, etc.?

Discuss the reasons and specifics of your product/service pricing. Define your sales model, explain why you chose your pricing model, and list estimate selling prices for your products. For example,

- **Sales model:** "One-off" sales (or price per unit)
- **Pricing model:** I chose this pricing model because I am selling individual products. Other retail businesses, like Fabletics, offer a subscription based pricing model, but they offer a much larger product inventory. I did not think it would provide any additional benefit to use anything other than one-off sales.
- **Selling prices:**
    - $18.99, T-Shirt with our signature cut style, no pocket design
    - $20.00, T-Shirt with our signature cut style and pocket design 1
    - $25.00, T-Shirt with our signature cut style and pocket design 2

6. Partnerships

Who are your partners? Do you have any strategic partnerships that give you advantages?

Discuss who you want to bring on as potential partners. You will define who can help you sell your product or services, determine how to make your products, describe what was your logic for selecting your partner, create a communication plan, think through a backup plan and backup partners. For example,

- **Partners:** I will partner with High Quality Cuts to cut and print my T-shirts.

- **Vendor/Manufacturer:** High Quality Cuts will cut and print my T-shirts in the styles I design.
- **Logic for partnership:** They have a lot of experience with national T-shirt manufacturing processes, allowing me to select a variety of different 'pre-made' cut styles or custom styles. They are also established in the San Francisco market and therefore reputable.
- **Partner communication:** I have made the initial call to High Quality Cuts. They requested design samples for both the cut style and logos so they can give me a manufacturing quote.
- **Backup plan:** If High Quality Cuts has a really high quote, I will have to find another manufacturer. I have already found a couple more companies I would be interested in partnering with.
- **Backup partners**
    - Manufacturing alternatives: Soft Cotton, San Fran Cuts
    - Distribution alternatives: I will hire employees to drive and/or bike to deliver my customers' orders.
    - Marketing companies: Currently, not needed. I will create and run all social media marketing campaigns myself.

7. Operations

How will you run your business?

Define the tasks and actions that need to happen to launch and run your business successfully. You need to present a realistic timeline, determine your biggest expenses, define your plan to hire employees, determine if you will need to rent a location to house your store or products, and decide if you want to create a trademark or copyright (also known as intellectual property). For example,

Timeline

- Three months before launch: Ensure inventory is on time for launch. Ensure the website or selling platform is live and functional, continue testing with sample users to fix bugs and issues.
- One month before launch: Begin marketing my business to incentivize "pre-orders."
- One month after launch: Ensure all orders are delivered on time, continue marketing.
- Six months after launch: Evaluate demand forecast and modify business plan as needed.
- One year after launch: Consider expanding and hiring one or two more people.
- Two years after launch: Re-evaluate business plan.

Business Costs

- Inventory, actual t-shirts
- Delivery, hiring one or two additional employees to deliver t-shirts in the local San Francisco area
- Marketing, monthly social media marketing budget

Hiring Employees

- I will find employees by asking friends and family first since I only need one or two more people to help me fulfill orders on an on-call basis.

Legal

- Lease agreements: Currently not needed. I might need to look into it if the first year goes well, order volume increases, and I can no longer store my inventory at home.
- Intellectual property: I want to trademark my company logo and copyright all original T-shirt designs.

8. Risk Mitigation and Exit Strategy

What are the biggest risks and obstacles? How will you minimize risk?

Demonstrate how you will prepare for some of the typical obstacles new businesses have to overcome. You should outline your plan for complying with relevant regulations and keep in mind that every business is subject to local, state, and federal regulation. For example,

- **Legal requirements:** San Francisco requires a small business license.
- **Sales:** I expect to sell X T-shirts in the first six months to offset my costs. If I sell less than X, I will not make any profit. If that happens, I will X.
- **Non-payment from customers:** Because my business is online, purchases will not be completed if credit/debit card information is not processed, so this will not be a problem for me.
- **Failed key suppliers:** If my suppliers deliver my orders late, I will contact my customers immediately and look into my backups, compensating customers for time lost.
- **Exit strategy:** I will consider selling my business three years after launch if the right offer is on the table.

9. The Team

Who are the people on your team? What are their roles and responsibilities?

Define who, if anyone, is helping you launch your business. After describing who the key people are, you will want to describe how you will organize each person's role and responsibilities for the efficient operation of your business. You will define who is currently involved, what their time commitments are, and how much they have or are willing to invest financially. For example,

- **Current team:** My sister and I

- **Time/Financial commitments:**
  - My sister is not spending any time developing the business, but has loaned me $5,000 to start. She expects to be paid back within the first year after opening or receive 10 percent ownership.
  - I am developing the business part time, after work, and have invested all my savings.

We want you to be aware that the financial (sales and pricing) sections of your business plan will be examined closely by those interested in joining you, investing in the venture, or lending you money. They will want to know how you will use invested funds to create a successful business. Make sure your business plan is thorough and as accurate as possible.

Business Valuations

When lenders or investors evaluate your business to decide whether they will give you money to help it grow, they're looking at the current performance and the future potential of your business. The facts and projections of your business plan demonstrate past and current performance. Lenders and investors use that information to calculate the value of your business, against which they'll decide the amount of money to loan or invest. If you plan to sell your business, this valuation guides the selling price.

The baseline for calculating the value comes from revenue multipliers. Most companies receive a valuation of one to two multiples of revenue; for example, if your revenue average of the past three years is a million dollars, you could sell your company for between one and two million dollars. Tech companies often get much higher valuations; they make 10 million dollars in recurring revenue and can sell for 70 million, or a seven times multiple of revenue.

The I'll-Never-Leave Trap

Most entrepreneurs who have sold their business say they wish they had thought about their exit strategy—how they would leave their business—from day one. An exit strategy can look like selling the business to another entrepreneur, merging with another company, or becoming a public company that's traded on the stock market (known as an Initial Public Offering or IPO). In each of these strategies, you would turn your business over to others and step away, or exit.

As much as you love your idea and your business, at some point most entrepreneurs get the itch to start something new, it's just part of the DNA of an entrepreneur. Entrepreneurs who think about setting up their business itself as a product to sell someday tend to make better short- and long-term decisions. Entrepreneurs with an eye to the future maintain an objective stance and don't conflate the business with their own identity. They see the value of their contribution to the business and see the current business as a stepping stone to the next one.

DISCUSSION GUIDE

Use the following questions to write your business plan. You may have already answered these questions in previous discussion guides; the business plan puts all your answers in one place.

- What product or service do you provide that people need or want?
- Who is your customer?
- What is the current demand and growth potential for your target market?
- Who are you up against?
- What is your strong competitive advantage and unique selling point for your business offering?
- How will you reach your customers?

- What platforms do you plan to use to execute your sales?
- What is your marketing budget?
- What do you charge and why?
- Which sales and pricing model do you use: single-time, recurring subscription, free and premium memberships, etc.?
- What are your revenue projections?
- Who are your partners?
- Do you have any strategic partnerships that give you advantages?
- How will you run your business?
- What is your timeline?
- What are your business costs?
- Will you hire employees?
- Do you have proprietary or intellectual property to protect?
- What are the biggest risks and obstacles?
- How will you minimize risk?
- Who are the people on your team?
- What are their roles and responsibilities?
- What is your estimated value of your business?
- What is your biggest challenge to writing a business plan?
- Who will you ask for help or where will you gain the knowledge to overcome your challenge?
- What is your exit strategy?
- Did working on your business plan reveal any gaps or misalignments in the different parts of your business?
- How will you fill those gaps or bring all the pieces into alignment?

Pitch Deck

If you've created a business plan following the steps we outline above, your pitch deck will be surprisingly easy to complete. Investors typically ask to see your pitch before they ask to read your business plan. This presentation is your opportunity to convince an investor that your idea is worth their time and money and that you have the right team and partners to make it happen.

The 10 slides we recommend here follow the same structure as a business plan. You want to include just a few bullets on each slide and you will talk through the details when presenting your idea to potential partners, lenders, or investors.

Slide 1 – Cover: Display the name of your business with your tagline and logo. Consider adding your company name and logo discreetly in one of the corners of each slide.

Slide 2 – Problem or opportunity: Describe the problem you solve or the pleasure you provide.

Slide 3 – Value proposition: Explain the value of the pain of the problem you solve or of the pleasure you provide.

Slide 4 – Secret sauce: Describe the unique magic of your business. Show a prototype or diagram if possible.

Slide 5 – Business model: Outline how you will make money, describe your customers, and your marketing and sales strategies.

Slide 6 – Launch plan: Describe how you will launch your business without going broke.

Slide 7 – Competitive analysis: Detail the existing competition in the market.

Slide 8 – Management team and partners: Outline the key people in your company, your board of directors and advisors (if you have them), and key partners.

Slide 9 – Financial projections and performance: Provide a three-year forecast of your expenses and revenue, including performance metrics like the number of customers.

Slide 10 – Current status, timeline, accomplishments, use of funds: Describe the actual state of your business and your plans for the next six months. Detail how you would use any investment funds you receive.

Some entrepreneurs customize each presentation by adding a footer with the date and the name of the person being presented to; this is a nice touch if you plan to leave a copy of the slide deck with the audience.

Investors are busy people who make rapid decisions. They see thousands of pitches and quickly recognize an idea with legs and an entrepreneur who has the confidence and competence to make things happen. We recommend creating a spoken presentation in two layers. Prepare a high-level conceptual explanation of each slide of no more than two minutes per slide, and then prepare a deeper level presentation for each slide that includes more detail. Investors may give you a limited amount of time to present; you can ask them which parts of your business they're most interested in and go deep on those sections while staying high level on others, or go through your entire high-level presentation and then answer their specific detailed questions, perhaps returning to the relevant slide.

You must practice repeatedly until you know every bit about your business without having to refer to written documents or notes. That said, you want to fully understand your message—not repeat it by memory—so practice talking through each slide with different levels of detail and with different words so you can respond to questions in an informed and spontaneous way.

DISCUSSION GUIDE

- Which sections of your pitch do you feel most confident speaking to?
- Which sections of your pitch feel shaky?
- Who will you practice with to build your confidence?
- Did preparing your pitch reveal any gaps in your idea?
- How will you fill those gaps?

Entrepreneurship shouldn't be lonely. In fact, we believe in building business together. In our final chapter, we discuss working with a mentor and developing a fruitful mentor/mentee relationship.

CHECKLIST

✓ Create a business plan to determine how much money you need to start and grow your business.

✓ Look for partners (if applicable).

✓ Look for donors who can help your business and to whom you offer a benefit.

✓ Identify and choose appropriate funding sources for your business.

✓ Create a long pitch deck to show to potential lenders and/or investors.

✓ Practice giving your pitch presentation orally.

✓ Apply for a loan (if that's part of your plan).

✓ Identify and pitch investors (if applicable).

CHAPTER 14

Building Businesses Together

When Should You Read This Chapter?
You can read this chapter at any point in your entrepreneurial journey. You may want to read it first so that you can find a mentor or peer and go through the Discussion Guides together as you read forward. Or read it when you are ready to work with a mentor to learn behaviors that will help you get the most out of the mentor/mentee relationship.

We place high value on human relationships at Skysthelimit.org. Our business model relies on mentor/mentee and peer relationships, and that's why the subtitle of our book and the title of this chapter is Building Businesses Together. When you start thinking about creating a business and taking the first steps, your relationship with mentors is one of the earliest and most important you can form. Remember, your own learning and professional development account for 20 percent of the 40/40/20 Rule. Mentors can help you build or develop qualities you admire in others, acquire skills or knowledge, and improve habits or behaviors.

A mentor can be a peer or someone with more experience than the mentee, who helps a mentee reach positive outcomes. Mentors offer many kinds of support and an entrepreneur may have more than one mentor, depending on the guidance and expertise they seek and the stage of their business. If you recruit more than one person to mentor you, then you will have access to even more experiences and networks than if you only have one mentor. Support comes in different forms:

- **Emotional support** in the form of empathy, encouragement, or compassion. This type of support helps build self-esteem and confidence.
- **Tangible support** is physical, concrete, or practical such as reviewing job descriptions or business plans, coaching, and making connections to other people.
- **Informational support** involves providing advice, helping with decision making and time management and developing plans to achieve goals.
- **Companionship support** means spending time doing activities together, celebrating success, and meeting regularly.

The mentor/mentee relationship goes both ways—we believe that mutual benefit is key to all healthy relationships. As a mentee, think about the value you bring to the relationship. Plan to give back in the future; as you move forward in your entrepreneurial journey, you, too, can mentor others. Ralph Waldo Emerson said, "Every person I meet is my superior in some way. In that, I learn from them."

Discover why a mentor would be willing to help you. Dale Carnegie said, "Every act you have ever performed since the day you were born was performed because you wanted something." Maybe for mentors it is an opportunity to learn, get inspired, to pay it forward—so many possible reasons. Mentoring relationships are voluntary—no one owes you anything. We generally recommend being authentic, showing appreciation, and a willingness to not only grow but to continuously show that growth to your mentor.

Finding a Mentor

Sometimes mentorships happen casually. Maybe you start off as friends or colleagues and a natural mentor/mentee relationship develops. Sometimes the mentor sees potential and promise in a mentee and believes it's worthwhile to nurture the relationship by sharing their experiences or becoming a sounding board for their ideas. However, in many cases the mentee has to actively seek out the experience and advice of a mentor. So, how can you find a mentor?

There is nothing wrong with asking for help and, in fact, most people are willing and excited to provide it. Look to your immediate network of colleagues, friends, and acquaintances and identify people who have knowledge or skills that could help you grow. Knowledge alone, however, doesn't make someone a good mentor. Look for people who seem to have a great work/life balance and are passionate about their field and craft, as this often translates into a desire to teach. If they have prior mentoring experience, that's a great sign that they would mentor again. Likewise, if they have been mentored, they'll understand the value of a mentorship to someone just starting out.

Tell your family, friends, and peers that you're looking for a mentor, describe the type of support you seek, and ask for recommendations. Attend industry or professional networking events to meet others in your field, and ask people you meet with for mentor recommendations. Look in places outside of your business, too. For example, business people generally like to stay active, so consider joining fitness classes or a gym. Social media networks give you the chance to find a mentor outside of your city. Follow people who you want to learn from and start a conversation through comments. As your interactions increase, you'll feel more comfortable reaching out to people you don't have personal connection with.

Many people express fear at the prospect of asking a total stranger for help as a prospective mentor. Remember: People like helping other people, particularly if you express your gratitude and if you show you continuous growth. By asking a prospective mentor for help, you're letting them know you admire them for their experience and expertise. Many people feel validated knowing their experiences and insights are valuable to others. Some people don't have the time and inclination to be mentors, but as you ask around, you'll be surprised at just how receptive many people are.

If you haven't identified a potential mentor in your current network, sign up at Skysthelimit.org to find one. We believe that success shouldn't be determined by the community you happen to be born into, so we built Skysthelimit.org to connect our community of entrepreneurs and supporters across geographic boundaries. Through virtual meetings and digital resources, we connect young entrepreneurs to each other and a community of supporters.

As you identify people who you believe could be a good mentor, start setting up in-person or virtual meetings with them. Send them an email or message asking for 30 minutes of their time to learn more about their experience, and be specific in your request. We suggest the following guidelines to find a mentor.

Prepare for the First Meeting

Before you seek a mentor, it's helpful to think about what you'll bring to the table. First, you should think about your own values. You should also consider your personal work style and how it might fit with different mentoring approaches. Think through your past approaches to work and projects: Do you need structured, directive guidance, or do you prefer gentle supervision? Finally, you should think about any knowledge and skill gaps you'd hope that your mentor could fill.

Once you've given thought to your values, work style, and needs, spend some time setting SMART goals (as discussed in Chapter 8, Strategy) and defining the type of support that would be most useful in helping you reach your professional and business goals. Well-defined goals prepare you to identify areas where you lack knowledge and in turn identify the right type of mentor you seek. Creating specific, written goals for three months, one year, and five years can be helpful for you personally, and it can also help you clearly communicate those goals to a potential mentor.

Goals should relate to the knowledge and skill gaps identified and they can be specific or broad. Setting goals will help you present your needs to potential mentors. A mentee who is clear about the advice they need and sets specific, time-bound goals demonstrates that they are responsible for their own growth. Showing this can make a mentor more likely to want to invest time and energy in helping you develop and reach your goals.

1. Contact the person that you would like to interview, you can either call or email them.
    - Briefly tell them how you found their contact information.
    - Mention why you have chosen to speak to them.
    - Be clear about the purpose of the interview.
    - Convey the parameters of the interview—day, time, place, duration.
2. Arrange the day, time, place, and duration for the meeting. Make sure you include a way to reach each other if plans change, so include an email or phone number.
3. Before the interview, prepare a list of your goals and questions—we offer interviewing tips in the next section.
4. During the interview let your potential mentor know that you'll be taking notes. Be enthusiastic and interested. The active listening skills you developed to interview customers apply here, too.
5. Thank your potential mentor for their time and willingness to meet you.
6. After the interview, reflect on your meeting:
    - Did you feel like you had a good rapport with them?
    - Did you perceive that they were available to you in terms of having some time to be helpful?
    - Do they seem knowledgeable and well-networked in your desired field?

- Would they make a good mentor for you?
- What are some things you might say, so you can follow-up with this person in the future?
- Do you feel like you and this person had similar interests?
- Do you have other ideas about follow-up questions to think about or ask yourself?

Mentor Interview Questions

This is your opportunity to find out if the prospective mentor has the expertise to help you and if you'll be a good fit. The interview should help you form your expectations about what the mentor wants from you and what you want from the experience. Ask questions that encourage your potential mentor to respond with an explanation, and then ask follow-up questions based on the person's responses and for clarification when you need it. The questions below help guide the conversation although you'll choose questions relevant to your needs:

- Given my current entrepreneurial pursuits, I'm interested in learning more about what you do. What was your path to becoming a business owner? For example, what school, training, and work experiences did you have that helped you to get to where you are today?
- What is a typical day at work like for you?
- What are some things that you find challenging about your work?
- How do you manage these issues that are challenging?
- What types of work or life experiences made a difference in your life?
- What types of social or extra-curricular activities are important to you?
- If you could change anything about your professional journey, what would you change or do differently?

Show a genuine interest in getting to know your potential mentor, and give them the opportunity to get to know you better. This makes it more likely that they will develop a true interest in you and your development, and want to be an advocate for you. Rather than asking them to mentor you at the first meeting, we suggest having a follow-up meeting at which time you can ask them to be your mentor.

If they agree, move ahead with scheduling your first mentoring meeting and setting expectations.

If you send an email to a potential mentor and never hear back or they said they were unavailable, you should still express gratitude for their consideration, and understanding of their inability to meet you. You want to ensure the relationship is not damaged. Ask for recommendations for other people who may be a good potential mentor. If they can recommend someone, ask for an introduction to that person or if you could use their name to contact the referred person.

Remember that a mentoring relationship should mimic the process that you use to build other types of relationships. It can take several meetings for you and your prospective mentor to get to know each other—we suggest being specific with what you want to cover in the next meeting and be okay with taking it one meeting at a time! The most enduring relationships can take a long time to form, and some relationships can be just one meeting. Both types can help you on your journey, and both can be valuable to prospective mentors.

DISCUSSION GUIDE

- What specific challenges would you like a mentor to support you on?
- What qualities and experience would you look for in a mentor?
- Who might you ask to be a mentor?
- Who could provide referrals to potential mentors?
- Do you "know" people through social media who you would like to have as a mentor? What steps can you take to reach out to them?
- How will you present your request to potential mentors and what will you say or write?

Defining the Mentorship

A mentor-mentee relationship, or mentorship, is a system of semi-structured guidance whereby one person shares their knowledge, skills, and experience to assist another person to progress in their own life and career. A mentorship can be a short-term arrangement or it can last many years.

Mentoring is more than giving advice or passing on experience in a particular area or situation. It's about motivating and empowering the other person to identify their own issues and goals, and helping them to find ways of resolving or reaching them—not by doing it for them, or expecting them to do it the way you did it, but by understanding and respecting different ways of working.

Mentoring is a mutually-beneficial, voluntary relationship between two individuals: the mentor and the mentee. The mentee will absorb the mentor's knowledge and have the ambition and desire to know what to do with this knowledge. The mentor decides the amount of help and guidance the mentee needs, and the mentee should take the initiative to ask for help or advice. The mentee will practice and demonstrate what has been learned.

Getting help and being mentored is not a one-way street, and mentees have a lot to offer to a mentor in a mentoring relationship. The point is to understand that each will bring something positive to the relationship just by being who they are. To be involved in a mentoring relationship is a privilege for both participants, and as a result it is important to be gracious and thoughtful toward each other.

General Ground Rules

The most successful relationships happen when the people involved establish ground rules and boundaries for their interactions. We suggest the following as the foundation of a strong mentoring relationship:

- Avoid inquiring into each other's personal lives too far, but be vulnerable to the extent you feel it is appropriate and safe. If personal things are relevant to the business, however, bring them up. Often, an entrepreneur's business and personal life are solidly intertwined.
- Mentor and mentee cannot make excessive demands on each other's time and will use an agreed-upon method of contact.
- The mentor will assist the mentee in achieving the agreed objectives but will let the mentee run their business independently.
- Both parties will review their relationship and the mentee's business progress on an agreed-upon cadence, typically monthly.
- Anything said during the course of a mentoring meeting is confidential to the parties involved and should not be repeated without the express consent of those individuals. You can find a Confidentiality Statement template at Skysthelimit.org, if needed.
- Remember, if you are an entrepreneur seeking support from a mentor, it is your business—you decide what is best for you and your business. Trust your instincts on whether to follow advice or not. You know your business best.

A ground rule that applies to all relationships is applying active listening. We discussed this idea in Chapter 3, Customer Development, in relation to the customer interviews but it's worth mentioning again. Active listening means being deeply engaged in and attentive to what the speaker is saying and requires far more listening than talking. Both mentor and mentee should practice active listening. Your goal as an active listener is to truly understand the speaker's perspective (regardless of whether you agree) and to communicate that understanding back to the speaker so that he or she can confirm the accuracy of your understanding. You can remember the rules of active listening with this acronym:

Look interested
Inquire with questions
Stay alert
Test your understanding
Empathize
Neutralize your feelings

Mentoring develops the person as well as the business. The mentor provides challenges as a positive lever to drive the mentee's improvement. The mentee who adopts a play-to-win attitude—where winning means learning even in the face of failure—will gain the most from the mentorship. When the goals and objectives the mentee set out to achieve are met, celebrate success and be willing to let go as the mentorship comes to a natural end. At this point, the mentee will have gained and established independence and self-reliance.

Many mentorships become long-term professional relationships as the mentee progresses in their career.

Mentoring Meetings

Because the mentee and mentor have met and agreed to a mentorship, active mentoring begins right from the start. We've provided a list of suggested questions for the first meeting in the Discussion Guide at the end of this section. Mentor and mentee will set rules and boundaries for their relationship, discuss the mentee's most critical SMART goals, and work on a plan to solve the most pressing challenge.

The mentor doesn't do the work for the mentee, but helps the mentee navigate challenges by asking thought-provoking questions and offering insight based on their experience. In addition to the SMART goal framework for defining big goals, we find the 5Cs framework useful for addressing specific challenges related to meeting those goals, and the Gradual Release model to shift the actions from mentor-guided, to collaborative, to mentee-independent.

The 5Cs Framework

Challenge: The mentee explains the problem they're struggling to solve.

Choices: The mentor will help mentee think through the available choices or options to overcome the challenge.

Consequences: The mentor will support the mentee to examine the consequences of those choices, looking at the advantages and disadvantages. The mentor guides the mentee to explore each option in more detail.

Creative Solutions: Once the best choice has been determined, the mentor discusses creative solutions with the mentee. This is a mutual and collaborative approach. The mentor can help by sharing any knowledge and expanding on their own experiences to arrive at a practical solution. Wherever possible, the mentor should encourage the mentee to develop their own solution to the challenge. If the mentor has 'ideas,' this is the time to share them. The mentor must balance the 'PUSH PULL' mentoring approach. If in doubt, the best approach is always to PULL, which encourages the mentee to take responsibility for the solution.

Conclusion: The session ends by asking the mentee to sum up the key points of the meeting and to describe what will happen next. Creating SMART goals can provide a concrete way forward. The mentor should encourage the mentee to act upon the agreed solution, and the mentee should feel empowered to take these actions forward.

Once the tasks or actions the mentee will do are defined, we suggest using the Gradual Release model, also referred to as "I do it, we do it, then you do it." When confronting a practical challenge, like how to post a Facebook ad or how to design a website, the Gradual Release model provides a way to move from mentor-centered instruction, to collaboration, to mentee-centered, independent practice. As the entrepreneur acquires the new information and skills, the responsibility of learning shifts from mentor-directed instruction to mentee processing activities.

The Gradual Release Model

Step	Mentor	Mentee
I do it	• Provide direct instruction • Establish goals and purpose • Model • Think out loud	• Actively listen • Take notes • Ask for clarification
We do it	• Instruct interactively • Provide support (as needed) • Check, prompt, clue • Provide additional modeling (if needed)	• Ask and respond to questions • Work with mentor • Complete process with mentor's guidance
You do it	• Allow entrepreneur time and space to figure things out • Provide feedback • Assess level of understanding	• Work alone • Rely on notes or other resources for clarification before asking mentor • Take responsibility for the outcome

DISCUSSION GUIDE

- Use these questions as a guideline to get to know each other for your first mentor/mentee meeting.
    - Ask each other to share a brief background. Where are you from? What is your favorite thing to do? What is your story? What are your top three strengths? Why did you sign up to be a mentor/mentee?
    - Why are you building this business?
    - What does success look like for your business?
    - What are your top three strengths?
    - How would you describe your communication and working styles? Casual? Professional? Warm and Friendly? Straight to the point?

- Some housekeeping questions to establish your cadence and boundaries:
    - How often will we meet and for how long?
    - Will it be the same time and day for each meeting, i.e., every other Tuesday at 4 pm?
    - How will we communicate outside of the meetings and how quickly can we expect a response?
    - If one of us needs to cancel, how much notice do we need to give? How will we communicate that need?
    - When will our mentorship end, i.e., a date or a milestone reached?
    - Are there any business topics that should remain off limits?
    - Are there any business topics that should remain confidential?
    - How will we provide feedback to each other?

- What are three specific SMART goals the mentee wants support on achieving?
  - What is your specific goal?
  - How will you measure success?
  - What are the advantages and/or potential barriers to achieving your goal?
  - How is achieving this goal relevant to your overall business objectives?
  - How long will it take you to achieve this goal?
- At each session, in addition to the questions in the Discussion Guides, use the following questions as guidelines for the mentoring conversation:
  - What is the mentee's current challenge?
  - What choices does the mentee have to respond to the challenge?
  - What are the consequences of each of these choices?
  - What creative solutions does the mentee have to overcome any of the negative consequences?
  - What is the conclusion?
  - What action will the mentee take before the next meeting?
  - What will the mentor do before the next meeting, if anything?

Mentee Best Practices

The most successful mentees are those who are motivated and feel empowered to plan and manage the direction of their professional life. They take responsibility for their development, learning, and professional growth. Further, they come to the mentor/mentee relationship open to coaching, feedback, and guidance from the mentor. Use the following as a guideline to strengthen your relationship.

- Take responsibility for reaching out to your potential mentor to meet and talk.
- Take the initiative and offer ideas for how you two might spend time together. Planning ahead of time will make it much easier to develop shared expectations for your mentoring relationship later on.
- Set realistic expectations about how often you plan to meet and how you will communicate. Be flexible. Establish your goals and types of activities. Determine information that will or will not be kept confidential, i.e., if your mentor is well known in your field, can you discuss your mentoring relationship or not.
- Show respect for your mentor's time, interest, and expertise. Mentors have personal and professional lives and showing an interest in them is an important part of building the relationship. Although the focus is typically on you and your needs, you also want to be sensitive to the needs of your mentor. If something important is happening in your mentor's life, show an interest, be caring, and supportive. Remember that relationships are a two-way street. If you have to cancel a meeting, reschedule with ample notice.
- Give your mentor feedback about their impact. It can be very rewarding and satisfying to a mentor to help a young entrepreneur achieve their personal, professional, or educational goals. Acknowledge the advice your mentor gave you and let them know about your accomplishments and how they have contributed to your success. Share updates about successes, challenges, and milestones along with examples of your work.
- Share updates about your professional and personal life. Give your mentor background information about you including your accomplishments, interests, hobbies, resources, life experiences, and challenges. Provide your mentor with up-to-date contact information, particularly if you move or change your email address or phone number.

DISCUSSION GUIDE

- What expectations do you have of your mentor and the mentorship?
- What value can you bring to the relationship?
- How will you provide feedback to your mentor?

Mentor Best Practices

Like any relationship, the mentee/mentor relationship is built on trust, and trust grows over time. Mentors will increase trust by keeping their conversations and other communications with the mentee confidential, honoring scheduled meetings and calls, consistently showing interest and support, and by being honest.

Considerate mentors usually don't give advice in the first or second meeting, but rather use those first meetings to get to know their mentee and establish rapport. Indeed, the best mentors share their experiences instead of advice. While mentees often want to hear about the mentor's experience, it's better to reserve those discussions until after the mentee has had a chance to thoroughly explain their issue, question, or concern.

Active listening creates a positive, accepting environment that permits open communication.

Share Experiences Instead of Advice

It's as straightforward as it sounds!

Determine Goals and Build Capacity

As a role model, mentors should have their own career and personal goals and share these, when appropriate, with their mentee. As part of the conversation, mentors can help mentees identify and achieve their career and personal goals. Mentors help develop a mentee's capacity for learning and achieving by doing the following:

Assisting them with finding resources such as people, books, articles, tools, and web-based information.

Imparting knowledge and skills by explaining, giving useful examples, demonstrating processes, and asking thought-provoking questions.

Helping them gain broader perspectives on their responsibilities and organization.

Encourage

Giving encouragement is one of the mentoring skills most valued by mentees. Mentors offer encouragement by commenting favorably on the mentee's accomplishments. They communicate their belief in the mentee's capacity to grow personally and professionally and reach their goals. Mentors respond to mentee's frustrations and challenges with words of support, understanding, encouragement, and praise. Just knowing that someone else has been there can be tremendously helpful.

Inspire

Mentors inspire their mentees to excel by sharing personal vision or those of other leaders. Mentees benefit from learning about experiences, mistakes, and successes others have encountered on the road to becoming a successful business owner. Mentors talk with their mentee about inspirational and motivational people and events. Mentors introduce mentees to colleagues who could be additional useful contacts or inspiring models.

DISCUSSION GUIDE

- What characteristics and needs would you look for in a mentee?
- How will you encourage and inspire your mentee?
- What professional experience can you draw on to best mentor your mentee?

CHECKLIST

- ✓ Define the SMART goals that a mentor could help you achieve.
- ✓ Identify traits you want in a mentor.
- ✓ Reach out to your network to find a mentor.
- ✓ Conduct interviews and ask someone to be your mentor.
- ✓ At the first meeting, make a plan and set expectations for the mentoring relationship.
- ✓ Get mentored!

Conclusion

Congratulations! Just by reading this far you've achieved a milestone that many entrepreneurs won't. If you've completed any, some, or all of the Discussion Guides and Checklists, take a moment to recognize your effort. Share your accomplishment with others—make that social media post that declares you are an entrepreneur, have a party with your friends and family to celebrate your efforts. You've come a long way but there's plenty of road ahead of you to travel, so don't stop here.

If you haven't already, join the Skysthelimit.org community, reach out to fellow entrepreneurs, and meet a volunteer mentor. Review the Checklists at the end of each chapter to determine the work you've already done and the tasks that remain. Wherever you are on the entrepreneurial journey, look ahead to your next steps and talk to peers and mentors about your questions and challenges.

There are no limits on who can become a great entrepreneur. You don't have to have a college degree, a bunch of money in the bank, or even business experience to start something to achieve your goals. You do need focus, humility, drive, energy, creativity, a willingness to learn, and a willingness to fail. Most importantly, however, you need a valuable product/service and customers willing to pay you more than it costs you.

Entrepreneurs build businesses for their own satisfaction and gain but the defining reason, as we stated at the beginning of the book, is to create value for a group of people in a way that sustains a profitable business. In its simplest, most distilled definition, entrepreneurship means creating value—for your customers, for your family, for yourself.

You're ready for this: Go out and create value for your customers and yourself—the sky's the limit!

Acknowledgements

We have so many people to thank.

We want to thank our wives, Caity Connolly Ghirardelli and Hannah Cary-Wallis, first and foremost, for being incredibly supportive partners along the way, we wouldn't be where we are without you! We especially thank you for tolerating our endless stream of entrepreneurial conversations and facilitating our passion.

To our friends and co-creators at Accenture—John Downie, Colleen Landino, Lucy Murdoch, Mathew Edwards (ret.), Natt Fry (frmr), and Jill Huntley—thank you for investing so much time, treasure, and care in the global vision of Skysthelimit.org.

To Nick and Anastasia Vasilius, and so many other friends, family, and family friends who seeded our work over a decade ago, we couldn't have launched without you. And to the many, many generous donors who make our work possible year in and year out.

To our wonderful partners, including those at Goldman Sachs, especially Clif Marriott, and PNC Bank—Richard Bynum, Sally McCrady, Susan Blasko, and Sharon Cercone (ret.)—thank you for making this ongoing work possible.

To our mentors, Fabio Rosati, Claudia Viek, Richard Hogan, Michael Grano, and Peter Bloom.

A big thanks to all the team and board members at Skysthelimit.org, past and present, and all the entrepreneurs who have put your trust in us to support your entrepreneurial journey.

To our dear friends Brad, Joel, Omar, and so many others, especially the DPE crew, who have helped do this work over these many years.

To Nic's sister, Tatiana Cary, whose lifelong commitment to serving others and understanding their lived experiences has helped shape and open our aperture to the world.

Thank you to the wonderful, talented people who helped pull this book together, especially Barbara Boyd, Rosie Spinks, Samantha Skal, and Carla Green.

Finally, we need to thank our labradors Gus and Whistler, and Leeloo the vizsla, for their pawfect support when things got tough and a brisk walk was needed.

About the Authors

Nicolas Cary

After an international upbringing, Nic worked as an educator before becoming a founding team member of the tech company PipelineCRM.com, where he focused on product development and management. He then moved abroad and became the co-founder and CEO of Blockchain.com. In his day-to-day job, Nic is responsible for bringing new adopters into the crypto ecosystem. A fascination with tech, money, and politics led Nic to become deeply passionate about helping people reinvent their relationship with money, and entrepreneurship. Founded in York, Blockchain.com has raised over $1 billion in venture capital, and achieved a valuation over $14 billion. A trilingual communicator, Nic is the Founding Commissioner of the Blockchain Commission for Sustainable Development and co-author of *The Future is Decentralised*. Nic is also the Co-Founder and Chairman of SkysTheLimit.org where he concentrates on fundraising, digital strategy, and growth. Regularly cited in the global press as one of the earliest crypto and digital asset industry experts, Nic was named the European Digital Leader of the year in 2015 and honored with a Professional Achievement Award in 2017 by his alma mater, the University of Puget Sound. A proven leader, investor, public speaker, and brand ambassador, Nic focuses on designing performant cultures that persevere in adverse markets.

Bo Ghirardelli

A lifelong social entrepreneur, Bo Ghirardelli was born and raised by a family of entrepreneurs with strong humanitarian values in Oakland, California. He loves entrepreneurs. He knows that talent is distributed equally, but opportunity isn't. Early on in his career, Bo served as a public middle school teacher through Teach For America and as a business development consultant with the Peace Corps in North Africa. Bo has been the founder of four organizations, two not-for-profit and two for-profit, that collectively employ over 50 people. He has spent over a decade as the Co-Founder, President, and CEO of Skysthelimit.org, a tech non-profit that provides business mentoring, startup grants, and training to underrepresented young adult entrepreneurs across the country and beyond. Seeking to close the opportunity gap in entrepreneurship, over 80,000 entrepreneurs have signed up on the platform, over 80 percent of whom are BIPOC, 68 percent women, and 85 percent low-income when they join Skysthelimit.org. Bo spends his time building partnerships, working on the design of the platform and curriculum, fundraising, and leading the executive team. He has an MPA in Nonprofit Management from University of Washington. Bo also speaks French and some Moroccan Arabic, and has lived in France, India, Dubai, and Morocco. He loves traveling, skiing, hiking, forests, scuba diving, and cooking.

Printed in Great Britain
by Amazon

57096264R00215